11764

# PLAIN
## TALK
### ON
# Philippians

# PLAIN
# TALK
# ON
# Philippians

## *MANFORD GEORGE GUTZKE*
### PH.D.

**ZONDERVAN**
**PUBLISHING HOUSE**  OF THE ZONDERVAN CORPORATION
GRAND RAPIDS, MICHIGAN 49506

PLAIN TALK ON PHILIPPIANS
Copyright © 1973 by The Zondervan Corporation
Grand Rapids, Michigan

Library of Congress Catalog Number: 73-2657

Eighth printing 1981
ISBN 0-310-25611-9

Grateful appreciation is expressed to the following for permission to quote from their Bible translations:

DIVISION OF CHRISTIAN EDUCATION, NATIONAL COUNCIL OF CHURCHES OF CHRIST IN THE UNITED STATES OF AMERICA. *The Revised Standard Version of the Bible.* Copyright © 1952 and 1971 by The Division of Christian Education, National Council of Churches of Christ in the United States of America.

TYNDALE HOUSE PUBLISHERS. *The Living Bible.* Copyright © 1971 by Tyndale House Publishers.

ZONDERVAN PUBLISHING HOUSE. *The Amplified Bible.* Copyright © 1965 by the Zondervan Publishing House.

*Printed in the United States of America*

# CONTENTS

# PLAIN
## TALK
### ON
# Philippians

## Chapter 1

## SALUTATION

### (Philippians 1:1, 2)

*Do you have any idea what is the most meaningful term you could use in referring to a preacher of the Gospel?*

> Paul and Timotheus, the servants of Jesus Christ, to all the saints in Christ Jesus which are at Philippi, with the bishops and deacons: grace be unto you, and peace, from God our Father, and from the Lord Jesus Christ (1:1, 2).

This could ordinarily be counted as just a salutation, but these words used in the opening of this epistle, although formal, are actually very meaningful. Notice how this phrase "servants of Jesus Christ" is used — "Paul and Timotheus, the servants of Jesus Christ." In that phrase, all the attention is focused on the Lord who controlled them. They were His servants only. This emphasizes that Paul and Timothy were not doing things on their own initiative for the Lord. They were not organizing work, and turning it over to the Lord, to show what great thing they had done for Him. Nor were they working on their own in their own wisdom and strength. They were doing as they were led to do by the Lord. They were the servants of Jesus Christ. It is Jesus Christ who came into the world to seek and to save the lost and He is still doing that. The living Lord is actively at work saving souls. The whole idea of spreading the Gospel is that we might be His servants because God is working through us in the people who listen, working in them to prepare them to where they could believe that they might be saved.

These two, Paul and Timothy, were the servants of the Lord Jesus Christ in what they were doing. They only wanted to do what the Lord wanted them to do. They knew that moment by moment He would lead them. "To all the

saints at Philippi." This word "saints" comes from the same
root as the verb "sanctify," and means "one that has been
set apart for a specific purpose." When a soul becomes a
believer, that person is translated out of the natural into the
spiritual. Each born-again person is a saint. This word, as
Paul used it, is for all believers, but it especially emphasizes
the fact that they have been separated to the Lord. They
have been called out from the world and set apart in a
special way for Christ Jesus. If they belong to the Lord
Jesus Christ they are His, they have put their trust in Him.
He has called them out of this world away from this situation, into a fellowship with Him to do His will and His will
only. They are no longer their own. They have been bought
with a price.

"With the bishops and deacons." The word "bishop"
means "overseer," an "undershepherd," "leader." This is a
person who has responsibility over others in spiritual things.
The deacons were the "servants" — the servants of the
church. They were men given the assignment of carrying
on certain activities in the name of the church as a whole.
The Apostle Paul is saying here he is sending his message
to all the saints — the common people in the church — together with their leaders and with their workers.

"Grace be unto you, and peace." Grace comes from God
toward man, and is the undeserved kindness and favor of
God toward him. It is God's attitude toward mankind,
prompting Him to do for man what man needs, but what
man cannot earn, and does not deserve. But there is another
meaning to the word "grace." It is "the inward enablement"
in the believer to do the will of God. When a person belongs
to the Lord Jesus Christ and is led by the Holy Spirit in his
life, he is going to be led into things that are contrary to
human nature. He will be led into denying himself and
yielding when he does not feel like it. He will be led to
accept and to endure suffering. He will be led into these
things, and he won't have the grace, the strength to go
through with it. He does not have it within himself to do or
to be like that. He will need help from God. That help from

God is called grace. In the believer, it gives him the power and the strength to do the will of God. "Grace . . . from God our Father, and from the Lord Jesus Christ."

"And peace." The word "peace" can be used in various ways. Peace exists when a disturbance is taken away, when a conflict has been removed, when a quarrel is ended and the opponents are reconciled. Since I can have peace with God, one wonders why I would ever be against Him. This is because of sin. God has one great controversy with the human soul: man is a sinner. Man has done wrong, and "the soul that sinneth, it shall die." Man is under condemnation of death because of sin, and this causes a tension between him and God. In Christ Jesus, there comes "peace with God" about sin. He will forgive me, cleanse me, and change me. He will carry my sins away. He has "cast all my sins behind [his] back." God will remember them no more against me forever. "As far as the east is from the west, so far hath he removed our transgressions from us."

"Peace with God" will not come to everyone. Anyone can have it, but only those who believe will receive it. One must reach up to take from God what God offers us in Christ Jesus. Just because a man understands that Christ Jesus died, and then goes on about his affairs and never turns to accept the Lord, never yields himself to the Lord, such a man need not think for one moment that his sins are going to be forgiven. As Paul writes, "Being now justified by faith, we have peace with God." When the Lord Jesus is in the soul, He rules; and when He rules, He can say to the waves of the sea: "Peace, be still." He can say it inside my heart and in yours.

"From God our Father." This expression recognizes the new birth. He is our Father because we are born again. "And from the Lord Jesus Christ," who is the Son of God into whose hands the Father has given all things, including judgment and the right to raise the dead. So "peace, from God our Father, and the Lord Jesus Christ" was the salutation the Apostle Paul gave to these Christians living at Philippi.

## Chapter 2

## THANKS FOR FELLOWSHIP

### (Philippians 1:3-5)

*Can you understand what is the most important service one believer can undertake for another?*

Paul is writing to these believers in Philippi. He writes: "I thank my God upon every remembrance of you." In these words the Apostle Paul is telling the believers at Philippi that he personally was thankful to God for each one of them. Paul had been blessed by the Philippians. They had been kind to him. They had sent him support. He appreciated them, but he gives all the glory to God. He was profoundly obligated to God for what the Philippians had done for him. He understood that they were doing this as God led them. He knew that God was responsible for what happened. Paul had been personally blessed by these believers; but, let me say again, he gives all the glory to God, not to the Philippians. We are to take that to ourselves. If someone does something for us, we can appreciate that very much and we may be grateful to that individual, but let us not stop thanking there. We should lift up our hearts and our minds and give thanks to Almighty God who moved that person to do for us. The Apostle Paul was conscious of this, and he said: "I thank my God upon every remembrance of you."

"Always in every prayer of mine for you all making request with joy." Paul prayed repeatedly for these young believers. We do not know how often, but they were in danger. They needed help, and Paul prayed earnestly for them. Every time he thought about them, his heart was filled with thanksgiving to God. What a wonderful thing that they believed! What a wonderful thing that in believing they had been so faithful! What a wonderful thing that they

12

had contributed to the work, in the name of the Lord Jesus Christ. Paul was grateful for all these things. "Always in every prayer of mine for you all making request with joy." Paul was delighted to be praying for these people, making request that they might be blessed, that they might be strengthened.

You will remember in reading other epistles of Paul what his praying would be. He would pray that they might have more knowledge of the things of Christ, that they might come to know the hidden things of God. He would pray that they might even come to know the love of God which passes knowledge. He would pray that they might in these things grow in grace and in knowledge. He would be praying for these young Christians that they would be kept faithful, that they would be kept strong, that they would be guided by God. He would pray that God would watch over them, and not allow them to be tempted above that they were able. All of this praying would be constantly going on, and Paul was delighted every time he was doing it. He made this request for their blessing with joy.

This leads me to remember that when the apostle would be in prayer, he would be looking into the face of Jesus Christ. As he looked into the face of Jesus Christ, he would rejoice when he would think of all the mercy and goodness of God that was in Christ Jesus. He would think of all the grace of God that was in Christ Jesus, and it would fill him with joy. Then he would ask of the Lord: "Now share some of that with those young believers over there in Philippi, those new Christians. Be with them and strengthen them." This is the way Paul would be praying for them. "Making request with joy, for your fellowship in the gospel from the first day until now." What gave Paul his inward sense of gratitude to God was the fellowship of the Philippians in the Gospel.

The phrase "for your fellowship in the gospel" has a practical note in it. That "fellowship" did not mean simply that they had the same attitude, and that they said the same words, or that they belonged to the same group of people. It meant more than that. Their "fellowship in the gospel" would mean that as Paul preached the Gospel, they shared. When Paul was seeking to win other people, they cared. As Paul would be preaching and teaching, they would pray. They were the kind of people who entered into his ministry with him. They gave him the means so that he could travel. They even sent him servants that would help him. They did everything they could that would help him along his way, because he was their spokesman.

In this same way we can support our missionaries. We can support them with prayer, and with concern. We can support them in faith. We can think about them. We can ask the Lord about them. We can pray God's blessing on them. We can share with them in all that they face, and we can pray with them in all that they are experiencing and enduring. Then we can give to them of our means, so that they may be able to go on and do their work. In this way we can have fellowship in the Gospel with our missionaries.

This is the way you can have fellowship in the Gospel with your pastor. How I hope you are praying for him. Let me suggest to you as far as your own family worship and your own private worship is concerned, that you actually make prayer for your pastor a part of that fellowship. You could make that praying more meaningful if you would specify one thing in particular. For instance, since you know that next Sunday morning your pastor is going to preach, and you even know what subject he is going to discuss, because he let you know about it, you could start praying about it. You could start praying about the people who will hear him. Do you know families in your church that need blessing? You could start praying for them. Do you know Sunday school classes in your Sunday school program that need strengthening, or do you know young people's work that needs help? I could go on and mention many other things. In any one of these you could actually take part, and so have fellowship in the Gospel. This fellowship then would be an occasion for thanksgiving to God. It is a marvelous thing for a preacher to have help from other people while he is trying to spread the Gospel.

Paul writes,

> I thank my God upon every remembrance of you, always in every prayer of mine for you all making request with joy, for your fellowship in the gospel from the first day until now (1:3-5).

When he writes "from the first day until now," we are to understand that these believers had been staunch supporters. We could do this too. Regardless of congregation or denomination, whatever our church, we can pray to Almighty God. If certain developments should take place in the church activity, or certain changes should be made in church procedure, we can pray. There may be things in our church life that we feel are not as they ought to be. We can pray.

Often we might find that our pastor would be very glad to know that we are praying for him. Some of the things that are bothering us may be bothering him too. We could be among those who can always be counted upon to do our part.

We may be encouraged to remember that if the Apostle Paul felt this way about the Philippians, we can be sure that our Lord in heaven will feel that way about us. If we want to share in the ministry of the Gospel of Jesus Christ, doing what we can to see that it gets out, and that people get to know that God sent His Son into the world to seek and to save the lost, that whosoever believes in Him shall never perish but have everlasting life, then let us pray that this message will go far and wide, and that it will call people that they might be saved.

*Chapter 3*

## CONFIDENCE IN GOD

### (Philippians 1:6)

*Do you know the sufficient reason for expecting a Christian to be faithful throughout his whole life?*

> Being confident of this very thing, that he which hath begun a good work in you will perform it until the day of Jesus Christ (1:6).

This is the way the Apostle Paul refers to his own attitude when he is praying for the believers at Philippi. He has no fears about the outcome. So often when we are thinking of praying for people, we are unaware of their need or direction. How should we pray for them when we do not know what they are going to do? Or perhaps we are asked to pray for a certain pastor. We hesitate, not sure we agree with his preaching. But that is not the basis on which we should pray. We do not pray because we have such confidence in the people that we think that our praying for them is going to be worthwhile. We pray because we have confidence in God.

Salvation is of God. Paul had no fears about those believers at Philippi, that they might fall by the wayside. It was true they were just human beings. They could falter as quickly as anyone. But Paul's confidence was not in the believers as such. His confidence in the work of grace that was growing in them was in the Lord. "Being confident of this very thing, that he which hath begun a good work in you will perform it until the day of Jesus Christ." Paul understood that those people had been saved by the grace of God when Christ Jesus died for them and carried away their sins. They were now being saved by the grace of God for God was daily forgiving them and keeping them in His grace and mercy. They would be saved one day: saved body, soul and spirit completely, taken into heaven by the power of Almighty God.

Paul's confidence was in God. He believed in the grace of God. "Marvelous grace of our loving Lord, grace that is greater than all our sins." "Where sin abounded, grace did much more abound." Paul was confident that the grace of God would be greater than any sin these people might commit. Then there was the power of God. To be sure, these Philippian believers might face hard times. They might be called upon to go through difficult and troubled times, but God was almighty. God in His power could keep them, and Paul had confidence in the faithfulness of God. When God gives a promise, He stands by it. He is not a fair-weather friend, here today and gone tomorrow. No! When God takes hold, He stays to the end. Paul's confidence was in God, and because he had confidence in God, he could say "being confident of this very thing, that he which hath begun a good work in you will perform it." When Paul prayed, he looked forward with confidence.

Paul knew that these believers might face persecution. In those days among those people, that was often the case. Sometimes people lost their lives because they believed in the Lord Jesus Christ. Paul knew that they could have suffering coming to them because of their witness. He knew that death would threaten, and on occasion death would come. He knew that suffering would come to some of them because of their testimony. If they dared to say they belonged to the Lord Jesus Christ, their families and neighborhoods might turn against them. There might be suffering but God would be faithful.

In 1 Corinthians 10:13 Paul wrote that God would not allow believers to be tempted beyond what they were able to endure, but with the temptation would provide a way of escape so they would be able to bear it. The writer of the Book of Hebrews said that God would be able to save to the uttermost those who would come to God by the Lord Jesus Christ, seeing He lives to make intercession for them (Heb. 7:25).

These passages bring to our mind the undergirding that was the strength of Paul's confidence. When Paul considered all this, and when he thought about these people for whom he was praying, that they were just young believers, he realized that they did not have a long history and background like the Jewish people had in dealing with God. They were relatively new in the faith, but he had confidence. "He which hath begun a good work in you" — God had sent His Son to die for them.

God had given His Son to die for sinners. Are you a sinner? Then God gave His Son to die for you. You may ignore it. You may neglect it. You may walk away from it, but you can never change it. He gave His Son to die for you. It does not make any difference who you are or what you have done. "Though your sins be as scarlet, they shall be as white as snow; though they be red like crimson, they shall be as wool" (Isa. 1:18). This is the promise of God. In the fullness of time, God sent forth His Son, born of a woman, born under the law to save and to redeem those who were under the law. Not only did He begin a good work when He sent His Son, but He regenerated those who believed. It is true for anyone — "whosoever believeth in him should not perish, but have everlasting life." The person who believes in the Lord Jesus Christ will be born again, not of the flesh but of the Spirit. He will be regenerated. God regenerates you once for all, and once regenerated you will be alive in the Spirit; and then He is in you. He will strengthen you. That life that begins in Christ Jesus will never die.

Another thing that God has done for every believer is to send His Holy Spirit into the heart. Are you a person who is trusting in the Lord Jesus Christ? Then I can tell you that because God gave His Son to die for you Christ Jesus has carried your sins away. They are gone. As far as the east is from the west, they have been taken away. He has cast all your sins behind His back. There is nothing now against you because Christ Jesus died for you, and there is in you a new "thing." "Therefore if any man be in Christ, he is a new creature: old things are passed away; behold, all things are become new" (2 Cor. 5:17). You may not be so conscious of it, but it is true. There is something new in you that will never die — it was put there by the Lord Jesus Christ Himself. Then God sent His Holy Spirit to be with you to guide you, and in addition to that God watches over you in His providence as you live your life day in and day out.

God is watching over you and keeping you, and He will freely forgive you. That is the good work that He has begun in you. "He which hath begun a good work in you will perform it." He will do it because you have put your trust in the Lord Jesus Christ. You are believing in Him as you are down here living in this world right now. The Lord Jesus Christ Himself is alive in heaven. He is the living Lord at the right hand of God and in the very presence of God. He is your Advocate. He is interceding on your behalf and that is why God is able to save you to the uttermost because you come to Him by faith in Christ Jesus. Christ ever lives to make intercession for you. And so, not only will Christ Jesus in the presence of God pray for you, but God has given His Holy Spirit to be in you, and the Holy Spirit of God in you will strengthen you from within. He will take the things of Christ and show them to you. He will strengthen you day in and day out, and He will comfort you. By His grace and by His providence, by giving you inward strength to endure and by watching over you to make sure that the load will not be too heavy, nor the way too hard, He will watch over you.

Now it may be true that you are in obscurity, that your life is being lived in spiritual darkness. You may feel all alone, but there is a day coming when you will be face to face with Him in all His glory and He will look upon you with thoughts of pleasantness and peace. He gave Himself to die for you and He is coming again. Listen!

> Let not your heart be troubled: ye believe in God, believe also in me. In my Father's house are many mansions: if it were not so, I would have told you. I go to prepare a place for you. And if I go and prepare a place for you, I will come again, and receive you unto myself; that where I am, there ye may be also (John 14:1-3).

This is the promise of the living Lord Jesus Christ. Are you a Christian? Do you truly believe in Him? Well, have one thing in mind right now: the Lord will come in God's own time, in triumphant glory, and you will be brought through into the fullness of blessing by the power of God.

# Chapter 4

## IN MY HEART

### (Philippians 1:7, 8)

*Can you understand that those who have gone through trials and suffering together are very dear to each other?*

Even as it is meet for me to think this of you all, because I have you in my heart; inasmuch as both in my bonds, and in the defence and confirmation of the gospel, ye all are partakers of my grace. For God is my record, how greatly I long after you all in the bowels of Jesus Christ (1:7, 8).

In this way the Apostle Paul is indicating his attitude toward the believers in the city and around Philippi. He thanked God for them whenever he thought about them, as he requested blessing for them in every prayer. He expected the blessing of God to come upon them always. He thinks it is the proper thing that he should do so, and indicates a deep personal concern and affection. That is the way you would feel about someone who was very close to you.

Not only were they interested in his career and service because they remembered him as the man who came and preached to them, but also they were glad to hear about him and to think he was successful in his work. They hoped he would overcome all his difficulties, and not only that, but they shared with him: whatever his problem was, they joined him in it.

One is reminded of the incident in the Book of Acts when Peter was put in prison by Herod. Herod had expected to bring him out after Easter and put him to death to please the Jews. While Peter was in prison we read that the church gathered in the house of the mother of John Mark and continued in prayer all night for him. I have been led to feel in my own heart and mind in thinking about that, that the people were not so much praying that Peter should be re-

21

leased from prison, as they were joining him in spirit while he was in prison, and sharing with him in his danger and in his expected death, for he certainly expected to be put to death (John 21:19).

When the Lord Jesus came to Mary and Martha on the occasion when Lazarus had died, He went to the grave where they had put him away. When He was there and saw them weeping and felt their sorrow and their grief, He groaned in Himself in His spirit. Then are recorded these marvelous words, the shortest verse in the Bible: "Jesus wept." He knew what He was going to do. He knew that He was going to raise Lazarus from the dead. But when those people were suffering so much, and were feeling so badly about the loss of their brother, He wept with them. Such heartfelt sympathy belongs to the very nature of Jesus Christ.

Paul is saying that these Philippian believers shared with him in his work. They had gone along with him. When he was in jail, they suffered with him. It was not only they knew he was in jail; they shared his experience and entered into it with him. When he answered the accusations against him by defending the truth of the Lord Jesus Christ and setting forth the Gospel, they joined him in his witness. They were praying for him and sharing with him when he stood up before the world to tell about the Lord Jesus Christ. When he got answers to prayer, when he was involved in things and prayed to Almighty God, they joined in prayer. They joined him in everything, and this aroused in him a special love for them.

When a believer is involved in witnessing or in serving others, when he is trying to live the Christian life, most other people will pass him by. Even people who are interested in him, people who are sympathetic with him, people who approve of him, and who probably hope he will succeed, have a tendency to pass by and leave the task with him. It seems only natural and common that they will be going on about other things. This can be seen in something as simple as when a woman is cleaning and caring for her home. It is natural for others in the home to go about their own affairs and leave the cleaning to her. If you are that woman, you will know how often the road gets dreary when you are alone; and you know how often deep down in your heart you wish someone would notice and share the burden with you. What a wonderful thing it would be if there was someone who would share and help you with your tasks and problems! Something like this happens when a person comes to church, sits in a comfortable place, listens to a good message, and then goes out and does not contribute anything. The believers in Philippi were different from anything like this: they really cared about the apostle and his ministry.

Paul goes on to say, "For God is my record, how greatly I long after you all in the bowels of Jesus Christ" (1:8). This phrasing reflects the current psychology of that day. In the times when the New Testament was written, the psychology of the day felt that the emotions were grounded in the visceral organs. Today I would say, "I long after you all in the heart of Jesus Christ," which would mean the same thing. In other words, Paul had special affection for his comrades, those who joined him in his service.

## Chapter 5

## ABOUNDING LOVE

### (Philippians 1:9, 10)

*Have you ever realized that love will abound more and more as a person knows the facts involved and exercises good common sense?*

In the description of the life in Christ the word "love" occurs many times. We talk about loving God, about loving one another, and loving the poor. In the New Testament, when the word "love" is used, there is little sentiment or emotion involved. Actually the word "love" indicates a way of doing things. It could be simply put this way: when one person acts in order that another may benefit, that is love. "For God so loved the world, *that he gave* his only begotten Son, that whosoever believeth in him should not perish, but have everlasting life" (John 3:16).

A deeper richer meaning of this word in describing daily living in faith is seen in Philippians. Paul writes:

> And this I pray, that your love may abound yet more and more in knowledge and in all judgment; that ye may approve things that are excellent; that ye may be sincere and without offence till the day of Christ (1:9, 10).

Another translation puts it this way:

> And it is my prayer that your love may abound more and more with knowledge and all discernment, so that you may approve what is excellent, and may be pure and blameless for the day of Christ (RSV).

Or again:

> My prayer for you is that you will overflow more and more with love for others, and at the same time keep on growing in spiritual knowledge and insight, for I want you always to see clearly the difference between right and wrong, to be

inwardly clean, no one being able to criticize you from now until our Lord returns (*The Living Bible*).

Or a fuller translation:

And this I pray, that your love may abound yet more and more *and* extend to its fullest development in knowledge and all keen insight — that is, that your love may [display itself in] greater depth of acquaintance and more comprehensive discernment; so that you may surely learn to sense what is vital, *and* approve *and* prize what is excellent *and* of real value — recognizing the highest and the best, and distinguishing the moral differences; and that you may be untainted *and* pure and unerring *and* blameless, that — with hearts sincere and certain and unsullied — you may [approach] the day of Christ, not stumbling *nor* causing others to stumble. (*Amplified Bible*).

These four versions are responsible translations of the original Greek text. In reading them a richer grasp of the meaning of Paul's words can be secured. In each of these translations "love" is involved in "knowledge." If you really want to do for anyone, as a mother wants to do for her child, or a husband wants to do for his family, or one friend wants to do for another, it is important for each to know all that he or she can learn. It is intelligent action that helps others. We have heard it said that "the way to hell is paved with good intentions," and while this is a rather sober and harsh statement it does express an important truth. Good intentions alone will not help, but intelligent performance will. Love is involved in good common sense. So Paul prays that their "love may abound . . . in knowledge and in all judgment."

The next sentence is extremely important: "That ye may approve things that are excellent." Not everything is alike. Some things are good. Some things are evil. A good way of translating this is to say "that you may distinguish the things that differ." One thing is different from another. Some people are big; some are little. Some are strong; some are weak. Some are right; some are wrong. You must try to see the difference. The believer should distinguish the things that differ. He should recognize the things that are vital, the things that are really important.

If people really knew the truth about God they would not be tempted to be such fools. It is the fool that says "in his heart, There is no God." It is a foolish person who acts as if there were no God. Such conduct does not make sense. If God is, then it makes sense to pay attention to Him. If Christ Jesus really died for sinners, who would not come to Him? If He really rose from the dead to enable a person to be delivered, who would not want to be delivered? If a person really believed that Jesus of Nazareth was now in the presence of God praying, who would not want Him to pray for them? Any believer can read the Bible, pray, and note the testimony of other Christians, and so see clearly that there is a difference. A believer should distinguish the things that differ. He should recognize the things that are vital. He should accent and emphasize the things that are good, because some things are excellent and are vital, and it is a matter of intelligence to know this.

Paul says that he prays for them.

> And this I pray, that your love may abound yet more and more in knowledge and in all judgment (1:9).

Another translator puts it this way:

> I just want you in your desire to help other people to learn things, know things, and have good sense. Exercise good common sense and especially in this. That you will approve the things that are excellent, that you will distinguish things that differ, that you will recognize the things that are vital that you may be sincere (1:9, 10).

The word "sincere" means a condition that is like a window pane that is clean, so that you can see through it plainly. Thus a believer is sincere when he is absolutely honest as daylight, inwardly clean and pure and without offense. This word "offense" means "a cause for stumbling." To say that a believer is "without offense" is to say that he is not stumbling nor causing anyone else to stumble. Every believer in Christ should seek to make sure that anyone else knows perfectly well what he stands for, and what he stands against. Thus he "may be sincere and without offence till the day of Christ."

One day the Lord is coming, and when He comes there will be a judgment. He will come to judge the quick and the dead. At that time no one will have to figure out what is right and what is wrong. Christ will let us know. But now while we are in this world, we will need to study, to learn, to pray, to seek to understand in every way we possibly can. For that we need to have an inward urge within us that others might know Christ Jesus and His will for their life. We need to care for others for Christ's sake.

## Chapter 6

## FILLED WITH FRUIT

### (Philippians 1:11)

*Do you think the manner of life lived by a believer is any credit to him?*

> Being filled with the fruits of righteousness, which are by Jesus Christ, unto the glory and praise of God (1:11).

This is part of the petition that the Apostle Paul makes for these believers at Philippi. He prays that their love might abound more and more in knowledge and all judgment so that they might approve things that are excellent, distinguish things that differ, that they might recognize things that are vital, in order that they might be sincere, genuine and without offense, giving no one reason to stumble to the day of Christ. The reason they would be without offense, and the reason why he wanted them to be so blessed with having an operation of love in their hearts, was because there would be results. "Being filled with the fruits of righteousness, which are by Jesus Christ, unto the glory and praise of God."

The Bible refers to the natural man as being wicked. In Hebrew "wicked" means "out of the way," suggesting deviousness, something crooked. The natural man is false, crooked. He has in him the disposition to lie. The Scriptures tell us plainly that all have sinned and come short of the glory of God. In the fifty-third chapter of Isaiah it is written, "All we like sheep have gone astray; we have turned every one to his own way." This is the natural man.

The wonderful thing to remember then is how in Isaiah it is written:

> Let the wicked forsake his way, and the unrighteous man his thoughts: and let him return unto the Lord, and he will

have mercy upon him; and to our God, for he will abundantly pardon (Isaiah 55:7).

It is true that the natural man is crooked, devious, out of
the way, but he can be saved. Christ Jesus came into the
world to reconcile, to bring that estranged person back to
God, to restore the relationship between God and His
creatures, to save that which was lost. He is the Son of
man who came to seek and to save the lost.

Christ Jesus came to bring a right relationship. He came
to make man right. The word "right" means straight up and
down, perpendicular, no deviation, no leaning one way or
another. This is suggested in the book of the prophet Amos
where he speaks of seeing himself with a plumb line. When
he went to judge Jerusalem he would hold that plumb line
there to the city to see if it were straight up and down.

Jesus of Nazareth who was made in all points like we are,
took upon Himself a human body and in His earthly career
was righteous. That is, He was right all the time in all His
dealings. In the plan of God, each believer in Christ Jesus
shares in that righteousness of Christ. It is this which leads
us to trust and to accept Christ. To willingly yield ourselves
to Him is right in the sight of God. This is why righteousness
is by faith. Righteousness, namely a man being and doing
right before God, is the consequence of his exercising his
faith in the grace of God. Thus the believer is right by the
very grace of Christ who is in him. This results in being right
in action and conduct, which is the fruit of righteousness.

When a man is right, he will honor God. He will worship
God. A man who is right with God will confess his personal
sins. He will acknowledge the law of God to be true,
righteous and holy. He will accept the judgment of God on
himself that he is not what he ought to be. He will look
upon God as high, holy, righteous and lifted up. He will
have his trust and confidence in God. And all this will take
place in the believer.

Any human being turning his back on God is not right.
Anyone choosing to live as if there were no God is not right.
In fact, the Bible will reveal that he is a fool. But, if any

person simply turns to God, acknowledges Him, sees Him as He is, he looks into the face of Christ Jesus and is made right. All he ever needs to do is to turn his eyes upon Jesus and to look up into His wonderful face. If he will turn that way to God and will look upon God, he will experience what the children of Israel experienced in the Old Testament when they looked upon the serpent that was raised in the wilderness. Everyone who looked upon that serpent was healed immediately of the plague with which he had been smitten. So it is with the believer. One look at Christ Jesus is enough. "There is life for a look at the Crucified One: there is life at this moment for thee."

The believer, because he has the grace of God in his heart through the Lord Jesus Christ, will have an attitude toward God that is acceptable and which will honor God. He will bow down before Him. He will worship God and he will ascribe praise and glory to God. Furthermore, he will seek to please Him. He will humbly realize that he is a sinner in the sight of God, and worthy of God's condemnation. He will repent and certainly not be casual about his sin. The wonderful thing is that if he will confess his sins, God is faithful and just to forgive him his sins and to cleanse him from all unrighteousness.

If a man is right in his soul, he will have a certain attitude toward Jesus Christ. He will understand and believe that Jesus of Nazareth was really the Son of God, that He was really God Incarnate in human form here upon earth. The believer will understand that the death on Calvary's cross was for him. Christ Jesus bore his sins on Calvary's cross. He will believe that Christ Jesus was raised from the dead, is really alive now in the presence of God interceding on our behalf. Christ Jesus is waiting in heaven until God's time comes when He will return to this world.

Then, too, there will be a rightness in his attitude about the Holy Spirit. He will know that the Holy Spirit is real, that He is true and that He will do the things that have been revealed in Scripture about Him. One can study John

14, 15 and 16, and know what the Holy Spirit will do in the believer.

If a man is right in his heart, so that he is filled with the fruits of righteousness, he will have a certain attitude toward other believers. He will care about them, be considerate of them and love them. He will also have a certain attitude toward unbelievers. He will seek in every way possible to bring people to believe in the Lord Jesus Christ. All of this in that man will be the fruits of righteousness which are by Christ Jesus, not by his own efforts and not by his own works.

"Unto the glory and praise of God." As far as that believer is concerned, he has nothing personally of which to be proud. All the praise and the glory goes to the Lord Jesus Christ. The believer has no reason to take any credit to himself. Everything that is right in his conduct belongs to the Lord. All praise and all glory belong to God the Father and the Lord Jesus Christ, our Savior.

# Chapter 7

## UNTO THE FURTHERANCE

### (Philippians 1:12)

*Have you ever noticed how often it happens that the very calamity that brought trouble becomes the source of blessing?*

> But I would ye should understand, brethren, that the things which happened unto me have fallen out rather unto the furtherance of the gospel (1:12).

All the things that happened to the Apostle Paul certainly caused the Gospel to advance. The life of any believer is often marked by difficulty. Some of the worst experiences involve other persons. Often it appears that when the Gospel is hindered by some difficulty, this actually works out for good. An example is recorded in the Book of Acts, after the martyrdom of Stephen. There was so much persecution that the believers fled everywhere from Jerusalem throughout the whole Mediterranean world. But everywhere they went they told the Gospel story. I have often thought that you could think of the believers in the church at Jerusalem as a pile of red hot coals where there had been a fire. I think of someone trying to put out the fire by using a big scoop shovel to scoop up all those red hot coals, and then throwing them away far and wide, not realizing that in so doing he was just spreading the fire everywhere. Wherever those coals would fall a new fire would burn.

Another difficult situation that seemed so unfortunate took place when Paul and Barnabas differed with each other in their judgment about whether or not Mark should go along on their second missionary tour. The contention was so sharp that they separated and went their separate ways. Someone might say, "Wasn't that too bad? Just think of what they could have done if they had stayed together." But what actually happened was that there were two missionary groups going out instead of one.

We could take Paul himself as an example. Let us recall to mind certain things about Saul, the Pharisee, who became Paul the Apostle, and what we know about his life. We know that when he became a believer, this came as a surprise and a shock to everyone in the early church. They were so frightened of Saul that they would not listen to this testimony of his becoming a believer. The result was that he spent three years in Arabia. No one has ever described what happened to Saul in those three years. But any person with spiritual understanding of the Gospel will feel sure that those three years would have been years of deep experience in the Lord, and of learning the ways of God. They would provide a private, silent time alone with God in which he learned much of the Gospel that afterwards he preached everywhere. Another instance to note occurred when he and Barnabas went out to preach in a certain city. The Jews would not listen to him because he was not one of the regular teachers. But when the Jews shut their doors and refused to listen then missionaries came to the Gentiles. The result was that many thousands of Gentiles became believers. One could wonder why the Lord would do things this way. It may be that we human beings just need to be broken out of a certain spot before we are willing to go some place else.

The same pattern can be seen when Paul was telling the Gospel story. He was arrested for preaching the Gospel, and it would appear everything was against him. But when he was thrown into prison the record shows what the result was. He preached to the governor. He never could have gotten in to the governor, never could have gotten into that courtroom to tell the Gospel story; but when he was brought in as a prisoner and was accused of certain things, he was allowed to give his testimony. And then he gave one of the most wonderful testimonies for the Gospel there is on record.

There was the time when some young men got together and vowed they would neither eat nor drink until they killed Paul. He appealed to the governor that he might go before Caesar; as he was a Roman citizen this was his privilege. As a result, Paul had the opportunity to talk to the top officials in the Roman government.

While on his way to Italy there was a storm at sea. It was so violent that one could be inclined to think that the elements were opposing Paul. Certainly the ship was threatened with sinking and that would seem to be the end of his career. But it turned out that he had an opportunity to witness to the captain and to all those people on that ship. In all that happened which seemed to be against him, he was able to serve to the honor and the glory of God.

Even when he was actually brought to Rome, he was unfairly kept in prison. There was no real charge against him. He was not kept in tight custody. He was allowed to have visitors come and go, and in all that time he preached the Gospel. Before he finished his course he had the opportunity to stand before Caesar and give his witness and testimony. Paul was often unfairly persecuted. Often he was stoned, beaten, left for dead. Yet he always bore witness to Jesus Christ — he preached the Gospel.

At this time when he was writing to the Philippians, he was in prison for preaching. But Almighty God was on the throne. While Paul was in prison, he preached, setting an example that inspired others, causing many people to witness for the Lord Jesus Christ. In prison he was in danger of being killed, but he was patient, he was meek, he was quiet and firm and persistent and kept telling the story and kindly sharing it with everyone. When they saw Paul in chains many other Christians began to speak out boldly in the name of Jesus Christ. Paul rejoiced that the name of Christ Jesus was so honored. He said even if they killed him everyone would talk about it. If they did not kill him, he would preach, so either way the Gospel would be told to the glory of God.

Can you see how something like this is happening today? In recent years some have criticized the text of the Bible, saying that the Bible is not really true. The result has been that many people have studied the Bible who would never otherwise have studied it. When believers are shaken they begin to read and study, and to discover the Word for themselves. Perhaps it would be helpful if Christians suffered some for their faith. It seems that when believers are opposed and are persecuted for Christ, the Gospel becomes central to their interest and concern.

## Chapter 8

## MY BONDS ARE MANIFEST

### (Philippians 1:13, 14)

*Do you realize that it often takes opposition to bring out the truth?*

> So that my bonds in Christ are manifest in all the palace, and in all other places; and many of the brethren in the Lord, waxing confident by my bonds, are much more bold to speak the word without fear (1:13, 14).

It is sadly true that we often neglect the very thing we appreciate the most. Do you remember hearing people say we never miss the water until the well goes dry? We take things for granted as long as we have them. The moment we are in danger of losing them, then they become important. Take, for instance, our health. What a wonderful thing it is to be healthy. Yet, as long as our body is well, we ignore it. We neglect it until we are sick and then we are so anxious to have help. It often happens that when a person has heart trouble so that he begins to take care of himself, he outlives other people who are careless. Another example would be our home. If a home has father, mother and children all getting along, growing up normally, with the usual problems that families have, it is surprising how easy it is to take all that for granted. So far as Dad is concerned, the family just counts on him. So far as Mom is concerned, they just count on her. The whole fellowship in the home can be endangered by trivial little things that do not amount to a hill of beans; until death comes, and one is taken out. Oh, how empty the home is when that one is gone! How little we appreciated it when that one was here!

I have sometimes thought that we believers may well suffer from lack of persecution. We have it too easy and simple. On every side there are churches to which we can

go Tragically many believers even feel they are doing something extra if they go to church. Yet even now in the world
there are believers who cannot go to church except under
pain of suffering. There are those who would be beaten if
they announced that they belonged to Christ. There are
young people who would be whipped and abused. Some
would even be put to death if they would say that they
believed. Yet in those very communities you often find a
level of consecration far above what we have amongst us.

It was my privilege one time to be in a foreign country
among people where being a believer brought real danger.
If you were known to be a professed believer you would be
in danger of suffering persecution. People would not sell
you anything. They would not let you into their houses. They
would not buy anything from you. They simply would turn
their backs on you in any way, shape, or form. Anything
could happen to you as a believer in that situation. Do you
know that in that particular community the believers lived
a spiritual life far beyond anything I knew here at home. It
made me ashamed of myself. I heard of congregations that
made it a rule, that if you missed attending church service,
you were expected to explain why. If you missed three
times, you were brought before the officers of the church
and your membership would be suspended. This was true
not only for the Sunday services, but also for the Wednesday
evening prayer meeting. That was in a community where to
go to church was a danger. Sometimes it is the opposition
that actually brings out the truth.

Paul found that to be true. "So that my bonds in Christ
(my chains) are manifest in all the palace." "My being in
chains because I am a believer was manifest in all the palace,
everyone in the government knew." The people would ask,
"Why is that man in prison?" Because he is a Christian.
What does that mean? He preaches the Gospel. He became
a case in point. He was an example set up before the whole
community and every time they did anything to him, other
people saw it and the name of Christ was spread abroad.
Paul's meek patience, his steadfast faithfulness inspired

others. There were many of the brethren in the Lord. When they saw what happened to the great apostle, they were encouraged to speak up, even if the same punishment happened to them. "Waxing confident by my bonds." They were much more bold to speak the Word without fear.

Our country now is being treated to an exhibition of something that never before would have been dreamed; young people themselves are actually testifying to faith in the Lord Jesus Christ. I know some of them and I know they go out of their way to talk to other people about the Lord. They will talk about the things of the Gospel and will bear their witness and testimony before anyone. Such young people are made bold by criticism and/or opposition. We can only praise Almighty God for His overruling providence. God is in heaven. He sees all that goes on down here, and you and I will have to realize that God knows better than we do. We all know perfectly well what God wants; He wants the Word spread. He wants people to know about the Lord Jesus Christ. If it is going to take opposition, controversy and trouble to challenge young people to witness, then let it come, because in the meantime the Gospel will spread. Souls will be turned to the Lord and will believe in Him and be saved.

## Chapter 9

## SOME OF ENVY — SOME ALSO OF GOOD WILL

### (Philippians 1:15-17)

*Can you see how controversy about the Gospel actually would be helpful in evangelism?*

It is a common thing to express sorrow and grief over arguments about religion. Can these arguments actually be good for us? The human being, as he is, is lost. He is a sinner. If we just leave him alone, he will be destroyed. Christ Jesus saves people from this condition. "Christ Jesus died for them." That is glorious. That is wonderful. Human beings generally are indifferent about these things. It is as if spiritually they are asleep and usually they do not want to be awakened. Normally, people do not want to hear that they need to be saved, or that they need to be changed. They want things left the way they are. Paul writes, "Awake thou that sleepest, and arise from the dead, and Christ shall give thee light" (Eph. 5:14). One regrets to say that as some pastors are called to certain pulpits, the basis of the call seems to be that they will preach to the congregation in such a way as to make them feel better, but apart from that just leave them alone.

This may help us to understand the providence of God who permits controversy about religion. Paul understood this as he writes:

> Some indeed preach Christ even of envy and strife; and some also of good will: the one preach Christ of contention, not sincerely, supposing to add affliction to my bonds: but the other of love, knowing that I am set for the defence of the gospel (1:15-17).

Think of it. Paul said he was glad such controversy was going on. "Some indeed preach Christ even of envy and strife

. . . the one preach Christ of contention, not sincerely, supposing to add affliction to my bonds." There were those in Paul's time who were opposed to the Gospel. They actually wanted to stop its being preached, but their opposition only resulted in advertising the Gospel.

During the early years of the church those who believed in Christ were persecuted. The persecution in Jerusalem was so severe that many of the disciples fled for their lives. They left the city and went in all directions. The Scripture records that they went everywhere preaching the Word. It has been said that the blood of martyrs is the seed of the church; so that actually opposition has never stopped the Gospel.

"Some also of good will . . . the other of love, knowing that I am set for the defence of the gospel." In answering opponents, people who actually do believe in speaking up and answering critics, tell the truth and so the truth is preached. In my own lifetime I have seen this happen. When I was a boy, one of the most definite ideas expressed in some communities was atheism. I grew up in a small community and observed life there. In those days every small town had its village atheist. Some man would become notorious and obnoxious because he openly advertised the fact that he did not believe. Everyone was shocked and fascinated, so they would come and listen to him. As I listened to such men, I found they brought out aspects of the Gospel I had not considered. They did not mean to, but in discussing what they claimed was wrong, they actually told what was right.

Another attitude I encountered was agnosticism or skepticism, as when a person does not believe what he hears. It is true that if you are an honest man and do not know for sure, doubt will grow. This is exactly how I got started. I was not certain the Gospel I heard was true or false, and so I began to study.

A little later when I became a Christian I encountered a great wave of Biblical criticism. It was said the Bible contained mistakes and was self-contradictory. But do you realize what Biblical criticism forced a great many people to do? It forced them to read the Bible. Some of the greatest preachers were produced a generation ago in the midst of the criticism in America. They were men who preached the Bible as it is.

Later in my college life I encountered the theory of evolution. This idea first became current among scientific people, but it finally got into the colleges, and is now abroad even in the church. There are persons who sincerely think that natural processes will actually produce that which is acceptable to God. This is of course contrary to the Bible message which is that God will save you by His grace through Christ Jesus, and only that way. But even the theory of evolution has caused men to go back and consider the Gospel and study it.

Then again there has been great argument and discussion over the inspiration of Scripture; questioning who wrote what is in the Bible and how they did it. It is true that the Bible was written by men, and because men are faulty, the critics argue therefore the Bible is faulty. This simple superficial argument catches hold in people's minds. But it is not true, and is clearly refuted by the experience of people who have actually tested the Bible. Some have tried it out in their own experience, and because they have tried it out they can tell the whole world: "I tried it out. I tasted and I saw. I know the Bible is true. 'This poor man cried, and the LORD heard him, and saved him out of all his troubles'."

In our day and time there has been a large movement to get all the churches together in a big church union project that is commonly called "ecumenical" activity. The implication of this has caused many to study and state what they do believe. Even more recently there has come into the foreground what is called the "charismatic" movement. Many are distressed and get into controversy about this matter of the gifts of the Spirit. With all its faults this interest has resulted in people digging into the Bible to find out what the actual promises are; and a great many people today are far more spiritually minded than they were before.

Above, beyond, and through all these controversies is the simple truth of the Gospel of Jesus Christ. He died on

Calvary. His body was raised from the dead. He ascended into heaven. He sent forth His Holy Spirit on the day of Pentecost. He is praying for us now and He is coming again. One way or another as the controversies go on, discussion brings this out to the foreground; and Paul would say: "I rejoice to think that in everything, whether in envy or in good will, Christ is preached."

## Chapter 10

## CHRIST IS PREACHED

### (Philippians 1:18)

*Do you think there is any real hindrance in spreading the Gospel because there are so many different denominations?*

What then? notwithstanding, every way, whether in pretence, or in truth, Christ is preached; and I therein do rejoice, yea, and will rejoice (1:18).

Paul has just said that there were many different voices being heard in his day and time. Some of them were opposed to him, some were for him. He rejoiced because they were all talking about Christ. The more they argued and the more they contended, the more they talked about Christ, and so he comments: "What then? notwithstanding (in spite of all the controversy), every way, whether in pretence, or in truth (those who are opposed to it, those who are for it), Christ is preached; and I therein do rejoice, yea, and will rejoice." Paul was a great missionary and preacher, and in his lifetime he was involved in much controversy. In Philippi where he had been preaching there were many different voices. Some of them were in opposition to him and here Paul sets us an example. He was not disturbed by this opposition. Actually, he could see with joy that this actually publicized the message, the very people who talked against the Gospel had to tell the Gospel while talking against it.

So the Gospel spreads even in our situation today. We have a story to tell to the nations, and we want to tell people far and wide that Christ receives sinful men. On every side this truth is being indicated. Many people speak of the Lord Jesus Christ. We even speak of Him in the way we date our events. When we say A.D. 1972, we mean "the year of our Lord." Even in the days of the week we observe Sunday as the Lord's Day, the Sabbath. Despite the fact that there are different opinions as to which day should be taken as the Sabbath, the Lord's Day, we all agree one day in seven is to be given over to God. In every town there are churches and cathedrals. Why? Because of Christ. There are often chapels. Why? Because of Christ. We have meeting houses that do not call themselves by any name but they are where the people meet to worship. There are ministers of the Gospel. Some wear robes and others do not. The public sees all this, and knows that those men are ministers of the Gospel. There are pastors of churches, and there are evangelists who come and go with the Gospel, and there are missionaries going far and wide with the Gospel. There are service centers. We have downtown missions — rescue missions. We have hospitals to care for the sick. There are orphanages to take care of orphan children and children from broken homes. There are sanatariums to take care of the sick. There are rescue homes to take care of those who are outcasts, the unwed mothers and people of that nature. All these various institutions operate in the name of Jesus of Nazareth, in the name of Christ. The Red Cross is known all over the world and it got its idea from the cross of Calvary. There is also the Community Chest, with the local community seeking to help the poor being carried on by the inspiration that comes out of the churches.

We could further think about the holidays we have. We have the Easter holiday: everyone knows that is the time of the resurrection. The lilies that you see, the anthems that we sing, and the praise we give, are all in celebration of Easter time. Thanksgiving time, thanking God for blessing, is a national affair. Christmas time, with its carols and all the singing that is done about the Babe of Bethlehem, speaks of the reality of Christ Jesus. Whether or not it is ever adequate or satisfactory, and even though sometimes we can regret what is being done, in it all Christ is being preached. In all these different ways His name is being kept before the minds of the people.

Then we can think of the various denominations. There

are probably about three hundred denominations in our country. Some people feel this is bad. If there were just one, the situation would be vastly different. With those three hundred different voices being raised as they are attention is drawn by the very fact that they differ with each other. It is like the leaves on a tree. Do you think it would be better if the great oak tree would have one big oak leaf and that would be the foliage of the tree? Would that really be an improvement? As a matter of fact, every tree has many leaves. In the case of the oak tree they are all alike, every one of them has an "oakness" about it. They are similar to each other, but there are many of them, even as there are many branches. By the way, where do you look for fruit? Fruit grows on the new branches. It is the small little branches, the twigs, that have fruit on them.

In addition to the denominations, we have recently heard about Campus Crusade. We also know of Inter-Varsity, Young Life, Navigators and Faith at Work. There are many different special projects, of which I have named only a few. Some of them are local, some of them are statewide, some of them are regional, some of them are national, and some of them are international. Take for instance, the marvelous testimony of the Gideons all around the world. In all this variety the Gospel is widely presented to all men.

There are also evangelistic meetings, from the Billy Graham meetings on through the many different varieties that are large and small all around the country. They too present the truth that there is one way to God, and that is through the Lord Jesus Christ. There are retreats, spiritual life retreats, Gospel retreats and rallies. The name of Christ Jesus is being lifted up on all sides. I realize that often the naming of His name may not be sincere. I am sure that many times it is not adequate. We could all pray that the Lord may forgive us as we think about that. We may not even be adequate ourselves when we are writing about this, but I will tell you one thing: the name of Christ is being talked about, and ideas are being spread around and talked over, so that even the people who differ have to argue about it. When they go to the Scriptures to find grounds for their argument, the things of Christ are being noted.

Also we have independent efforts of all kinds with independent churches. We have independent missions. We have special crusades going on all over the world. Can we say with the Apostle Paul, "What then? notwithstanding, every way, whether in pretence, or in truth (adequately or inadequately), Christ is preached; and I therein do rejoice, yea, and will rejoice"? Always His great name is being lifted up; that name which is above every name! We rejoice to remember that at the name of Jesus every knee shall bow and every tongue shall confess that He is Christ, to the glory of God the Father.

## Chapter 11

## TURN TO THY SALVATION

### (Philippians 1:19)

*Do you realize that blessing in the life of any believer is dependent on the prayers of others and on the Holy Spirit of God?*

For I know that this shall turn to my salvation through your prayer, and the supply of the Spirit of Jesus Christ (1:19).

It is such an easy thing in trying to understand Christian living to develop misleading ideas about the promises of God. There is a reason for that. It is easy to forget that many of the promises in the Bible are spoken directly to believers. It is such a common public practice to assume that one can take anything in the Bible and offer it to anyone. In our generosity we are glad to share the Gospel with everyone. We wish all men were right with God, and so we are inclined to offer the promises of God to all men without having the authority to do so. I cannot promise blessing to a man who is walking away from God. There is no blessing for him. If I were honest, I would tell him he is headed for destruction. It is such an easy thing to emphasize "being saved by faith"; that has such a good ring to it and it sounds so fine when I say it. I like to affirm "It will not cost you anything; you can really have it." When I do this in such a broad, easy way, I omit the aspect of obedience. Believing in God involves obedience. "Abraham believed God, and it was accounted to him for righteousness," I know. But how did he believe God? He believed God when he obeyed God and went out from where he was into a land where he had never been. He went out not knowing where he went. Abraham believed God when he took his son and offered him up as a sacrifice to God. He believed God and acted on

47

that basis. Because he acted, his faith was fulfilled. So when we say that we are saved by faith, we mean faith that is exercised in obeying God.

The same is true as we speak of being forgiven. Some will say it is such a hard thing to forgive other people, and such a hard thing to forgive oneself. And they reason this is one reason why the sinner cannot believe the forgiveness of God. But being forgiven of God is a simple procedure. It means that your sins will not be brought up against you. God will remove them as far as the east is from the west, and will remember them no more against you forever. That kind of forgiveness is given to people who repent. It is simply not true that a person can be forgiven of God while he is cherishing his sins. How foolish can a person be? Just as I would not blame the blind man for stumbling, so it is understandable that the sinner would grasp at any straw in the dark. However, we who know the truth should tell him. The truth is, whoever confesses his sin is the one who will be forgiven. If any man hides them, if any man covers up his sins, he will not prosper, but the wrath of God will abide on him. Make no mistake about it as far as sin is concerned, the first thing I must do is repent, and I must confess my sinfulness to God. The person who will be forgiven is the humble and the contrite heart. Such a person will be forgiven! Praise the Lord! If he is humble, he will admit the truth. If he is contrite, he will in the presence of God be sorry that he has committed such sin. He will then repent in the presence of God and so he will be forgiven.

We talk about having communion with God and sometimes we sing about it. Sometimes one gets the impression that a sinner could walk down the street and saunter along with God any time he wished. Wait a minute! Who can walk with God? How can two walk together except they be agreed? The person who can walk with God is the person who has come out of the world, has separated from the world so that he can walk with God. We read:

> Be ye not unequally yoked together with unbelievers: for what fellowship hath righteousness with unrighteousness?

and what communion hath light with darkness? And what
concord hath Christ with Belial? or what part hath he that believeth with an infidel? And what agreement hath the temple
of God with idols? for ye are the temple of the living God;
as God hath said, I will dwell in them, and walk in them;
and I will be their God, and they shall be my people.
Wherefore come out from among them, and be ye separate,
saith the Lord, and touch not the unclean thing: and I will
receive you (2 Cor. 6:14-17).

Anyone willing to turn away from sin to the things of the
Lord will find that he can walk with God.

Now let us come back to the Apostle Paul, a consecrated
servant. This man Paul is writing to the Philippian believers
and telling them that he realizes that the blessing he needs
will come to him because, first, they are going to be praying,
and second, the Holy Spirit is going to be working. It never
occurred to Paul to think that he could earn it. Paul never
for one moment dreamed that he was so good that it was
going to come to him. No! It will come in response to faith,
his own faith, the faith of others and the grace of God.

Paul had just been talking about how he was glad that
Christ was being preached everywhere, as they were fellow-
shiping with Him. On the basis of that confidence, he is
convinced that this is going to turn to his salvation through
their prayer and a supply of the Spirit of Jesus Christ. Notice
those two things. In spite of all controversy, and in spite of
all the people who were opposing him, all the opposition, if
the other believers would pray, and the Holy Spirit would
work in him, Paul was going to have victory. Intercession
on the part of others and yielding to the Lord on the part of
himself, would actually be involved in victory. "For I know
that this shall turn to my salvation."

Paul's eternal destiny is not in focus here. He is not talking
about whether he is going to go to heaven or to hell. These
words convey a broader, more contemporary meaning of
the word "salvation." Right now, while he is here in this
world, the Lord is going to do things for him because other
people are praying for him and because the Holy Spirit is
working in him. For instance, Paul is in prison. What is he

facing? What could happen? Being in prison, not being able
to go on with his preaching, not knowing what the future
would have, could be discouraging to him. What would be
the victory? To be strong in the face of that discouragement.
That strength would come when other believers would pray
and the Holy Spirit would work in his heart.

As a matter of fact Paul, in prison, was in danger of being
condemned to death. He could be executed.

If a person knew that any day might be his last, what
would he need? He would need to be kept strong. How
could he be kept strong? By exercising his will power? No!
By gritting his teeth? No! By taking a good grip on things?
No! Then how could he be kept strong? Other believers
could pray for him and the Lord could work in him when he
is yielded to Him. For that matter Paul could be released.
If they should let him out, what would happen then? If
Paul was let out, he would preach. For that he needed to be
ready to preach. How would Paul be ready? Because he was
so good? No! Because he was so strong? No! Because he was
so smart? No! But because the other Christians were praying for him, and the Holy Spirit was working in him. The
desirable, favorable outcome would occur if intercession was
being made, and he was yielded to the indwelling Holy
Spirit of God. Paul did not count himself being personally
able to do these things, but he did have faith in the presence
of the Lord in his own soul and he had confidence in God's
power and willingness to answer prayer.

## Chapter 12

## CHRIST SHALL BE MAGNIFIED

(Philippians 1:20, 21)

*Do you know how a sincere believer in Christ would know personal victory in living?*

Each believer in Christ Jesus expects blessing. This is proper. God has promised to bless, and the believer knows it. Paul knew that he was engaged in a vast spiritual conflict between the forces of light and darkness. Christ on the one side with him, and Satan against him. The battlefield was in the souls of men. Paul was engaged in this great spiritual warfare. He knew that in this assignment he was to witness and to preach. His business was to tell men what God had done, is doing, and would do in and through Jesus Christ.

Paul faced a hard prospect. Things were not going easy for him. He had been persecuted, thrown into prison and was in danger of being put to death. This was his prospect, but he expected victory through Christ. The victory that the Apostle Paul expected would not be measured by human values. He did not expect wealth or a life of ease. The expectations of the Apostle Paul were spiritual and eternal.

We read:

> According to my earnest expectation and my hope, that in nothing I shall be ashamed, but that with all boldness, as always, so now also Christ shall be magnified in my body, whether it be by life, or by death. For to me to live is Christ, and to die is gain (1:20, 21).

You will remember he was in prison with the possibility of his being put to death. There were restrictions and he was under a guard. He was separated from his supporters. He was under the shadow of the fear of death. I am sure that Paul was not afraid to die but he would not have wanted his life to have ended that way. There were churches that needed his guidance, believers that needed his encouragement. All over the Mediterranean world where he had been there were people wishing they might see the Apostle Paul and wishing they might hear him again. Paul faced the frustration of being shut up in prison while these people were out there needing, hungering, thirsting for the very things that he had to give.

Paul had a hope, so he said "according to my earnest expectation and my hope." Paul's hope was that he would never be ashamed. When Paul writes "that in nothing I shall be ashamed," he means he hoped he would never be embarrassed because what he believed in did not work. He expected victory. He expected that he would never be disappointed in Christ. He was absolutely sure about one thing: Almighty God would be watching over him, and in the presence of God was the living Lord Jesus Christ praying for him. He hoped that the Lord would prove able to keep every confidence he had put in Him. This is similar to how he felt when he wrote to Timothy: "I am persuaded that he is able to keep that which I have committed unto him against that day" (2 Tim. 1:12). His hope was centered in Christ Jesus.

Paul also had an ambition. His ambition was to magnify Christ in his body. Paul had an ambition to use his body in such a way that it would magnify Christ, either in life or in death. How could he magnify Christ in life? He could minister the Gospel to others. He could take that body of his and go out and teach. People would beat him. They would throw stones at him. They would abuse him. But he would endure it and he would not fight back. He would let them do this, because he wanted to magnify Christ in his body. He would be preaching Christ. Then again, he would be meek. When people would mistreat him, he would not retaliate. Then he would be humble. He would actually count others better than he was. He would be quiet and humble and he would have patience. He would not allow himself to take offense when people said things to make him feel disturbed but he would have patience and he would expect answers to prayer.

In these expectations did you notice there was not a thing said about money or health. There was nothing about power. There was nothing that was to his personal advantage. All he wanted was that he might be found a faithful, willing, humble, meek servant of the Almighty God in Christ Jesus. If he lived, that was exactly what he was going to do. Thus his ambition was that he would magnify Christ that way in his body.

How could Paul magnify Him in death? Suppose death came, what could Paul do? Paul would have in mind that he would want to be able to pass out of this world with joy. He would want to be able to die in quiet triumph. The Apostle Paul would want to be able to walk out of this world with his shoulders back and his head up. Death could not hurt him. His persecutors could take his life, but they could not touch him. His hope was in God. His expectation was in eternity.

Paul wrote:

> Truly the signs of an apostle were wrought among you in all patience, in signs, and wonders, and mighty deeds
> (2 Cor. 12:12).

That is how he wanted to live, and in death he wanted a quiet triumph and a glorious release. Paul's ambition was that he might be walking forward into death with his face lifted up as if he were walking into the sunlight, as if he were walking into the dawn of eternal day. This would be possible in Paul because he would be strong in faith and so he could say:

> According to my earnest expectation and my hope, that in nothing I shall be ashamed, but that with all boldness, as always, so now also Christ shall be magnified in my body, whether it be by life, or by death. For to me to live is Christ, and to die is gain.

## Chapter 13

## IN A STRAIT BETWIXT TWO

### (Philippians 1:22-24)

*Can you see how a believer could tire of this old earth and long for heaven?*

As Paul wrote this letter from prison he was in danger of death. Even if he were to be released from prison, he would face controversy and strife which could ultimately end in death. He could see that dying now would bring him a glorious release into joy. As a pastor and minister of the gospel, I have seen people who were ready to die, who were not anxious to stay down here. As a mature Christian, Paul knew that in this world he would never have final victory. But Paul knew his place in heaven was sure. The Lord Jesus had spoken His Word:

> In my Father's house are many mansions: if it were not so, I would have told you. I go to prepare a place for you. And if I go and prepare a place for you, I will come again, and receive you unto myself; that where I am, there ye may be also (John 14: 2; 3).

Paul believed this word for word. He realized that living down here, when he could be up there, was actually playing a losing game.

The Apostle Paul was separated from everything as far as this world was concerned. His personal interests were all secure in glory. He had laid up his treasure in heaven and he yearned to go there; but he knew that while he was here, he was helping many by his testimony. This is true for the believer today. He may face life that daily has in it suffering and frustration. Some older people have shared with me their own experience, and admitted that the days down here were dreary. The long nights were weary. They have just

54

ached to go home, often wondering why they were left here. Sometimes it was possible for me to help some of these people by suggesting that while they were here they could be praying for their loved ones. While they were here, their sons could be remembering them. While they were here, their daughters could have in mind that they would be praying for them. This would be helping their own young people. So it was with Paul. Paul knew that as long as he was here in the flesh, there would be some believers who would be encouraged by his presence. This brought Paul into a dilemma, which he expressed in these words:

> But if I live in the flesh, this is the fruit of my labor: yet what I shall choose I wot not. (This old English word means "I don't know for sure." What am I to choose?) For I am in a strait betwixt two (I am right in a tight spot between two great, big, important things), having a desire to depart, and to be with Christ; which is far better: nevertheless to abide in the flesh is more needful for you (1:22-24).

This left Paul in a difficult situation. It seems almost as though he had some choice in the matter.

As a pastor I have been at the bedside of persons who had this very feeling. I remember so well a certain woman who felt in her heart that staying here in this world was not going to get done what she wished. She yearned for a certain blessing to come upon her son. I remember how she asked me the question, "Do you think it is possible that if I were to be taken away the Lord would be able to get into the heart of my son?" Under the circumstances I had to say, "That is quite possible." She said, "Well, I was thinking so." Within a matter of a few months, on Christmas Eve, we were at prayer meeting at the church when word came over the telephone during the prayer meeting that I should come immediately to her home. Several doctors were there and they said that she did not have long to live. When I arrived, she was dying. She had asked me very earnestly to promise to pray for her son. I had hesitated to assume this task, but I was her pastor. So in good conscience I had said, "Yes, I will do that." Now she reached out one hand and took mine.

She drew me over close to her, and whispered, "Will you remember?" I said, "Yes." I knew she meant, "Will you remember to pray?" When I said "Yes," she pushed me away. She had never opened her eyes, and she passed away within the hour. The blessing that she had asked for came immediately. Her son was blessed from the day of her death. The very thing she would have given her heart to see happened. He was blessed with the grace of God for the rest of his life. Actually he did not live much longer. But when I think back on that incident, I have to think about that stout, staunch believer in God. She had dealt with God about her son. She put the matter into God's hands and trusted in Him, and He granted her the desire of her heart.

If there should be anyone reading these words who is wondering why you are here suffering, or in trouble, when you cannot do the things you were once able to do, while you are here look up and pray. Pray for your loved ones. Pray for your preacher. Pray for the Gospel. Pray for the missionaries. While you are here, pray for a larger share in His work.

When you look at what Paul was facing, you can understand his dilemma. If he had gone to be with the Lord, he would have had a glorious release. But if he stayed here, he would be helpful to other people. It was when Paul realized this that he felt he would be staying here for the sake of others. Could we take this man, Paul, as an example for ourselves? I will ask you, Why not, if we are ready to meet the conditions? Paul had all his hopes in Christ. We could be like that. We could quietly get to the place where we want above everything else that Christ Jesus should be magnified in our bodies and we could have a sure conviction about heaven.

I remember so well a young girl in my congregation. She was dying at the time. She lingered some months but she knew that she would never get well. I remember a very earnest conversation I had with her when she smilingly looked into my face and said, "Well, pastor, there are lots worse things than dying." I have never forgotten that from that day to this. When I preached her funeral services a few days later in a crowded church, I used as my text, "If you loved me, you would rejoice when I said, I go to be with my Father." Such assurance is possible. If you and I were to come to the place where we would have no more confidence in the flesh, with no more big ideas about what we are going to do and accomplish, and so with no interest in this passing show down here we could have this frame of mind. I have seen believers facing death with an expectation of joy to be present with Him.

Sometime ago it was my privilege to visit a friend in the hospital who was facing a very serious operation. It was said he had a sixty percent chance of survival, a forty percent chance he would not get through. My heart quaked within me as I wondered what to say. When I got to his room I was delighted to find that he was strong in spirit and smiling. He shook hands with me and talked with me about his coming operation. "You know, doctor, this could be serious." I said, "Yes, I know." He said, "You know, they say I have three chances in five to get through, two in five I won't get through," and then with a wonderful smile he looked into my face from his bed and said, "You know, doctor, I can't lose. I just can't lose." I didn't really know what he meant. Then he said, "If it should happen that I am among the forty percent so that I am one of those who is not coming through (lifting up with his hand toward heaven), you know I have a ticket straight home." My heart rejoiced. He went on to say in triumph: "If I stay here, I am going to buy some more of your tapes and listen to them." I reminded myself I was not seeing the Apostle Paul in prison at Philippi. I was seeing a meat salesman in Miami, Florida, who had found out the wonderful truth of the Lord Jesus Christ. Any believer anywhere can put his trust and his confidence in Christ in life and in death. I will never forget that man with the look of joy on his face when he looked into my eyes and said, "If I should be among those that don't come through, I have a ticket straight home." And he had! And you and I can have this.

*Chapter 14*

## TO ABIDE IN THE FLESH

(Philippians 1:24, 25)


*Do you realize that a person might be left in this world longer than he wants to stay because of what he can do for someone else?*

Normally, a person would want to live as long as possible. I think that is natural and healthy. Occasionally, there can be situations in which someone would like to die. They might say that they would like to go home. This is sometimes true with the older Christian who has nothing to fear about going, and only a lot to dread about staying. A person can be just so old and feel so increasingly helpless and weak that staying here becomes a burden. There may also be those who are ill, with no prospect of recovery. One's heart goes out to those people. Sometimes this feeling may be caused by trouble. A person can be in so much trouble that he honestly, sincerely wishes to God that he was dead.

Paul understood all this very well, for while in prison writing to the Philippians, he wrote of having a desire to depart and be with Christ, which is far better. This did not mean necessarily that he was morbid or weak. A person, even a good person, can get downright tired. There is no doubt Paul was tired in his situation.

This is how I understand the famous incident in the Old Testament of Elijah, the prophet, under the juniper tree, when he said, "Lord, take my life." I do not think Elijah was necessarily scared or morbid. I think personally Elijah was tired of the whole business. He had been through the most strenuous experience on Mt. Carmel facing those 850 prophets of Baal. The king and all the people were against him. He called upon Almighty God, and God answered him with fire from heaven. Now it was all done. The victory was

58

won. The issue had been resolved. The people had been persuaded and Elijah was ready to go home, especially since, as you will remember, Jezebel was after him to kill him and he was running away.

Here is an interesting angle, Elijah was running away from Jezebel so she would not kill him, but he asked God to take his life. He did not want to let it be known that this woman who was an idol worshiper could destroy a prophet of God, so he would rather have God take him. "Lord, take my life." The response of the Lord to Elijah's prayer could be put in language something like this: "I have several more errands I want you to run. I want you to go and anoint a certain king to be king of Israel, and I want you to anoint a certain man to be king of Syria, and I want you to tell Elisha to take your place." Elisha responded and began to follow him, and he went to the palace and anointed one to be king of Syria and anointed another to be king of Israel. Then the record tells the story! God took him home in a chariot. That is not the way you would treat a man who lacks faith or is disobedient.

There is nothing wrong when some grandmother who has reared her family so they are grown and busy, and all her friends have been called home, has the feeling deep down in her heart, "I'd be happy to be gone." But note what Paul writes:

> Nevertheless to abide in the flesh is more needful for you. And having this confidence, I know that I shall abide and continue with you all for your furtherance and joy of faith (1:24; 25).

No one lives to himself alone. My reason for living is others. That is why God has me here. It is tragic how many live only for themselves. My reason for living as a member of Christ is other people. If I am a husband, it may be my wife. If I am a father, it may be my children. If I am a citizen, it may be my neighbor. In anything I am doing, my reason for living and acting in this world is other people.

When I was pastor, I had a member in my church who was well past eighty years of age. I remember visiting her one time, when she asked earnestly, "Pastor, why am I here? I want to go home. All of my loved ones are over there. I believe in God and I believe in heaven and it would be better than this. I am just a burden to people." She lived with her son where she had a room in his house. She had a daughter-in-law and grandchildren. I asked: "Do you care about your son?" She answered immediately, "Of course I do. I love him." "Do you care about your son's soul?" "Yes, I do." "Who loves your son as you do?" She didn't know that she could name anyone. "You have a daughter-in-law, do you care about her?" "Why, yes." "Does she have any needs?" "Yes, she does." "And your grandchildren—who has as much time as you? Your son is standing in the need of prayer. Your daughter-in-law is standing in the need of prayer and you know the Lord helps." I was blessed to see that woman actually get a vision of serving in praying. I remember telling her: "You don't have to think that when you pray once, you are finished. You can pray again and again and again."

By the way, you and I can pray for people who belong to us. We need not pray only for those who are nice, for the good ones. Then who should we pray for? Our people. They are ours and God has us here for that very reason. We need to pray for others not just once a day, but again and again and again.

There are sins to be forgiven. As you think of those you love, you can pray to Almighty God, "Keep that boy. Keep him wherever he goes. Guard that girl. Guard her from danger. Strengthen that son of mine who is carrying a load. Give grace to that daughter-in-law to endure certain experiences she has, and give a new heart to that relative who doesn't even turn to God." Pray for them. And then thank the Lord for the blessing received. No one else is doing it. You can do it. Praise God for His goodness and mercy. If you are one of those people who feels that your day here in this world is done, lift up your eyes, look round about you. They are all right here. Who else will remember them? You can remember them. Paul realized that his staying here in this world was not because of himself but because of others.

## Chapter 15

## REJOICING MORE ABUNDANTLY

### (Philippians 1:26)

*Can you see how every work of faith, every answered prayer increases the joy of the believer?*

That your rejoicing may be more abundant in Jesus Christ for me by my coming to you again (1:26).

Philippians has been called the "Joy Epistle." Of all the letters written by the Apostle Paul in the New Testament this one has more to say about joy and rejoicing than any of the others. It is here we find the word "Rejoice in the Lord alway: and again I say, Rejoice." Have you ever considered what it means to rejoice? Suppose I repaint the house. This assumes the house has been painted or I could not repaint it. The same is true in order to rejoice, a person must first have joy. It is only when one has joy in the Lord that he can rejoy in the Lord, and we say "rejoice."

There are certain conditions that make joy possible. One of these is to find what has been lost. You will remember the famous parable of the Lost Sheep, how the shepherd went out to find his sheep and when he found it he put it on his shoulders and carried it home. Then he called his neighbors, "Rejoice with me; for I have found my sheep which was lost." Luke tells us that there is joy in the presence of the angels of God over one sinner who repents. The next parable in Luke 15 had to do with the woman and the lost coin. She swept the house diligently seeking for this coin until she found it. When she found it, she called in the neighbors, "Rejoice with me, for I have found the piece which I had lost." Luke goes on to say again, "Likewise . . . there is joy in the presence of the angels of God over one sinner that repenteth." The third parable is that of the

Prodigal Son. Remember the joy that the Father had when his son returned different than when he left. He was a changed man, so there is joy in the presence of the angels of God over one sinner who repents.

You can have joy when you think of being redeemed from bondage. It is the joy that a prisoner has when he is released from prison. Or you can have joy when you have something restored. For example, if you were blind and your sight was restored, you would rejoice. Another condition that makes for joy is harvest time, the joy of the harvest. It is the joy the farmer has when he reaps the wheat; the joy the gardener has when he reaps the vegetables, the beans in the garden or the apples in the orchard. This gives joy. Then again there is such a thing as having joy when you are in good health, when you feel well with no aches and pains. That will give you a sense of joy. Another occasion that calls for joy is fellowship. When you are with your friends you have a time of joy and of gladness.

These conditions which make joy possible are all implied in receiving the Lord Jesus Christ as your Savior and committing yourself to Him. Abounding joy resounds to the praise and glory of God. When the heart is filled with joy and gladness, the lips express praise and thanksgiving to God, the name of God and of the Lord Jesus Christ is exalted, is lifted up, and this is always something that is pleasing to God who would like to see the name of His Son raised up above every name. Abounding joy in the heart and soul resounds to the praise and glory of God. To have Paul rejoin these Philippians after he had been in prison would be an occasion of rejoicing. As you know, this whole letter was written by Paul when he was in prison. He told them if they would continue to pray for him, he believed that it would work out that God would restore Paul to them and this would be an occasion of much rejoicing.

In 1:26 we read these words: "That your rejoicing may be more abundant in Jesus Christ for me by my coming to you again." He had been in prison, his life had been in danger, he might have been killed and now Paul says that if it should be the will of God, in the providence of God, that he should be released and returned to them, their rejoicing would be more abundant.

The natural person is inclined to find joy in the things that he possesses. If he has many things he wants to rejoice. If he has more he wants to rejoice more. Many people would feel that if they were just rich, and they had things, therein they really could have joy. Do you recognize the weakness in that? Can you see the weakness there is in putting your joy, having your joy, in riches? Riches can be lost. The Lord Jesus said a man's life consists not in the abundance of the things he possesses. Then again sometimes people find joy in prestige, in fame. Their names are mentioned, their pictures are in the paper and people are making a big fuss over them. That is a dangerous business. Fame is fleeting. Fame is a hard taskmaster.

Some people have joy in their power. They like to win. There are people who have their joy seeing a ball game. The trouble about winning any game is that the other fellow or team has to lose. The person who gets ahead of others you may think has something to joy about. What about all the others who are behind? It is a poor business to get your sense of joy because you are ahead of other people. There are those who seek joy in their appearance. Others seek joy in owning trinkets: clothing, homes, cars or jewelry. You would be surprised how many people seek pleasure and joy in the way in which they appear, what an impression they can make on other people. You and I know a person can lose things.

One is reminded of the occasion when Mary and Martha were before the Lord and Martha was complaining because Mary was taking time to listen to the Lord. Martha was worried about the house and about getting things done. She complained to the Lord about it. You remember the Lord Jesus said this: "Martha, Martha, thou art careful and troubled about many things . . . Mary hath chosen that good part, which shall not be taken away from her."

This is the way it is with the believer. If you have your

joy in the Lord, you will never lose it. You will find by looking into His face that peace and quietness will come into your soul. You will rejoice in the things of Christ Jesus and you will never lose them. They will always be with you in life and in death and on into eternity. You will never lose out when you put your hope and trust in the Lord Jesus Christ.

## Chapter 16

## YOUR CONVERSATION

### (Philippians 1:27)

*Did you know that the one characteristic recognized as being truly Christian is mutual love and esteem?*

> By this shall all men know that ye are my disciples, if ye have love one to another (John 13:35).

Why is it so significant that these Christians should love one another? It is not natural. Men naturally care for themselves. You will find men justifying themselves, alibiing as long as they are seeking that which is to their own benefit.

This is so different from becoming a believer: "If any man will follow after me, let him deny himself, and take up his cross, and follow me." Thus the first prerequisite of becoming a believer is to deny self. It is true, all over the world, that the first law of nature is self-preservation. For many, it is "me and mine and let the devil take the hindmost." But the Scripture says, "If any man will follow after me, let him (first) deny himself." That is the number one step — to deny my ego and then when I have denied myself, I can accept Christ in my heart. The whole business of becoming a believer is to yield myself into the hands of God and to be born again. The new creature in me wants to be well-pleasing in the sight of God. I will receive the Lord Jesus Christ into my heart not only as Savior but also as Lord.

In this letter to the Philippians Paul is concerned about their morale. He is concerned about how they feel. He wants them to be strong in their faith, willing in their spirit, ready in their frame of mind for commitment to the Lord. Paul wants their rejoicing to be more abundant in Christ Jesus. He wants them to be strong in the Lord and now he goes on to say in verse 27 that this will depend upon their manner

65

of life. Notice how he uses the word "conversation." In the original language it means "manner of life." So Paul writes:

> Only let your conversation be as it becometh the gospel of Christ: that whether I come and see you, or else be absent, I may hear of your affairs, that ye stand fast in one spirit, with one mind striving together for the faith of the gospel (1:27).

If a believer wants inwardly to be strong in his spirit and ready to serve God, he must have an attitude toward all other believers in which he shares with them that he stands fast in one spirit with them, with one mind striving together for the faith of the Gospel. This would be the appropriate thing as it becometh the Gospel of Christ, and why? Because anyone in this frame of mind is no longer interested in self. Thinking of oneself is just as natural as breathing. Thinking of oneself is as natural as taking a drink of water if you are thirsty. It is not natural to deny yourself and think of someone else, but it is spiritual.

The believer does not earn any merit by such conduct. He turns his heart over to the Lord. He looks up into His face and God tells him that He gave His Son to die for him. The believer then looks up at the Lord Jesus Christ and in his own heart and mind he decides, he chooses. He yields himself over to God. From now on, he belongs to Christ Jesus, and his action is Christ's idea and not his. He is not running his own affairs. The Lord is running them in him. The believing person is no longer committed to himself. He is no longer in bondage to himself. Self is crucified, he joins Jesus on Calvary's cross. Christ will join him in the resurrection. Just as surely as he dies with Christ, the Lord will raise him from the dead. Now yielded to God, God will send His Holy Spirit into his heart, and the Holy Spirit of God will take the things of Christ and show them to him. The Holy Spirit of God in the heart of the believer mediates the mind of Christ in each one of the believers. "Let this mind be in you, which was also in Christ Jesus." It is the operation of the Holy Spirit of God to take the things of Christ and make them active and real inside the believer and in that way he can actually "stand fast in one spirit," which will be the Holy Spirit. "With one mind," which will be the mind of Christ, believers will be striving together for the faith of the Gospel.

Hold out your right hand in front of you. Look at it. Wiggle your fingers. Let them move around. What do you actually see? You see five fingers but one hand. Each finger in a different place, but one hand. Each finger moves differently. They are not all the same length and they do not all have the same strength. They do not all work from the same angle but they work together. Have you ever hurt a finger? It seems to be in the way of all the others. It will be sore, stiff and lacking in coordination. To be able to do things normally with the hand, those five fingers must work together, as when each of them is healthy and well, and responding to the mind of the man. So it is with Christians. Paul would say, "Let me hear from you people that you are all working together with one spirit and with one mind, striving together for the faith of the Gospel. Then I will know that you are actually believing in Christ." What Paul has in mind is that then they will be strong and so will be able to withstand things that happen to them because of their testimony.

## Chapter 17

## IN NOTHING BE TERRIFIED

### (Philippians 1:28)

*Can you see how firm convictions of a believer would make him seem hopeless in the eyes of the world?*

The world may admit that the believer in Christ may disagree with the world but it cannot accept the idea that the believer may be right. They are willing to give him the liberty of his own opinion, but privately they want it understood that he is wrong. The assurance of a believer is based upon the fact that he believes Jesus Christ is God, and he has the promise of Jesus Christ that He will save him. This is an annoyance to the world.

I can remember years ago when I was just a young believer, that in my home community I had occasion to tell people what it meant to me to be a believer. Sometimes, one of the neighbors would ask, "Well, Manford, what do you think it means, now that you have become a Christian?" I would answer, "For one thing I am going to go to heaven." Then they would say, "You mean to say you are sure you are going to heaven?" "Yes." "You must think you are pretty good." "Oh, no. I am not good but Christ Jesus is good." "Well, if you think you are going to heaven, how can you be so sure?" "He said so." I was never sure they liked to hear me say that. The assurance of the believer is an annoyance to the world.

The world may feel that believers are critical of others, because they say there is only one way to be saved: there is only one way that is right, and that is the truth. So they say, "You say there is only one way to come to God." I say, "Yes, just one way. 'I am the way, the truth, and the life: no man cometh to the Father, but by me.'" It is not a matter of my being critical of other people. I am simply telling them how it is. There is no other way: that is the only way there is: "No man cometh to the Father but by me."

I remember some years ago when I was preaching, I was seeking to outline the Gospel. I was telling people, frankly, on that particular day, "You must be born again." One reason why I like to preach about that is that anyone can have it. Anyone in the world can have it. Whosoever will may come, and whosoever comes He will "in no wise cast out." But it is absolutely true that while it is wonderful to say, "Whosoever will may come," it is just as true to say, "Whosoever won't, don't." That is all there is to it. There is a bluntness about that that people dislike.

That afternoon my phone rang in my hotel room and I was told there was a special delivery letter at the desk for me. It was a local letter. As it happened the writer did not sign his name. The letter was annonymous, but it was a vicious letter. "You are unbearable, you are crude. You condemn everyone but yourself. You think that you are all right and everyone else is all wrong." The writer poured it on. Why? Because I had claimed that no one can come to God but the person who is born again. What could I say? I had told exactly the truth. "Whosoever will may come, and whosoever won't, don't." That is all there is to it. Just as surely as Christ Jesus is the way to heaven, it is just that sure that the person who does not go by the way of Jesus Christ will not get there. There is no other way but this. It is the way of the cross that leads home. The Christian simply bears witness and testimony. "Whosoever believes in him shall not perish, but have everlasting life." "He that believeth not is condemned already."

Paul spoke about this to these Philippians:

> together . . . that ye stand fast in one spirit, with one mind striving for the faith of the gospel; and in nothing terrified by your adversaries: which is to them an evident token of perdition, but to you of salvation, and that of God (1:27, 28).

This is exactly what the truth means. The believer actually belongs to God, and such assurance is a gift from God, even as it is the ground of his salvation. Just as surely as he is confident about Christ, just so surely he really and truly belongs to Him. As certainly as the believer trusts in Christ, just so certainly he will have joy and peace in his soul; and this is what Paul wanted the Philippian believers to have.

Paul writes:

> Only let your conversation (your manner of life) be as it becometh the gospel of Christ (act like a Christian): that whether I come and see you, or else be absent, I may hear of your affairs, that ye stand fast in one spirit, with one mind striving together for the faith of the gospel (1:27).

This involves no overt action or conduct on their part. Paul was referring to their personal testimony, their personal witnessing for God. What do they have to say about God? What do they have to say about the Lord Jesus Christ? Do they believe Christ Jesus died for them? Do they believe that their souls will be saved through Him? Do they believe that He is carrying away their sins? Do they believe that they are actually reconciled to God by Jesus Christ? That is their testimony. That is their message. That is what they are going to tell the world and they are going to hold to this: "in nothing terrified by your adversaries." "Whosoever believes in him shall not perish, but have everlasting life."

# Chapter 18

## THE SAME CONFLICT

### (Philippians 1:29, 30)

*Do you realize that if a person accepts Jesus Christ as Savior and Lord and is a real Christian, it will be impossible for him to escape suffering?*

> For unto you it is given in the behalf of Christ, not only to believe on him, but also to suffer for his sake; having the same conflict which ye saw in me, and now hear to be in me (1:29, 30).

Jesus of Nazareth lived a perfect life. He obeyed His Father always, and He suffered. He told us simply that the servant is not greater than the master. If the Lord Jesus Himself suffered, certainly any one following Him would suffer. Peter warned believers to expect suffering.

> Beloved, think it not strange concerning the fiery trial which is to try you, as though some strange thing happened unto you: but rejoice, inasmuch as ye are partakers of Christ's sufferings; that, when his glory shall be revealed, ye may be glad also with exceeding joy. If ye be reproached for the name of Christ, happy are ye; for the spirit of glory and of God resteth upon you: on their part he is evil spoken of, but on your part he is glorified. But let none of you suffer as a murderer, or as a thief, or as an evil-doer, or as a busybody in other men's matters (1 Pet. 4:12-15).

If any man hates his brother he is a murderer. You and I have a simple way of understanding these words of Peter. Just keep our nose out of other people's business. If we do stick it in and get it bumped, don't say we are suffering for God's sake: we aren't.

> Yet if any man suffer as a Christian, let him not be ashamed; but let him glorify God on this behalf. For the time is come that judgment must begin at the house of God: and if it first begin at us, what shall the end be of them that obey

71

not the gospel of God? And if the righteous scarcely be
saved, where shall the ungodly and the sinner appear?
Wherefore let them that suffer according to the will of God
commit the keeping of their souls to him in well-doing, as
unto a faithful Creator (1 Pet. 4:16-19).

If you should be conscious of personal suffering, of being
burdened, being depressed, you could always help yourself
by reading I Peter because Peter wrote his first epistle to
believing people to help them in the matter of suffering.

"The Son of Man is come to seek and to save that which
was lost" is true, wonderfully true, but that does not mean
there will be no suffering for those who believe. Paul knew
that these young believers in Philippi faced suffering. This
could come to them as a shock. So he tells them plainly:
faith is a privilege, and suffering is unavoidable. The way
of the cross leads home, and we are called to have "the
fellowship of his sufferings."

"Unto you it is given . . . to believe on him." Do you
realize that when you believe in Christ, you are saying all
things are from God? Be thankful to God. Inasmuch as all
things are from God, you practice stewardship about possessions and money as these things are not really your own.

God is over all, therefore prayer is timely. Paul writes, "I
will therefore that all men pray everywhere." Obedience is
proper because I believe in Him, and God is over all. I owe
Him obedience. Worship is involved because He should be
looked upon with worship and be praised. When I say I
believe in Christ, it is given to me to believe in Him. Because Christ is all in all, I will remember:

I am crucified with Christ: nevertheless I live; yet not I, but
Christ liveth in me: and the life which I now live in the
flesh I live by the faith of the Son of God, who loved me,
and gave himself for me (Gal. 2:20).

It is given to me also to suffer for His sake. Because I
believe in Him and name His name I will with Him experience rejection. He came to His own and His own did
not receive Him. I only need to put my hand in the hand of
the Lord and start walking with Him to find rejection. The

Lord Jesus could say "He that eateth bread with me hath lifted up his heel against me." On the occasion of the Last Supper he said to His disciples, "My soul is exceeding sorrowful unto death." He was suffering a deep grief. "One of you shall betray me." If I have some close friends who agree with me about the Lord, I should thank the Lord for them. If this should be the case with a husband and wife, that would be wonderful.

Then again, I will have in my suffering the experience of being forsaken. The Apostle Paul had that. He told Timothy "At my first answer no man stood with me, but all men forsook me . . . Notwithstanding the Lord stood with me, and strengthened me." And again we read, "And a man's foes shall be they of his own household." I will not only have these things happen to me, but I will suffer persecution, criticism, abuse, slander: people will say things that are not true. Destitute, despised, forsaken will be the experience of many persons because of their belief in Him.

When I hear the Gospel distorted, or error preached as truth, when I am grieved to think that the name of the Lord is not being honored, this is suffering for His sake. Sometimes I could be human enough to lean back and wonder "Why doesn't God end this whole business? Why doesn't He take away all this suffering?" I can almost sympathize with James and John who asked the Lord, "Lord, wilt thou that we command fire to come down from heaven, and consume them?" Then I can hear the Lord gently saying to me, "You don't know what kind of spirit you are. The Son of Man came not to destroy but to save men's lives." And so my attitude when I am face to face with this unavoidable suffering will be to "let both grow together until the harvest." You and I will be in this world, and this world will have evil in it. But Almighty God will hear us when we pray that He will keep us from the evil and keep us for Himself.

## Chapter 19

## LIKE-MINDED

(Philippians 2:1, 2)

*Do you know of any good reason why a believer should deny himself?*

The moment you become a Christian you do not begin "to sprout wings" right then. Actually when you accept Jesus Christ as Savior and Lord, your human nature is the same. What happened to you was not human. It was of the Spirit.

If a man were drowning in a lake, and a boat came along and rescued him, he would be no stronger after he was in the boat than he was when he was in that lake. His state would be better. Whatever a man's natural desires were before he accepted Christ, he would still have those natural desires afterward. Every human being has his own ego, his own self, his own interests. Accepting Christ does not change that, but if any man be in Christ, he is a new creation. Old things are passed away. All things have become new. It is true that when a person accepts Christ, he is now accepted by God. The moment that man (who had been drowning) was pulled into that boat his experience was different; I know. And the person who accepts Christ is accepted by God, and is adopted into the family of God, so that it is true about him, "you are not your own, you have been bought with a price." Now, as a believer, that person becomes a child of God, is now one of the family of God, is now a member of the body of Christ and enters into a new relationship with other believers, "members one of another."

This new relationship should now be openly demonstrated. The new believer must openly show the unity of the body of Christ. He should get in with other Christians. This is one of the greatest benefits and blessings that there

74

is in the congregational life of the ordinary church. It is fellowship with other Christians. Have you ever gotten in step with anyone while walking down a street? The moment you get in step with that other person you cannot do as you please anymore. You must keep up the rhythm and take the length of step, the speed, the tempo, that the other person is taking, to stay together. The moment that you are going to work together with anyone, you are no longer on your own. The person who believes in Christ becomes one of a company of people. They will be all around you. Paul says that it is very important that you maintain a fellowship with the other believers about you.

I want to share with you again my favorite illustration of unity in diversity, that is, how a number of different people can work together. Look at your hand. It has five fingers, each one different. Each finger is set in a different place, has a different strength, moves in a different way, and yet together they make up the hand which is probably the most wonderful physical structure on earth. The flexibility and the way in which a hand can be used for so many different things is marvelous. The hand is made up of a great many bones, muscles and nerves, set together in a certain way that allows flexibility. The fingers can move in various ways but each one of them moves from where it is. It has to stay in its joint right where it is. I think this is a wonderful illustration of the church, of the Body of Christ. Each member is different from the other, and yet altogether are one in Christ.

But why would any one believer willingly want to deny himself his own personal liberty that he might join in to live with other people? Paul writes plainly about this:

> If there be therefore any consolation in Christ, if any comfort of love, if any fellowship of the Spirit, if any bowels and mercies, fulfil ye my joy, that ye be like-minded, having the same love, being of one accord, of one mind (2:1, 2).

If you have any feeling of rejoicing in what Christ Jesus has done for you, that He gave Himself for you, that He will not fail to give you all the things that you need; if there is any fellowship of the Spirit, in that you now belong to the whole company of believers and you are never alone, you should gladly yield yourself to the demands of the Gospel. In the days when the New Testament was written, the prevailing idea of human nature was that the emotions were centered in what we call the visceral organs, the organs of the trunk of the body, and here the word "bowels" is used. We would say "heart." "I feel it in my heart." If we love each other, we belong together. In other words, if there is anything at all that is like sympathy where people have the same joys and the same fears and the same purpose, if you get any benefit out of that at all, then you should do this thing. On the basis of the blessedness of being a believer, I find myself wanting to, and willing and ready to, do this thing. Yielding self into the will of God, results in being likeminded, and this would give Paul joy when we have the same love, and of one accord, and of one mind. This is the result of having Christ in you, the hope of glory.

# Chapter 20

## LET US EACH ESTEEM THE OTHER
### (Philippians 2:3, 4)

*Do you realize that if a person is going to live in like-minded fashion with others, he must esteem those others better than he thinks of himself?*

When any person lives with others in a group, it is natural to make a comparison. I cannot help but wonder how I rate with them. You can feel this among all the activities of men. If two cars are approaching an intersection, what do you suppose is in the mind of each driver? "Will I get there first?" If two boys start to cross a lawn, they may just start walking, but if one starts to run, the other will run. This is natural. It is just natural to fall into rivalry. If a girl is with a group of girls, she wants to look better than the others. She makes comparisons. It is natural to fall into competition with others near me.

I can remember when I was in the Canadian Army in the First World War. I belonged to a service unit that was attached to a cavalry unit. In the military units we had the cavalry, artillery, infantry, and the Service Corps. Could you understand that among those various units, and especially between the infantry and the cavalry, there was the strongest kind of rivalry? In fact, they even became bitter in their competition with each other. Everyone in the military is familiar with this keen competition between services and units. This is natural enough, but it is bad in a home between husband and wife, and among the children. Such rivalry actually hurts people. It hurts home life. In such matters we stand in our own light so often.

Paul gave guidance for believers because the very thing I am talking about can happen with them. Even in the matter of public prayer there will be persons who are proud

77

of their praying. In the matter of preaching there will be ministers who are proud of their preaching. There will be people proud of their teaching. There will be people who are proud of their personal giving, their stewardship. All of these will cause individuals to act toward other individuals in such a way as to arouse competition, envy, rivalry, even strife.

Paul writes: "Let nothing be done through strife or vainglory." These are straight forward instructions: don't do it.

> Let nothing be done through strife or vainglory; but in lowliness of mind let each esteem other better than themselves. Look not every man on his own things, but every man also on the things of others (2:3, 4).

This is profound wisdom, extremely important. "Let nothing be done through strife or vainglory." If you are going to work in the church, do it humbly. If you are going to promote the Gospel, do it humbly in lowliness of mind. Think of yourself as being at the bottom of the ladder. "Let each esteem other better than themselves." This is especially true with reference to fellow workers, but it can be just as true with reference to neighbors. How will it be possible for you personally, to esteem every other person better than you are? How can you do it? Let me offer you two ideas. Ask yourself this question when you think about any person: If I had been born where she was born; if I had had for my father the man she had for her father; if I had had for my mother the woman that she had for her mother; if I had been brought up in the home that she was brought up in; if I had gone to the schools where she went to school; if I had gone to the church where she went to church; or if I had spent my Sundays the way her family spent their Sundays; if I had had the kind of preaching to listen to that she has had to listen to all her lifetime, isn't it possible that I might not be as good as she is? I might not be as far along as she is.

Or think of this possibility. If that person had been born in my home; if he had been born the child of my mother or the child of my father; if he had grown up in the high school I went to; and if that person had met the preachers that I have met, isn't it possible that that person would have been way ahead of where I am? It is quite possible to "esteem others better than" yourself. This is not to say such persons are better, but only to say that you will think of them as if they were better.

"Look not every man on his own things." Not long ago I saw the title of a Sunday school class: "Me-Third." Did you ever think of that for the name of a Sunday school class? You know what that means? The Lord first, others second and me third. That is good. Believe me, if you want to be happy as a Christian, you must get along with your fellow Christians. The way to get along with them is to consider them better than you are.

## Chapter 21

## LET THIS MIND BE IN YOU

### (Philippians 2:5, 6)

*Can you understand that a believer does not make up his own mind as to how he will do in serving God?* He is to receive the mind of Christ by the grace of God in his heart.

So often a person will say, "I am going to do my best from now on." A minister may make the earnest plea that people should commit themselves to the Lord. Some will be concerned and moved to say, "I am going to do better from now on. From now on, I am going to do the right thing." There are many who will strive earnestly. Some will try to do it by going to church regularly. Some will do it by giving a certain amount to missions. Some will do it by praying under certain conditions. And some of these people may become very proud of themselves. They can be thinking: "I have always gone to prayer meeting, and I have always been there when they had the church doors open. I take part in the singing. I take part in the praying. I take part in reading the Bible." And some persons will feel that if they can add up a score like that they should have a pretty good rating with the Lord.

Then, of course, there will be others who try but who feel that they fail, and are filled with despair. "I just can't ever do anything right." As if blessing depended upon that! Basically, the whole matter of committing oneself to God and walking with God is a matter of self-denial. That is all it will take. If I will deny myself, take up my cross that I can die to myself, and follow Him, He will lead the way.

This was demonstrated by the Lord Jesus Christ Himself, who, when He came into this world did not come to do any big thing. When we encourage our young people to be ambitious, and give them some great task to perform, I often wonder how many of us stop to look at Jesus of Nazareth. This is the One about whom Almighty God said, "This is my beloved Son, in whom I am well pleased." He engaged in no program. He was involved in no set of scheduled activities. He led no army. He managed no business concern. He wrote no book. He built no wall. In all the things that are ordinarily counted as human achievements, Jesus of Nazareth in this world, in the flesh, is not reputed as having done any one of those things. Yet the Lord from heaven, Almighty God, could say, "This is my beloved Son, in whom I am well pleased."

Then what was so outstanding about Christ Jesus? In what way was He so acceptable to God? We read:

> Let this mind be in you, which was also in Christ Jesus: who, being in the form of God, thought it not robbery to be equal with God (2:5, 6).

The word "mind" refers to the total complex of ideas that is found in the consciousness.

Each of us is in favor of this and against that. We are with these people, and are against those people. We do this; we don't do that. We think this is right; we think that is wrong. We think this is good; we think that is bad. These patterns make up our thought. We have certain landmarks in our consciousness. We have a set of values, things we count right, things we count wrong. It is this which makes up our mind. Such "mind" is not peculiar to me as an individual, for I may share the mind of my family. I may share the mind of my community. I may share the mind of my church. I may share the mind of my nation. Some people even share the mind of their generation. It is the way I think.

Now to "Let this mind be in you, which was also in Christ Jesus" means to let the ideas which Christ Jesus held govern your thinking. For a moment, let us look at Him. The name "Jesus" refers to His earthly form, the flesh. As "Jesus of Nazareth," He was the Babe born in Bethlehem, He was the One who grew up in the house of Joseph and Mary. He was the One who began preaching and teaching in Galilee and in Jerusalem, who traveled about in those hills and valleys mingling with the people, teaching them the things of the Gospel. He was the One they took and crucified, and put in the grave. He was the One who rose from the dead. He was the One who ascended into heaven. He was the One who came down and fellowshiped with His disciples for forty days. This was Jesus of Nazareth. He is now the One who is in the presence of God, and He is coming again. "This same Jesus, which is taken up from you into heaven, shall so come in like manner as ye have seen him go into heaven" (Acts 1:11).

The word "Christ" is His title. It indicates "the chosen One of God." This is the One who was promised in the Old Testament. The Old Testament prophets talked about the fact that the day would come when a certain Servant from God would come to do the work of God. What was the work of God? Building bridges? Building houses? Accomplishing big things in a social way? In an economic way? In a political way? No! What did Christ come to do? To reconcile men to God, to bring the soul of a man to God, that God might be in Him. Christ Jesus came into this world to affect things that would be eternal in their significance.

As far as this world is concerned, the Son of man had nowhere to lay His head. "The foxes have holes, and the birds of the air have nests; but the Son of man hath not where to lay his head" (Matt. 8:20). He was anointed of God to do something. He was to seek and to save the lost. He came to give His life a ransom for many. He came to shed His blood that souls might be saved, that sins might be forgiven, that men might be delivered. He died and He rose again and He ascended into heaven. He is coming again. He is praying for us now. All this is Christ Jesus.

"Let this mind be in you, which was also in Christ Jesus." What mind? This is stated in verse 6. "Who, being in the form of God, thought it not robbery to be equal with God" is Paul's version of the virgin birth. When you read this sentence of Paul, you can see why the virgin birth had to be. It was absolutely necessary, because the Son of God lived before. He was existing before He came into this world. This is not true of any human being as such. No one would ever claim seriously that I lived before I came here. This is where I started. But the Son of God was with God. He was in the form of God. He was pre-existent before the world began, before God ever created the heavens or the earth. "In the beginning was the Word, and the Word was with God, and the Word was God" (John 1:1). In the seventeenth chapter of John our Lord Jesus said words like this in praying to His Father: "Glorify thou me with thine own self with the glory which I had with thee before the world was." I repeat, this is Paul's version, this is the way he would put it about the virgin birth of the Lord Jesus Christ. Jesus of Nazareth was not a child of Adam. He never was in Adam's loins. Jesus of Nazareth received from Mary a body in which He would live, but He came from God. He did not think it was robbery to be equal with God. The Greek words mean He did not think it was a thing to be grasped, or He did not thing it was a thing to be snatched, or He did not think it was a thing to be held on to, to be equal with God. That is why the word "robbery" is used.

So we would say that if you want the believer actually to get along with other people, to be with them in a way where he can share with them, you want him to esteem others better than himself. You want him actually to have an outlook that will be acceptable to others. You want him to let the mind be in him which was also in Christ, with that basic commitment of self-denial, so that he will not hang on to himself. He will be willing to pour himself out, and to give himself a ransom for many that others might be saved, and to deny himself. This would be the first step in walking with the Lord.

## Chapter 22

## EMPTIED HIMSELF

(Philippians 2:7)

*Have you ever realized that no man lowers himself when he humbles himself in the presence of others?*

Jesus of Nazareth is one of the world's best-known persons. Quite apart from whether or not you believe Him to be the Son of God or accept all the promises of the Gospel, His achievements are so profound and so unique that He is entitled in your estimation to a top place among all men who have ever lived. It is reported that Napoleon on the Island of Elba, where he spent his last days, said, "Thou hast conquered, thou pale Galilean." Napoleon always said that Jesus of Nazareth had no armies and took no political position, and yet had far more men obedient to Him than he himself, the Emperor of France and the ruler of Europe, ever had.

This is all the more remarkable because the way that Jesus lived and died to accomplish His work was so different from what people could expect. He came to redeem. He came to over-throw the powers of evil. He came to rule that He might activate the will of God. He accomplished all this by first emptying Himself.

> But made himself of no reputation, and took upon him the form of a servant, and was made in the likeness of men (2:7).

"Empty" can be translated simply "emptied himself": "He made himself of no reputation." He emptied Himself of His glory. He never resigned His position. He never abdicated His authority. He never gave over His place as the Son of God, but He gave up His public prestige as it were. He gave up His glory, humbling Himself. He gave up His privileges as being the One on the throne with His Father. He was no longer to be seen beside His Father, but He never gave up Himself as He was in the plan of God. It does not say that He made Himself of no knowledge, because Christ Jesus knew what was in the hearts of men. It does not say that He made Himself of no wisdom. He always had the wisdom of God. It does not say that He made Himself of no virtue. He always was the perfect person. And it does not say that He made Himself of no strength. He always was the Son of God and could exercise the power that God gave Him. He did not empty Himself of His purpose. It is not true that He made Himself of no purpose. He always had in mind what He was to do; but He made Himself "of no reputation." He took upon Himself the form of a servant.

All of this will come to your mind perhaps more clearly if you consider it as demonstrated in the thirteenth chapter of John's gospel. There you will read the well-known incident of the washing of the disciples' feet. You remember the Lord with the disciples was present at what we call the Last Supper. While they were at the table, you will remember what He did. He rose from His place, laid aside His garments, took a towel, which is what a servant would have, and girded Himself. He wrapped a towel around His waist, took a basin, and filled it with water. Then He began to wash His disciples' feet. This was not nearly so striking and unusual an experience as it would sound to us in this country today. In that country people went barefoot or wore sandals. The roads were hot and dusty. If you had a guest and you wished to show unusual courtesy to that guest, you would not have brought him a glass of cold lemonade or a glass of ice water the way we would do, but a servant would come with a basin and rinse, wash, and dry the guest's feet. That could be a very refreshing experience on a hot dusty day.

So Jesus of Nazareth began to wash the disciples' feet. This task was the task for the lowest of the servants. We would call it a menial task to put a towel around the waist to wash the disciples' feet. We can understand just how shocking that would be, how exceptional that would be, and we can feel it when we remember what Peter did. When He came to Peter, Peter drew himself up and said, "No, Lord. You will not wash my feet." The Lord Jesus said to him, "You may not know what I'm doing now, even though you will know. But if you do not let Me wash your feet, you can have no part with Me." When Peter heard that he said, "Well, then, not my feet only, but my hands and my head as well." Then the Lord told him, "Anyone who has been bathed, who has been down to the public bathhouse, will not need to do anything when he comes home but to rinse his feet, because that is the part that got dusty." So the Lord continued and washed the feet of each of the disciples.

When the Lord Jesus was finished He set aside the basin and towel, put on His garments, and took His place at the head of the table. Then He said: "Ye call me Master and Lord: and ye say well; for so I am. If I then, your Lord and Master, have washed your feet; ye also ought to wash one another's feet." "I have set you an example"; that was the reason He did it. He took upon Him the form of a servant, but He never was a servant. He always was the Son of God.

One time my father-in-law tried to help me to understand this. He suggested that sometime, late at night, I might be in the rotunda of a big bank. While in this open place, I might see a scrubwoman carrying a pail with a mop, going about her evening tasks. A door might open and a well-dressed man might come in, whom I might recognize as the president of the bank. He might step over to the scrubwoman, whom he knows, and talk with her. After some conversation with her, he might pick up the pail and the mop, and carry them down the hallway for the woman. My father-in-law said very soberly to me, "When you see him walking with that pail, don't make the mistake of thinking that he is the scrubwoman. He is the President of the bank. That is what makes his act so important." In that way he tried to help me understand that when Christ Jesus died for me, I should realize that was the Son of God who died for me.

It is true that Paul says, "He was made in the likeness of men," but that does not mean He was made a man. Do you remember in the Book of Genesis how Adam was created? Do you remember that Adam was created in the likeness of God? In the image of God? And you know very well that Adam was not God. He was created in the image of God, in the likeness of God, and so when the Son of man was made, fashioned, in the likeness of men, He was not a man. He was the Son of God.

## Chapter 23

## HUMBLED HIMSELF

(Philippians 2:8)

*Do you understand that no man belittles himself when he is willing to serve in a humble place?*

In all the affairs of men, it is abundantly demonstrated that one trait of the really great person is that he is willing to take the lower place.

I can remember when as a lad I first began to read of the history of the Greeks and the Romans. I remember being fascinated by the story of one Roman general who had led armies to victory. He was entitled to high esteem and honor, but his political enemies sent him to be a humble farmer. This great man went to that task with genuine sincerity, accepted it with dignity, and applied himself diligently. He went to work as if that were the only thing he was to do in the world. There came a time in the course of his lifetime when the whole nation was in danger of being destroyed. The people came to this man and called on him to take charge. He left the farm, left the plow, and took over the army. He led them through to victory. The name of Cincinnatus has long been revered in Roman history as the man who took the low place and did a good job there, while he was being prepared to take the higher place and do a wonderful work there.

It makes you think of the wonderful story of Joseph in the Bible. He was rejected by his brothers, sold as a slave, then falsely accused and made a prisoner. Then in prison he was forgotten. It appeared as though everything was against Joseph. Then in the providence of God he was released from prison to become the head man in the whole Egyptian empire. It is a great story. It has in it a great deal of truth, and it prepares us in heart and mind for the world's outstanding example, the Son of God, who came to seek and to save the lost. He came into this world and was made flesh. He was "despised and rejected by men, a man of sorrows and acquainted with grief." It is said about Him in the words of Isaiah that there was "no beauty that we should desire him." We esteemed Him rejected by God, "smitten of God, and afflicted." Paul writes of this:

> And being found in fashion as a man, he humbled himself, and became obedient unto death, even the death of the cross (2:8).

What makes this so meaningful to us is that here is the pattern that you and I will be called into.

If Christ is to walk in me, if it is to be "Christ in you the hope of glory," a change must take place in me. From the inside I will be moved to humble myself, to become obedient to death, which means to self-denial, "even the death of the cross" in which I actually deny myself. Now look at these words as they are written: "being found in fashion as a man." He deliberately chose this route. Perhaps this example will help. A man's car is in the ditch, stuck in the mud. A man who has a tow truck comes to help the car out of the ditch. The man who is driving the tow truck must get down into the mud, if he is to attach his chain to the axle of that car stuck in the mud. He will have to get down in the mud, and he will do this in order that he may get hold of the car to pull it out. Or think of the person who is going to rescue someone from drowning. This cannot be done without that person getting wet.

So the Lord Jesus Christ, coming into this world to save me, came down and took upon Himself the form of man, the form of a servant. He was "found in fashion as a man." It is true that He was "the Word of God."

> In the beginning was the Word, and the Word was with God, and the Word was God. The same was in the beginning with God. All things were made by him; and without him was not any thing made that was made (John 1:1-3).

That is all true, but "the Word became flesh." He humbled

Himself in that way. He laid aside His glory; He took upon Himself the form of man and was made in all points like as we are. He could become tired and weary as we do. He was made "in all points tempted like as we are, yet without sin."

Christ Jesus humbled Himself and became obedient to death, even the death of the cross. You and I might not be inclined to realize what that death on the cross would mean, because we have appreciated the cross of Calvary so much, we have praised it so much. We have sung words and phrases and songs of worship and praise about the cross: "In the Cross of Christ I glory, towering over the wrecks of time." We have been happy to sing: "The Old Rugged Cross, so despised by the world, has a wondrous attraction for me." We are inclined almost to miss the horror and the shame. We need to tell one another that death on the cross was the death of a criminal. That was the fate that was reserved for the worst criminals. Christ Jesus was obedient to the point of accepting a criminal's death for Himself.

There is another evidence of His being God, another proof of His deity. He did not need to die. He would never have had to die. The Bible tells of Enoch, a man who walked with God and was not because God took him. We can all remember that Enoch was a man who did not see death because he walked with God. Jesus of Nazareth walked with God. We may think of Elijah. That man was taken to heaven in a chariot. Was he any more righteous, was he any more a servant of God, was he any more faithful to God, than Jesus of Nazareth? No! Jesus of Nazareth was taken to the cross of Calvary. We may think of Moses. We remember Moses went up on Mount Nebo, and there God took him. "No man ever saw his grave." We do not know what happened to Moses. We read later how Satan contended with Michael the archangel over the body of Moses. In the case of the Son of God, He was put to death on the cross, His body was taken down from the cross and put into a grave.

We may remember how Peter wanted to defend Him. Peter drew his sword and attacked, as it were, the whole

Roman army, but the Lord Jesus stopped him, told him to put up his sword, saying, "Thinkest thou that I cannot now pray to my Father, and he shall presently give me more than twelve legions of angels?" I often think to myself that the American version of that very statement would be something like this: "Don't you know that if I wouldn't let them, they couldn't lay a hand on Me?" Then He asked Peter, "How then shall the Scriptures be fulfilled, that thus it must be?" How is the work of God ever going to be done if I do not die and be raised from the dead? He came to deliver us from death, so He Himself died, was put in the grave and was raised from the dead. He did this by humbling Himself to death.

Paul is reminding the believers at Philippi that it may be their lot, if they have the mind of Christ, that they may be humiliated. They should be willing to humble themselves and to depend on the grace of God. However, the will of God may include for them personal humiliation. This will occur when other people actually press them down and hurt them and reject them and abuse them, for the servant is not greater than his master. If they did such things to the Lord, they might do it to His servants. The Lord Jesus set the example when He humbled Himself, taking the lowest place. But no one can say that at any point in His earthly career He was anything else than the Son of God.

## Chapter 24

## HIGHLY EXALTED

### (Philippians 2:9)

*Can you understand that nothing is really established unless God does it?*

Perhaps nothing indicates the weakness of man as much as his careless ignoring of the reality of God. It is enough to scare you that a man can live in this world as if there were no God. How foolish can a man be? There are natural objects all about us, and we think we know the world. We think about the earth and all it contains. We think about plants and animals. We think about men. Then we stop. How limited we are! What about the Maker? What about the One who made all these things? As we think about the processes of nature about us, the growing of the plants, the flowering of the blooms, the ripening of the fruit, the gathering of harvest, and as we think about the mountains and the oceans and the stars, and think about their movements and how orderly they are, how they move strictly according to plan, we cannot help but be deeply impressed by the wisdom and the power of the Creator. How tragic that even learned men will omit this context within which they do their seeing and their perceiving.

I remember some years ago reading the arguments of a very famous debater, Thomas Huxley, who was speaking in support of the theory of evolution that has been popularly ascribed to Darwin. At the time in my life that I read his material, I was just beginning to be interested in spiritual things. I thought this man had the last word. But I found that as far as the whole universe is concerned he had no theory about its origin to present. His material was actually a very limited statement. Yet this man was considered very learned. The very existence of the universe proclaims the reality of God.

So many persons live and plan as if there were no God. I wonder if such people would feel badly if I say they are acting foolish? Even without the light of Scripture, anyone can open his eyes and look about him, and have some feeling of the reality of a Creator.

This can be in the background of our minds as we think further on what Paul wrote about Jesus of Nazareth. The Lord Jesus lived in this world well-pleasing to God. There is no indication that He aimed to please any human being. There is no indication that He formed His life and shaped His conduct, so that some human being would approve Him. He was living always in the presence of His own heavenly Father. He humbled Himself under the hand of His Father. He accepted this world as it is, as being created by God. He came and took our form and our nature, so that He became obedient even to death. During the time He was here in this world, He set us an example, a pattern, and it is worth thinking about. He made no effort to secure anything for Himself. Never once is there any account of His doing anything for Himself.

But God the Father, the One whom the Son of God served, the One whom He loved, the One whom He honored, saw what His Son had done, and He took a hand in the whole matter. Paul tells about this in these words:

> Wherefore God also hath highly exalted him, and given him
> a name which is above every name (2:9).

Anyone who knows the history of the world will agree that the name of Jesus Christ is great. Actually, even today we measure time by Him. Our whole recording of time is divided into B. C. (before Christ) and A. D. (the year of our Lord). This was not by any plan on His part. This was not the result of any goal He had set, and not the result of any achievement He had performed. All we know about the Lord Jesus Christ is that He did all things to be well pleasing to His Father. He looked up to His Father and we read about Him:

> For the joy that was set before him endured the cross,
> despising the shame, and is set down at the right hand of
> the throne of God (Heb. 12:2).

In understanding the truth about Jesus Christ, we should remember that it was Almighty God who raised Him up. He did not rise from the dead by Himself. He was not that strong in Himself, or so self-contained, that He died and at a certain time made up His mind that He would rise from the dead. No! When He died He was dead, after He had committed Himself into the hands of His Father. The record is plain:

> Father, into thy hands I commend my spirit: and having
> said thus, he gave up the ghost (Luke 23:46).

He yielded Himself into the hands of God and God the Father glorified Him.

It is true about Jesus of Nazareth that He emptied Himself and made Himself of no reputation. He came to give His life a ransom for many. One reason I have for stressing this is that if you are walking in the Lord, you should not be surprised if the situation you are in demands everything you have, everything you are. You will never have enough, nor be enough to meet all the demands. You will need to be yielded totally, holding nothing back. Remember, your Savior emptied Himself. And so, if you are suffering even now, with people taking advantage of you because you want to act worthy of being a believer, but it seems that everything you are doing doesn't amount to anything, do not mind that. This will be our purpose, to lay ourselves out in the service of the Lord. We are to be like streams of water in the desert. Consider an oasis in the desert, where there is a spring of water coming up out of the desert floor. Where does the water go? It does not collect in a cistern. It is not collected in any pond. It seeps out through the soil. It makes the earth fruitful. The water from the spring sinks into the thirsty land and it is lost. The plants grow. It is thus we should think of ourselves totally given over to the service of the Lord. By humbling ourselves, in yielding, we qualify for God's gracious help. He will raise us up and we can enjoy His grace throughout all eternity as those who have been redeemed and saved by the grace and the power of God.

## Chapter 25

# THE NAME OF JESUS

## (Philippians 2:10)

*Do you realize that every creature will be brought to see the Son of God in His incarnate form as Jesus of Nazareth, as the most important act of God?*

It is tragic that people blandly assume that the only things that really matter are their personal concerns. It seems that each person feels "If I do not think about God, He does not exist." Human beings have the tendency to be arrogant and blatant in their self-conceit. Each one seems to think "The world is just what I make it." The believer understands that he did not make the world, and cannot sustain it or control it. Actually, as far as he is concerned in this world, he does have one significant opportunity. He can choose within certain limits which way he will go and what he will do. What is more important, he can turn to God or he can turn away from God. Everyone knows that men do not drop dead when they turn away from God.

Christ Jesus is the Son of God made flesh. He is the One who was born of a virgin. He is God manifested in human form. He was not of human origin and not the result of human ideas. In a sense Christ Jesus is like the sun, which is not the result of human invention. It is not that scientists got together and decided they would have a sun, and voted to put one up there. It does not shine as directed by man. Men do have something to say as to what they will do with it. They can open the shades and let the sunshine in, or they can close up the room and keep the sunshine out. The sun is, and men cannot do anything about it. They did not do anything to get it started, nor can they do anything now to modify its course. All this is of God.

In this context the truth implied in the question "What

think ye of Christ?" can be seen clearly. A person can accept
Christ as his Savior as He offered in the Gospel. A person
can come to Jesus Christ, and believing in Him can be
saved. That is the testimony of Scripture and of all believing
people down through the ages. But a person can reject
Christ. Staggering? Yes! Tragic as it may be, actually shaking
as it may be, the truth is that a person can actually turn his
back on God. God has reached out His hand to that person
in the Gospel, but he can ignore it. Man cannot change one
item about Jesus Christ. Jesus Christ is the Son of God and
in Himself He is God. Nothing can change Him. But a person can turn away from Him. As far as a human being is
concerned, a person can accept Christ and be saved. And a
person can turn away from Him and remain lost. But no-
body can avoid Him. Every human being that ever heard
the Gospel has been brought face to face with Jesus Christ.
That person may accept. He may reject. He may worship.
He may despise. All this has been done. No one should be
surprised if it happens again. It has happened in every
generation of people on the face of the earth, but the Lord
has not changed. The cross of Calvary has not changed.

Paul implies all this in his letter to the Philippians:

> That at the name of Jesus every knee should bow, of things
> in heaven, and things in earth, and things under the earth
> (2:10).

"Every knee should bow." This is the startling truth. Each
person will confront Jesus Christ as He is. In the Gospel
each soul confronts the Son of God in all His power, in all
His glory. "Whosoever will" may come to Him, receive Him
as Jesus Christ on Calvary's cross dying for him, and so come
into the presence of God. "Whosoever will" may come, or
that person may turn his back on the Lord, and refuse to
accept Him. The truth is plainly stated in Scripture, that as
far as that person is concerned, he will die in his sins.

Look at it again: it is the will of God that "at the name
of Jesus every knee should bow, of things in heaven, and
things in earth, and things under the earth." Every human
being is in that group "things in earth." Each person will

confront Him. Each person will come personally into the presence of God. He is coming again, and all will see Him face to face. The truth as revealed in Scripture, as recorded in the Bible, is that Jesus of Nazareth, as written in Matthew, Mark, Luke and John, is the One who was born of a virgin, lived in this world, performed miracles, taught the Word of God and went to the cross of Calvary and died and was raised from the dead, ascended into heaven, appeared again to His disciples and then actually poured forth the Holy Spirit into their hearts. It is the will of Almighty God that every human being will meet Him, will confront Him and will have to bow the knee to Him confessing Him as Lord.

It is true many have never heard, but God will deal in mercy and grace with them. The servant that knew little will be beaten with few stripes, but those who have heard, and many have heard and have turned away, such will bear their own burden. It is plainly written:

> For if we sin wilfully after that we have received the knowledge of the truth, there remaineth no more sacrifice for sins, but a certain fearful looking for of judgment and fiery indignation, which shall devour the adversaries (Heb. 10:26, 27).

The day of judgment is coming. The Scriptures make it clear that God has appointed a time when "every knee should bow . . . and every tongue should confess that Jesus Christ is Lord to the glory of God the Father."

*Chapter 26*

## EVERY TONGUE CONFESS
### (Philippians 2:11)

*Can you believe that Almighty God wants His Son to be honored by the minds and voices of men?*

The believer accepted Jesus Christ as the Son of God. For anyone who has confidence in the Bible it is clear that the Son of God was Jesus of Nazareth incarnate in the flesh. The believer worships Him in loving gratitude. He died for him. In his heart he rejoices in faith and praise to the Lord. The heart of every believer is lifted in praise and thanksgiving, not only that Christ Jesus died for him but also that He has patiently kept him. In all of this, the believer on earth is simply joining the innumerable multitude in heaven.

We have some idea of what is going on in heaven because of the Book of Revelation. It is written that John had a vision, that he saw the mighty angels. The record is that he saw mighty angels, the seraphim, the cherubim, heavenly creatures of all kinds, great multitudes, all bowed down in worship before the Lamb that was slain, the Lamb that now sits on the throne. While Jesus of Nazareth was here on earth even the demons recognized Him. They said, "We know thee, Jesus, who thou art, Jesus the Son of God." They asked Him to spare them. The demons recognized Him and they obeyed His Word. When He said, "Come out," they came out. John in his vision saw all heaven united in praise, as if there were one vast chorus, a choir extending over the whole of heaven, united, singing praises to God and honoring His name. God intends that all men, creatures of His, made upon the face of the earth, shall honor His beloved Son, the Lord Jesus Christ who came into the world to seek and to save the lost.

99

And that every tongue should confess that Jesus Christ is
Lord, to the glory of God the Father (2:11).

The word "tongue" is the expression, the conclusion, of the
mind. It is for every man to see and to recognize the work
and the power of the Son of God. The plan of Almighty God
is that this truth will be brought to the knowledge of every
human being on earth. Men will be confronted by the
reality that Jesus Christ, who was here on earth and lived
here some thirty or more years, was crucified, dead and
buried, arose from the dead, and ascended into heaven is
actually Lord. He is over all things. While He was here He
said that the Father had given all things into His hands.
"The Father judgeth no man, but hath committed all judgment unto the Son." Jesus of Nazareth knew that all power
had been given to Him in heaven and on earth. Because of
this, it is the will of God that every human being bow down
and recognize Him; that every tongue confess that Jesus
Christ is Lord to the glory of God the Father.

"Confessing" is simply saying out loud the exact description of what really is. If you want to confess, you will have
to give utterance to your own recognition of the truth. The
truth of the matter is that Almighty God was in Jesus Christ
reconciling the world to Himself; but Almighty God Himself was invisible, so He made Himself visible and presented
Himself to all mankind in the person of Jesus Christ.

Many think that Jesus of Nazareth was a good man, but
are not willing to think that He was the Son of God. God
wants it understood that Jesus of Nazareth actually is Lord,
meaning He is in control of everything. When I say "Jesus
of Nazareth," I mean "Christ Jesus incarnate." He is the
anointed One. He comes with all the power and authority
of God. This Jesus Christ was actually taken by wicked
hands and was crucified. He was raised from the dead and
ascended into heaven. This Jesus Christ shall so come in like
manner as they saw Him go into heaven. But this Jesus
Christ who died for us, who is interceding for us, who is
coming again for us, is actually Lord. He is in control
of everything.

> In the beginning was the Word, and the Word was with
> God, and the Word was God. The same was in the begin-
> ning with God. All things were made by him; and without
> him was not any thing made that was made (John 1:1-3).

That is the way it is written in John's opening verses in his
gospel. He goes on to say in the same chapter, "the Word
was made flesh," and this was "Jesus of Nazareth." He was
the Son of man come to do His Father's will. He came into
the world to seek and to save the lost. God wants all men
everywhere to recognize that this Jesus Christ is actually the
One in charge. God has committed all judgment to the Son.
Every human being is going to have to deal with Jesus of
Nazareth. Every human being will have to answer for the
deeds done in the body to Christ Jesus, who is the Judge of
all the earth.

Jesus of Nazareth said, "I am the door: by me if any man
enter in, he shall be saved. I am the light of the world." He
advised people to walk in the light, and not to walk in darkness where they would stumble. Again, He said "I am the
bread of life." He encouraged people to eat of Him, to
assimilate what truth He had to give, because it would
mean everything to them. All of these things are implied
in that name "Jesus." That Jesus Christ is Lord.

The word "Christ" was a title, and implies the promise
from Old Testament times. Whenever you have the word
"Christ" you have in mind the One whom the prophets
promised, the One of whom Moses spoke, the One the Old
Testament predicted was coming. This Servant is the Savior.
I put my trust in Him: He works it out. He is able to save
me to the uttermost because I came to God by Him. This is
Jesus Christ. Now what Paul is saying is that every tongue
must confess that Jesus Christ, the One who came to Bethlehem, the One who was the fulfillment of Old Testament
prophecy, that Jesus Christ is Lord. He is in charge of
all things.

Every person is going to meet the Lord Jesus Christ. You
may say, "Well, I think He will be merciful to them." What
would make you think that? He will be merciful to anyone

who is humble and repentant. "The humble and the contrite heart" the Lord will not despise; and He has appointed to all men everywhere to repent. Those who repent, and acknowledge themselves to be sinners, and come humbly before Him, will find that the grace of God is for them. The Lord Jesus Himself will receive them and keep them forever. God's plan is that Jesus Christ will be honored and confessed as the Lord by all men everywhere. Some will do it willingly, gladly, rejoicing, and some will do it in a sullen fashion; but they will have to admit it. It will be brought out before them when it is even too late for them to profit by it, but they will find out that He was actually the Son of God while He was here on earth. We can pray Almighty God to help us to understand this, and even now to share with our voices in the tribute to Him who was actually the King of Kings and the Lord of all. We saw Him and heard of Him in the fashion of a man, but He was always the Son of God.

## Chapter 27

## WORK OUT YOUR OWN SALVATION

(Philippians 2:12)

*Can you understand that when a person believes in Jesus Christ, there is something he must do?*

There may be many good reasons why so many people fall into error about being saved. We know there are many people in the world who are not interested, but I am just now thinking about those who really want to draw nigh to God. They really desire to have the blessing of God. The invitation is given to them very simply. "Come unto me, all ye that labour and are heavy laden, and I will give you rest." "If any man believes in me, he shall not perish but shall have everlasting life." It seems so simple, and yet people can make a very common, ordinary mistake right here. The Gospel is told to sinners. Most of these people have their own opinion of what it means to be saved. Very few realize that to be saved involves being changed.

Many people who hear the Gospel would like to have the blessing of God, but do not want to change their ways. Usually men simply want more benefits to enjoy. They want to live as they are living, except they do not want to hurt as they are hurting. They wish to avoid trouble. Many are inclined to think of the Gospel as a sort of fire escape in times of emergency. Actually, being saved is a good deal like getting into an elevator to go up to the tenth floor of a building. If you were on the ground floor and you wanted to get to the tenth floor, the elevator presents a marvelous effortless way. But there is one simple fact about going into that elevator. You have to get all in, and the door will be shut behind you, before you can go up. If a person tried to go up with one foot in and one foot out, the elevator would not even move. Some persons do not want to go up, it is

103

true, and some persons do not want to change. They simply want to enjoy more benefits, and wish to be relieved from some of the troubles they have.

Despite failure and loss, and in spite of defeat, the natural person does not wish to be changed. How often this is true! A person who has been addicted to liquor often endures trouble to keep the habit. Such a person might want to cut down a bit, but if you have had any experience with such a person, you will know sadly that person will never be cured. It is not until a person is born again that he will have the disposition to obey God. Obeying God does not come naturally. It is of the spiritual man. It is true that the Gospel says "only believe" but the further truth is that believing involves obeying. It is a tragic snare to think that believing is simply a matter of admitting something to be true. No! Even the demons will admit that God and Jesus Christ are real, but they are still evil.

Do you believe in fire insurance? Do you have your house insured? No? Then you don't believe in it! James gives a needed accent when he says simply that faith without works is dead. Every Christian person should read the Book of James often and especially the second chapter.

> But wilt thou know, O vain man, that faith without works is dead? Was not Abraham our father justified by works, when he had offered Isaac his son upon the altar? Seest thou how faith wrought with his works, and by works was faith made perfect? (James 2:20-22).

"Perfect" being complete, carried out.

Paul urged this truth upon the Philippian believers:

> Wherefore, my beloved, as ye have always obeyed, not as in my presence only, but now much more in my absence, work out your own salvation with fear and trembling (2:12).

This does not mean "work *for* your own salvation." It means work *out* your own salvation. You can only work out what you already have in. If you have your salvation in your heart, you can work it out, and this is what that Scripture means. If a man wanted to have a garden, he would need a plot of ground. He would have to work that soil to prepare it. Then he must plant, weed, fertilize, and kill the bugs if his garden is to be fruitful.

Perhaps you haven't gardened. Remember embroidery? A woman takes a piece of cloth and starts stitching with various colored thread. If she is going to do a piece of embroidery, she must first have the cloth. You can also notice there is a pattern printed on it. Sometimes only a faint color is used, but there will be a pattern printed on that cloth. Then the stitching is according to the pattern. We can say that she is *working out* the pattern on the cloth. The pattern was already stamped in it and her stitching is a matter of *working it out*. "Work out your own salvation with fear and trembling."

Why does it say "with fear"? Does that mean you need be afraid God is going to hurt you? No. In my own case I know what it is to be afraid I will stumble or make a mistake, so that I will fail. I "work out" my own salvation avoiding pride. I am not that sure of myself, so I am not absolutely confident what the outcome will be. As a believer I may be sure in the Lord, but I may not be cocksure about myself. I can work out my own salvation humbly with fear and trembling, which means to say that I would seek to obey God, conscious of my own weakness. He will lead me, and I will accept His guidance as I accept His will and try to do it humbly and faithfully, seeking to obey Him. The salvation of God in Christ Jesus will actually be produced, will be worked out in me. The believer actually believes in Christ by obeying Him.

## Chapter 28

## GOD WORKETH IN YOU

(Philippians 2:13)

*Can you understand that the believer does not need to decide how or what he should do as a believer?*

> For it is God which worketh in you both to will and to do
> of his good pleasure (2:13).

This is a wonderfully reassuring statement. Many young Christians have heard about living a yielded life. We are so inclined as believers to talk about the glory of walking with the Lord. We speak out freely of how wonderful it is. We describe what has happened to us without realizing that often the heart of the hearer can be filled with despair when he hears such glowing testimony. It is so easy to feel in one's own heart, "I could never do that." Then again when we hear about some person who has prayed and waited upon God, and has had some marvelous thing happen, we can have the feeling in our hearts, "I wouldn't know what to do." Let me say with reference to all such feelings, they can be only too true. Yet they all are quite beside the point. They do not refer to the real issue. Living will not be up to the believer, personally. It may be quite true that you could never do that, but you are not going to do it. It could even be true that you would be able to hold out, but you are not going to do the holding.

"It is God which worketh in you both to will and to do of his good pleasure." We have just studied through the verse preceding this, "Work out your own salvation with fear and trembling," and sometimes when people hear that, they feel despair. They say to themselves, "I will never be able to do it. If I am going to have to do that, I will fail, because that requires knowledge which I do not have. It requires virtue I lack. It requires faith I yearn for. I am just not up to doing that." But wait a minute! It is not up to you. Remember! "It is God which worketh in you both to will and to do of his good pleasure." The believer is not left to himself. God is watching over him, and God is working in him. The only contribution that you will make is your willingness, a yieldedness on your part.

God works on us by His providence. As we live our lives, we have certain things happen to us. Things can happen from the outside, and God controls all that in His providence. There will be times when circumstances are such that we can do nothing. If we can do nothing, we should sit still and see the salvation of the Lord. There will be other times when something ought to be done. In that case we should do it. "Whatsoever thy hand finds to do, do it with thy might." God in His providence is watching over us. We are exactly where we ought to be, and we will serve God in that very situation. "It is God which worketh in you both to will and to do of his good pleasure."

As I have said, this may come to us in providence from the outside. But even far more so it may come through His Word on the inside. As we get acquainted with the Word of God, He will guide us in and through His Holy Spirit. He will bring the words to us that we ought to have in mind and He will keep His Word. We will find out what the promises are, as well as what our duties are. We will find what God wants us to do laid out before us in Scripture.

Then again, God will work on us not only by His providence, by the circumstances we are under and by His Word which is the guidance we have in the Scriptures, but by His grace inwardly prompting us from the inside. He will prompt us like a fountain of water springing up out of our hearts. There will come the disposition to want to be well-pleasing in His sight. We will want to do His will. We will want to trust Him. In addition to that, there is His Spirit watching over us, hovering over us and guiding us along the way. We may keep one thing in mind, we are never alone. We should remember where we are, and think of where we will spend the rest of our days. God know where we are and He knows what the situation is and we can let our light shine there, and glorify our Father which is in heaven.

As we are thinking about this, let us look out into the world of nature. How is it that the lily is white? Or if it is a canna lily, how is it that it is red? How is it that violets are blue? How is it that the rose is pink? Does anyone go out and paint these? No. How is it that flowers grow and bloom? The bud will come out of the stem, and then burst open and become a bloom right there in front of us. How does that happen? All these things come from the inside out. Should we suppose He would do that with flowers and not do it with us? Should we think He would do that in the natural world outside, and not work in our hearts? He will work that way.

When we look at an oak tree, all the leaves on an oak tree are oak leaves. And while each one is different from the other, they are all enough alike to be recognized as oak leaves. Why is it that they are oak leaves? Why is this characteristic in all of them? This is simple: it was in the seed. Just in this way we have the seed, the Word of God. When the Word of God is in our hearts, we will be prompted from the inside by the Word of God to praise God, to trust God, to obey God, to call on God, to believe in God, to depend on God. Such action will come naturally to us.

I can remember some years ago seeing something happen in a practical way in a store, which came to my mind to suggest that the Christian life is something like that. I needed to get a pane of glass. I went to a hardware store where I wanted to get the glass. As I remember, it was something like 8½ x 10½. He didn't have a sheet just exactly 8½ x 10½, so I told him what the measurement was. He took a larger sheet of glass, and with a rule, he marked off 8½ x 10½. Then he took a glass cutting tool, and with it he scratched what the measurement was to be. When he scratched out a portion 8½ x 10½, he then took a small hammer and from underneath he tapped the pane of glass with his hammer with gentle taps. Each tap was a jolt. Each jolt put a certain tension on that glass, as if each tap of the hammer threatened to break the glass. Do you know what happened? When it broke, it broke exactly where he scratched it and I got my piece of glass 8½ x 10½. You might ask how is that like the Christian life?

The Scriptures are like that glass-cutting tool. I read the Bible and it scratches the surface of my heart and my consciousness in the likeness of Jesus Christ. The shadow of the cross is etched out, scratched out, on my heart. Then life comes to me with its strain and with its problems and with its jolts, as if it would just shatter me, as if I were going to break. How will I break? According to the sign of the cross that was etched into my consciousness in the reading of Scripture. That is exactly where I will "break." Providence does that. As a believer I need not strive, nor strain, nor run. All I need to do is to yield. I need to yield myself into the hands of God, for "it is God which worketh in you both to will and to do of his good pleasure."

## Chapter 29

## DO ALL THINGS

(Philippians 2:14, 15)

*Do you realize that God expects every Christian to be kind?*

The natural way of living is spontaneous, like water bubbling up out of a fountain, just as I please; that is natural. The believer is not natural, but spiritual. This one who is in Christ Jesus is led to discipline his body. Paul says, "I bring my body into subjection," and he says, "But I keep under my body, and bring it into subjection: lest that by any means, when I have preached to others, I myself should be a castaway" (1 Cor. 9:27). This great apostle illustrated in himself that, led by the Spirit of God, he would take his body and bring it into service. He put it under control, and then he used it to obey the directives that he received from the Holy Spirit. Why would Paul do this? Because he had in him the Holy Spirit of God, who had filled Jesus of Nazareth to overflowing. Here is the basis for all fellowship of believers. The reason they say the same thing is because their tongue has been brought under control, and led by one Spirit. The believer does not act by impulse. He has impulses, but he keeps them under control. A believer is not gracious to another person because he happens naturally to be a gracious person, nor is he generous and gives to the poor by chance. He is guided and led by the Spirit of God. The believer in Christ acts as he feels led, for he yearns to be well-pleasing in the sight of the Lord.

It is not easy nor simple for the believer. Perhaps you will think in your own mind, "The problem is that we are just not like Jesus of Nazareth. We have sin in us." This is true. We are inclined to think about Him: "He didn't have sin, so He just naturally wanted to do the will of His Father." Yes, He naturally wanted to do the will of His Father, I agree.

110

But when the will of His Father was that He should take His body to death, He faced a terrible prospect. It was only after hours of agony, you will remember in Gethsemane, that He prayed to His Father: "Father, if thou be willing, remove this cup from me: nevertheless not my will, but thine, be done."

The believing person lives humbly, meekly, gently, kindly, helpfully in this world. He certainly is not born that way. But now he is under control. Paul refers to this when he writes: "Do all things without murmurings and disputings." When he says, "do all things," he means "take charge, take hold of yourself, take hold of your mind, yes, and take hold of your mouth, take hold of your attitude, take hold of that face of yours because of the frown that comes so easily."

> Do all things without murmurings and disputings: that ye may be blameless and harmless, the sons of God, without rebuke, in the midst of a crooked and perverse nation, among whom ye shine as lights in the world (2:14, 15).

It is so natural for me to be dissatisfied with what I dislike. I can be dissatisfied with what that other person does. Some people fall into a snare and are habitually critical. They constantly find fault with others. But when that other person is a believer and is minded as I am to do the will of God, then there need be no problem. I can just go by what he does. I can go by what he says. I can go by how he acts. I can accept all his conduct because I know he is being led to act as he does.

Paul says, "Do all things without murmurings." Don't start fussing with each other. Don't start complaining about things. I must learn to get along with folks. "That ye may be blameless and harmless, the sons of God." I need have no share in doing what is wrong. I need not share in anything that is destructive. I am to be blameless in that no one can blame me for what happens. "And harmless." I am not to hurt anyone. "The sons of God." God treats all people alike. He makes the sun shine on the good and the bad, and the rain to fall upon the just and the unjust. So when I am giving to the poor, I don't check up on them. God knows them. I will not be quarreling with people. I will have no contention with people. I will do no damage to anything or anyone. If you and I will live that way, even our enemies will be at peace with us.

But this is the point: "without rebuke." I am to live and act in such fashion that no one may be able to find fault. This reminds us of the Lord Jesus. When the mob wanted to condemn Him and put Him to death, Pilate gave the classic word, when he said, "I find no fault with this man." Oh, that God would help us to be able to live that way! I may not win. I may not become rich. I may not be the person who is honored or glorified. I may actually suffer. Christ Jesus suffered death, but, oh! the honor and the glory that belongs to the person of whom they must say, "Certainly there is no fault in him, no fault in her."

"In the midst of a crooked and perverse nation." A crooked and perverse community, or a crooked and perverse world, where the normal way of living is devious, and is actually undependable. You remember how the prophet Isaiah said, "All we like sheep have gone astray; we have turned every one to his own way." When each one is acting selfishly and willfully, conflict is natural. "Among whom (among these crooked and perverse, arguing, contentious, disagreeable, discontent people) shine as lights in the world."

"Ye are the light of the world. A city that is set on an hill cannot be hid" (Matt. 5:14). So you will honor God and you will serve Him: you will obey Him, and let your good works be seen and known, that people may glorify your Father which is in heaven. This secret of living as a child of God is in obedience. The Holy Spirit will guide you into all truth. Here is a true statement: "For as many as are led by the Spirit of God, they are the sons of God" (Rom. 8:14). And again, "Wherefore by their fruits ye shall know them" (Matt. 7:20). Shall I not think with you that we can pray to Almighty God to help us? Help us do what? Help us to yield; help us to give in; help us to give up; help us to yield ourselves into the mighty hand of God. God will take care of us.

## Chapter 30

## WORD OF LIFE

(Philippians 2:14-16)

*Did you know that one of the marks of a believer is that he is concerned for the salvation of other persons?*

"Wherefore by their fruits ye shall know them" (Matt. 7:20). One of the fruits of believing in Christ is a concern for the spiritual welfare of other persons. If I am a believer and accept Christ Jesus as my Savior, so that I yield myself to God, and He works in me by His grace to regenerate me into His likeness, and gives me His Holy Spirit to dwell in me so that I have Christ in me, I can tell you one thing is going to happen to me. I am going to be thinking about the spiritual welfare and the soul's salvation of other people. I will be concerned for the people that I meet and the people that I have dealings with, especially the people in my home. I cannot help but be concerned about their spiritual welfare. They are human beings, and as such they need the grace of God. I know Christ died for them and that each one of them could be saved. As a believer in Christ Jesus, I have been regenerated as a child of God. There is that in me that comes from God by His grace and mercy. It is not because I am good, or strong, or smart, but because Christ Jesus died for me, because God is gracious, and because He has given the Holy Spirit to be my Guide, that these words apply to me.

The Lord Jesus said, "As my Father hath sent me, even so send I you" (John 20:21). As one who is sent, I am pushed along by an inward feeling. Paul wrote of himself: "The love of Christ constraineth" me (2 Cor. 5:14). As a member of the body of Christ, I care about the souls of other people. The Lord said to all who believe, "Go ye into all the world, and preach the gospel to every creature" (Mark 16:15). This inward disposition will be in me, especially with reference to all in my own family and those whom I hold dear. I would want each one of them to know that Christ Jesus died for him. Christ has made it possible for my loved ones to come to God, and has promised that He will receive them. He will give him the Holy Spirit. This is the wonderful truth of the Gospel: "Whosoever will, may come" and "him that cometh to me, I will in no wise cast out." These things help me to understand this word from Paul:

> Do all things without murmurings and disputings: that ye may be blameless and harmless, the sons of God, without rebuke, in the midst of a crooked and perverse nation, among whom ye shine as lights in the world; holding forth the word of life; that I may rejoice in the day of Christ, that I have not run in vain, neither laboured in vain (2:14-16).

When I say "the word" I think of the Word of God, the promises of God: These are written for us in the Scriptures. It was incarnate, the Word of God was actually in flesh in Christ Jesus, and it is declared to the whole world in the Gospel.

What are those promises of God? That I am to win every ball game? No. That I am to be rich? No. That I am always to be healthy and well? No. That I am to get some office that I may be running for? No. That I am to pass an examination? No. None of these is the Word of Life. The Word of Life is that God promises to save for eternity the soul that accepts Christ Jesus.

What does saving the soul include? Forgiveness? Yes. That God will forgive my sins. Regeneration? Yes. That I will be born again: that there will be a new being in me. That God will cleanse? I can actually be washed whiter than snow. The blood of the Lord Jesus Christ will cleanse me from every sin and I will be endued with the Holy Spirit. God will give His Holy Spirit into my heart. That is the promise! I can be filled with the Holy Spirit. All these promises are in what we call the Word of Life. It is the Word that has to do with living. It is not something that I am going to do by striving. No, this is something God will do, and He will do it in me because He promised to do so in His grace and in His mercy.

As a believer I step out before the world, and one way or another I am going to tell them all about Him. I am going to hold forth the Word of Life. That is why it is a good thing for me to have Bible reading. It is a good thing for me to sing hymns. It is a good thing for me to go to church. There the preacher will tell the Gospel. The people will repeat it. It is a good thing for me to go to Sunday school. The Sunday school literature somewhere will tell the story that Christ Jesus died for sinful men. All this is what is meant by "holding forth the word of life."

Just now, our whole country has been stirred by an exhibition of a great mass movement of presenting the Gospel. There has been a great campaign of evangelism preparation and training. There are evangelism schools and there are study classes all over the country for various kinds of evangelism: how to conduct evangelistic meetings, and how to do evangelistic visitation through the church services, how to do evangelism by private visitation, and by personal work. All that kind of activity is "holding forth the word of life." What all this means is that believers care about other people. They want them to come to know and to believe in the grace of Christ.

"In the day of Christ" means the day of judgment. This will be when Christ Jesus will come to judge the living and the dead, at His appearing and His kingdom. There is a day coming when the facts of life will be opened up, and all that is being done now will be shown for what it really is. Paul yearned that the Philippian believers would grasp this. Then he would know that he had not run in vain. What does he mean when he writes "that I have not run in vain"? Paul had tried by his example, by the way he had lived his life, by the things he had tried to do, to show forth the Gospel. His example in his own personal conduct did bear fruit in the lives of those he won, and this would show up in the last day. It would be obvious that the way he lived, the times that he had prayed, the times that he had preached, the times that he had endured, the times that he had suffered, had actually affected other people. He had done all these things for that very purpose, so that other people should learn about Christ. Some of that seed fell on good ground, and some people were turned to God. That was the hope cherished by the Apostle Paul.

Are you ready to think that for yourself? As you live your daily life day in and day out, will it have lasting effect for Christ Jesus? Do you have the hope that some day the things you have done, the trials you have endured, will yield consequences in other people? This is what Paul wanted.

If we are believers in the Lord Jesus Christ, and His Spirit is in our hearts, we will be inwardly moved, we will be inwardly impelled, we will inwardly feel that we are not satisfied unless we are doing something about letting other people know that Christ Jesus died for them and they could be saved. For God is no respecter of persons and whoever comes to Him will not perish but will have everlasting life. No wonder we say, "Praise the Lord!"

## Chapter 31

## JOY AND REJOICE

### (Philippians 2:17, 18)

*Can you see that in order to be able to rejoice, a person first must have an original experience of joy?*

It is a frustrating, discouraging thing to pray for others when one can see no result. There are so many of us who put ourselves out for people who do not seem to care. This is discouraging. We pray and pray, and ask and ask, and apparently there is no change in these people. This is especially true with parents, with husbands, or wives and friends. Caring for the wayward and rebellious is such a drain on the spirit.

But there is an answer! This is to be found in the way of the Lord. When we believe in Him and receive His Holy Spirit into our hearts, we will be led to go His way. The Lord Himself promised that if we would receive the Holy Spirit into our hearts, there would be within us "a well of water springing up." This is a poetic way of describing a fountain or a spring, water coming up from underneath to water the earth. No doubt we are all acquainted with what an oasis in the desert would be like. It is some spot where there is a spring in a desert area. The water comes up out of the ground in a pool, and then it spreads out. It seeps away into the sand, and it is lost. But here grass grows and palm trees flourish. There are results round about, even though the water is gone. This is much like the way it is with us when we care about others. We do for them, we care for them, we pray for them, and then we are gone. Our prayers and our witness are so much like water running out into the sand.

We may be reminded that we are told we are the light of

the world. A city that is set on a hill cannot be hid. Now it is a wonderful thing to be a light, because the light reveals and guides. Yet have you ever considered how helpless light is? It can reveal but it cannot decide anything. If there is no one traveling on that road that beacon shines in vain. It can shine and those who see can choose to disregard the guidance. This is so often the distressing case with believers who care for others, and who try to witness to them.

"You are the salt of the earth." In that connection we can understand the salt would be used as a preservative. However, if there were no food, the salt would be of no use. So it is with reference to us in our witness for Christ. We feel a helplessness in witnessing to other people. Sometimes we feel what we try to do is like pouring water into a leaky bucket: it just runs out. That seems to be unfair! It is unfair, but true. We will pour out, and be poured out, and gone. This is the way of the Lord. And the servant is not greater than his Master. If the Lord Jesus Christ could come into this world to His own, and His own would not receive Him, let me say very kindly and gently, we need not expect anything better.

What can we do then about witnessing to others? We can heed the Scripture. Paul would say "the love of Christ constraineth us." What we do is not being done on account of other people. What we do is being done on account of the Lord. If we look at others, we are sure to be disappointed. If we look at the Lord, we will never be disappointed. If we give to the poor because they are poor, we will be disappointed: we will be discouraged. But if we give to the poor because that is pleasing to the Lord, we will never be disappointed: we will never be discouraged.

Remember that the love of Christ caused Him to come for us. He gave Himself for us, He suffered for us, and He died for us. He always needed to look up into the presence of His Father to be strengthened. The Scripture says about Him, "Who for the joy that was set before him endured the cross, despising the shame." There was no joy in the cross. Remember in Gethsemane how He asked the Father,

Abba, Father, all things are possible unto thee; take away
this cup from me: nevertheless not what I will, but what
thou wilt (Mark 14:36).

The Apostle Paul could write:

Yea, and if I be offered upon the sacrifice and service of
your faith, I joy, and rejoice with you all. For the same cause
also do ye joy, and rejoice with me (2:17, 18).

This expression "offered upon the sacrifice" actually in its
form implies being poured out like a drink offering. The
worshipers sometimes would bring meat, and sometimes
they would bring cakes of meal, but at other times they
brought drink offerings, such as wine. They would bring
this offering before the Lord, and pour it out before Him.
It was offered "as unto the Lord." Paul is saying "if I should
be poured out on your account, I will joy and rejoice."
Think of some sweet-smelling perfume that you would be
glad to have poured around. Perfume is poured out and you
never get it back. The fragrance is for the sake of the people
who receive its pleasure. Paul is saying, "if I should be
poured out, so that I never come back again to myself; if I
should be spent on your behalf, I would joy and rejoice."
How could he possibly joy in such a thing? Because he
would be having fellowship with the Lord.

Paul's faith was in God. Paul's attention, his eyes, were
upon the Father. As Paul lived and served, he looked to
"Jesus, the author and finisher" of his faith. This enabled
Paul to joy in the Lord, and to think back on it, and rejoice
because he was able to share with the Lord Jesus Christ in
His own personal sacrifice and service for other people.
Remember, Christ gave His life as a ransom for many. In the
same way you can do for other people and be blessed because that is the way of the Lord.

## Chapter 32

## GOOD COMFORT

### (Philippians 2:19, 20)

*Do you realize that it is only a believer who would be inwardly moved to naturally care for the welfare of other souls?*

> But I trust in the Lord Jesus to send Timotheus shortly unto you, that I also may be of good comfort, when I know your state. For I have no man likeminded, who will naturally care for your state (2:19, 20).

Here is a good example of a concerned brother. You will remember that the Apostle Paul in writing this letter to the Philippians was a prisoner in Rome, facing possible execution. He was burdened with concern for the believers in Philippi. He realized that they might face real persecution, and he was concerned that in their new faith they should not falter. He could not rest, nor be comforted until he knew they were secure. Certainly Paul was in danger, but he wrote triumphantly: "For to me to live is Christ, and to die is gain." He had it all settled between himself and the Lord. But Paul needed a first-hand report about the Philippian brethren from a man whom he could trust to be truthful.

Often you will hear reports about people: what they are doing, whether their testimony is good or poor. But hearsay about other believers is not good enough. Reports that come from strangers are inadequate. Reports that come from rivals or competitors are unreliable. Reports that come from those who are enemies, who do not want believers to be doing anything at all, are false. In other words, if you want to get a report about anyone's work, for that report to be valid, for that comment to be helpful, it must come from a true friend.

Paul wrote, " I trust in the Lord Jesus to send Timotheus

unto you" because Timothy was a true friend of the Philippians. This particular passage seems to say that Timothy was perhaps the greatest Christian Paul knew. He said: "I have no man likeminded, who will naturally care for your state." We may well wonder how did Timothy turn out to be a man like this? Paul himself tells us enough to give us an idea.

> When I call to remembrance the unfeigned faith that is in thee, which dwelt first in thy grandmother Lois, and thy mother Eunice; and I am persuaded that in thee also (2 Tim. 1:5).

Timothy apparently was one of those persons who was brought up in the nurture and admonition of the Lord. There is no record of any dramatic experience of conversion. Apparently he did not have to be "turned around" because his mother and his grandmother took him by the hand, and led him in the way of the Lord, as a little child.

Many are concerned about conversion in becoming a believer. You may have heard about some being turned from darkness to light, and you may have wondered in your own case, whether your own experience could be genuine. It may be that you cannot remember a time when you did not believe in the Lord Jesus Christ. It may be that the first thing you ever heard about the Lord Jesus was "Jesus loves me, this I know, for the Bible tells me so." And you believed it even as a little child. You always thought of the Lord Jesus as your Savior and so you have continued that way. This consideration of Timothy as a believer may be of real help to you.

> But continue thou in the things which thou hast learned and hast been assured of, knowing of whom thou hast learned them; and that from a child thou hast known the holy scriptures, which are able to make thee wise unto salvation through faith which is in Christ Jesus (2 Tim. 3:14, 15).

Apparently there was nothing spectacular in his spiritual experience. There is no record of anything dramatic about his turning to the Lord, but would that make him any the less real? Which of the following do you think would be the more genuine? If you saw a doctor who by his skill as a physician saved the life of a desperately sick child on the one hand, and then you saw a mother who kept her child well by keeping it away from infection, would you discount the mother because her conduct was without excitement? Is a person any more healthy who has had smallpox and barely escaped with his life, than the one who through vaccination is immune from smallpox? The believer with godly parents, as Timothy had, has a great advantage. At the same time you can praise the Lord about this. Regardless of who his parents were or what his background was, it is wonderfully true: "Whosoever will may come."

# Chapter 33

## SERVED WITH ME
### (Philippians 2:21, 22)

*Can you see how willingness to be guided by those who know more is a mark of the truly great servant of the Lord?*

For all seek their own, not the things which are Jesus Christ's. But ye know the proof of him, that, as a son with the father, he hath served with me in the gospel (2:21, 22).

Paul continues his comments about Timothy. He has just said: "I have no man likeminded." There was only one of his kind. The characteristic of any human being is to be interested in self. That is the most natural thing in the world. This is natural in the flesh. It is not really spiritual in the Lord Jesus Christ. Christians are concerned that while they have Christ in them, they also have the old man around them. Paul's co-workers all manifested something of the flesh about themselves except Timothy. He was just an unusually advanced case of a spiritually-minded person.

Timothy had an unusual advantage. He had godly parents and grandparents. "I know the faith that was in your grandmother, the faith that was in your mother and I am persuaded is in you also." It is a wonderful blessing to have godly parents. Not all have had that advantage. You could say, "He knew about the things of the Lord from the time he was a child. He never had the experience of having to choose this when he was older." And this would be true.

Do you think it is that important to have to come out of darkness into light? I am one of those who came "out of darkness into his marvelous light." I am one of those who was walking along on a country road in the darkness of agnosticism and in walking across a little culvert that was not four feet wide, I stepped on it as an agnostic, and by the time I stepped off, I was in blazing light. I could believe in the Lord Jesus Christ. I had that kind of experience.

My good wife did not have that kind of experience. She never knew the day that she did not believe in the Lord Jesus Christ. When I was a young man, and was courting her in the fashion of the old days and I was very much distressed because she could not tell me when she accepted Christ, she was almost impatient with me. What I failed to recognize at the time was that my good wife had the experience of being born to a couple who prayed for her before she was conceived. All the time that her mother was carrying her, they made it a matter of regular prayer for this child of theirs. That child was brought up in the nurture and admonition of the Lord. I remember one time as a young enthusiastic believer that I was pressing this other person, this young woman, about her relationship to Christ. I asked her when she had accepted the Lord, and she couldn't tell me. Then I questioned whether or not she was a real believer. She was very hurt by that. But she also confronted me about this and said she did believe. I remember I asked her at the time, "When was the first time you ever heard of Jesus Christ? What did you think the first time you ever thought of Him?" She looked me straight in the face and said, " 'Jesus loves me this I know, for the Bible tells me so.' That is the first thing I remember about Jesus Christ. I believed it then and I believe it yet and there never was a time I didn't believe it." Fortunately, I hushed my mouth and, as I often tell my folks, instead of keeping on with that argument, we settled it. I just married the girl and was done with it. And so our children have grown up in a home where the father had a dramatic experience of conversion. I have told something about my experience in some booklets of mine, "Out of Darkness" and "Into His Marvelous Light," but I haven't told all the details because they are too dramatic. I still remember very well the exceptional experiences that were mine spiritually when I came to believe. It was like a lightning flash when I could suddenly believe. Our children had me as their father but they had a mother who could not remember a day that she did not believe.

Which do you think is the better? Some think the more spectacular experience is better. But I would say this. The person who has been nurtured in the admonition of the Lord has an experience that can be far more enduring. There is a great benefit and blessing in having godly parents and this was what Timothy had.

In speaking of the others, Paul said about them, "all seek their own." What would their own be? Would that not be their own satisfaction and prestige? They want to make something of themselves. They seek personal interests. "Will this help me? Will this advance me?" As long as any person has such in mind, he is a different person from Timothy. He is among those of whom Paul would say "all seek their own, not the things which are Jesus Christ's." What are the things that are Jesus Christ's? Would not that be the lost sinner? Christ came to seek and to save the lost.

If I really had His Spirit in me, wouldn't I be interested with Him in those lost souls, those sinners? Then again, wouldn't the Lord Jesus Christ be interested in worshiping God? Wouldn't He want me to worship the Father? So if I am actually belonging to Him, and I want to seek the things which are His, wouldn't I seek among other things how to honor God? That is what the Lord Jesus Christ did. Jesus Christ gave His life a ransom for many and came to lay down His life for people who did not appreciate Him. As I follow Him, I should be ready to do anything I possibly can to help other people. These would be the things which are Jesus Christ's.

Paul said of Timothy, "But ye know the proof of him, that, as a son with the father, he hath served with me in the gospel." He was willing to cooperate with Paul, willing to accept guidance from Paul. Isn't this what a believer would be? Do you realize that a believer would never be independent of other people's fellowship or judgment? He would prove everything by the Word of God. He would test everything by the Holy Spirit, but he would count on the brethren. "He hath served with me in the gospel."

The primary thrust of every fellowship among Christians

would be to tell someone else about Jesus Christ. It would be to tell the whole world about Jesus Christ. You and I could well study Timothy, this exceptional man for our own guidance.

> For all seek their own, not the things which are Jesus Christ's. But ye know the proof of him, that, as a son with the father, he hath served me in the gospel (2:21, 22).

And may the Lord help us to be faithful and to meekly, humbly share with other people in telling the story of the Lord Jesus Christ to the whole world.

## Chapter 34

## I TRUST IN THE LORD

### (Philippians 2:23, 24)

*Do you realize a person may have the fullest confidence in God and yet not know for sure what will happen to him tomorrow?*

The New Testament epistles tell us about Paul, the apostle, a man of great faith and yet a humble man. At the same time that he had great faith in God, he had great ability as a leader. Paul exercised his leadership in directing the activities of other men. He had a company of people with him in his missionary group that went out into the world to preach the Gospel, and yet he was careful to act only as he was led by the Lord. It could be said of Paul that whereas apparently his followers obeyed him, yet he obeyed the Lord.

Paul wrote about Timothy saying:

> Him therefore I hope to send presently, so soon as I shall see how it will go with me. But I trust in the Lord that I also myself shall come shortly (2:23, 24).

There seems to be no doubt that Timothy would have done whatever Paul told him to do, yet Paul himself was not absolutely sure what he should tell Timothy to do. A believer may be sure when he is obeying God, and yet not cocksure about what is going to happen tomorrow. Complete trust in God is quite proper. In fact, it is wonderful. The ability to trust in Him is given to us by His grace. God is worthy of our trust. His power and integrity is such that we can depend on Him. Even so, the trusting soul may not know what will happen tomorrow. This is expressed in the hymn: "I do not ask to see the distant scene, one step enough for me." The Lord teaches us to commit all to God, even though we do not know the future.

Abraham is the outstanding example of faith. When God called him, Abraham obeyed and "went out, not knowing whither he went." This is very important to remember. It will help us to understand so much about faith. It is true about us, any day we live, that we have not been over this way before. It is unknown to us what that day will bring forth, but it is not unknown to God. He wants us to trust Him. The Lord Jesus in speaking to His disciples told them very simply, "sufficient unto the day is the evil thereof" and told them not to concern themselves about tomorrow. They were directed to leave that with God. The believer is impelled to trust God; because though he does not know where he is going, he knows God, and God does know.

If I hesitate to follow, and am reluctant because I cannot see where I am going, do you realize what I am revealing? I am showing that I am depending on myself, and so I am uneasy. This is simply unbelief. I am cutting myself off from the help I need. I can believe in God without knowing what is going to happen. The very fact that I hesitate to plan, because I cannot see the future, shows that I am expecting to do it myself, and this reveals that I am really not trusting God. I hesitate to move forward, because I don't know where I am going. I don't know what is going to happen to me.

Some feel they cannot trust God because they do not have any clear guidance from Him. What do they mean? Do they mean they do not hear His voice? I am not talking about that. Do they mean they have not seen any vision? I am not talking about that either. Do they mean they have not felt any nudge on their shoulders? I am not talking about that. Such things would be wonderful if they came to pass, but they may never come to pass. However we do have the Scriptures. We do have the promises of God. God is all around us. As a believer, I should be trusting God, depending on Him. The will of God is probably to be found right in my circumstances. I am likely right now to be exactly where God wants me to be. All the way, through all the days of my life, everything is in the hands of God. Why do

I ever forget that? Because I am only a human being. I am so easily influenced by my own feelings. I need to deny myself. I need to humble myself under the mighty hand of God. I need to look up to Him and ask Him to give me grace to believe in Him. I ought to let God have His way and rest in His will. Then I could have peace.

Paul made his plans subject to God's will. He had his plans, as when he hoped to send Timothy to Philippi. Notice how he put it. "I hope to send him." He doesn't say he is going to do so. He "hopes" to send him. It is in his mind to do so. But this is going to be subject to God's will. "So soon as I shall see how it will go with me." He means to say, "When I see how the hand of God works out my affairs. I need to wait to see what is going to happen; but I trust, I really am expecting, that I also myself shall come shortly." There is not a flavor in all this of Paul saying, "I am going to come. I am going to send him. I am going to do this or I am going to do that." James talks plainly and simply about this matter.

> Go to now, ye that say, Today or to-morrow we will go into such a city, and continue there a year, and buy and sell, and get gain: whereas ye know not what shall be on the morrow. For what is your life? It is even a vapour, that appeareth for a little time, and then vanisheth away. For that ye ought to say, If the Lord will, we shall live, and do this, or that (James 4:13-15).

It is a good thing to trust in God. Paul longed to see those believers in Philippi, but he recognized it is not in man to direct his steps. Complete trust in God is proper. It is such an attitude which honors Him.

## Chapter 35

## EPAPHRODITUS

### (Philippians 2:25-27)

*Can you see that it is a mark of thoughtful concern for other people when one seeks to relieve their fears about his own state?*

Paul was a very busy man with a wide range of service. He had been in many cities preaching and had founded many new churches with converts that he had won from paganism. Yet Paul carried in his heart a memory of each group of people with whom he had served. He was constantly concerned for their spiritual welfare.

> Beside those things that are without, that which cometh upon me daily, the care of all the churches (2 Cor. 11:28).

Paul lived day in and day out constantly aware of situations as they existed in other cities where they had been affecting the converts that he had won: "the care of all the churches." Again he writes:

> For I would that ye knew what great conflict I have for you, and for them at Laodicea, and for as many as have not seen my face in the flesh (Col. 2:1).

Paul cared about them all. There were people even in that time who had never seen Paul but who had read what he wrote, and who had heard other people tell what he preached. And Paul was concerned about them all.

Paul seems to have had a personal interest in these believers who lived in the city of Philippi. These were new believers, young believers, and he had won them out of paganism. Now they were about to enter into a period of persecution. He was hoping that he would be allowed out of prison that he might see them personally, because he wanted to strengthen them. He wanted to be sure that they would not be without some personal touch from him. Since he could not come personally, he planned to send some of his helpers. "Yet I supposed it necessary to send to you Epaphroditus."

I have often wondered in the providence of God why He let some of the great men in the Bible have such extraordinary names. I find in Scripture the record of a man like Mephibosheth, with such a strange name, or again the record of a great king called Hezekiah. And here is a name that you could feel is one of the worst: "Epaphroditus." But I want you to note this man. Paul wrote:

> Yet I supposed it necessary to send to you Epaphroditus, my brother, and companion in labor, and fellowsoldier, but your messenger, and he that ministered to my wants. For he longed after you all, and was full of heaviness, because that ye had heard that he had been sick (2:25, 26).

This man was downhearted. He felt bad. His spirits were low. "Because that ye had heard that he had been sick." Epaphroditus was unhappy and distressed because the folks back home heard he was sick.

> For indeed he was sick nigh unto death: but God had mercy on him; and not on him only, but on me also, lest I should have sorrow upon sorrow (2:27).

This is how Paul indicates that God has a hand in matters when anyone is to leave this world; and if He does not want them to leave this world, they will not.

Epaphroditus was a man who was a great comfort to Paul. It would seem from the general context of this letter that the people in Philippi wanted to help Paul. No doubt they could have given him money and they may have done this. But they did more. They selected one of their young men who was an earnest, dedicated believer, and they sent him to help take care of Paul. Paul was by now an older man, and this young man, Epaphroditus, came along to help him out. Paul calls him "my brother." What a wonderful word!

Paul knew that the life that he had in him was the same as the life that was in Epaphroditus by the grace of God. He calls him "a companion in labour." In all that Paul was trying to do this young man Epaphroditus worked right along with him, suffered with him, went through everything he experienced as "a fellow soldier." This would mean that Epaphroditus would be ready to take the distress, the suffering, and the persecution, ready to stand up and testify and witness and suffer because of rejection. This would be soldiering.

Paul also says of him "but your messenger." In this Paul reminds them that they had sent him. "He came from you folks." "He that ministered to my wants." He is the one who helped me. Then Paul went on to say about Epaphroditus: "He longed after you all." Paul wanted them to know this young man missed their fellowship. Epaphroditus wanted to see them so badly that he "was full of heaviness." The young man was downhearted, low spirited: "Because you had heard that he had been sick." Because these former friends of his, the folks back home in the old church, were actually concerned about him Epaphroditus was concerned about them. In fact Paul goes on to say "and indeed he was sick nigh unto death." This young man practically worked himself to death in helping Paul to minister the Gospel.

Epaphroditus was a man who would be marked above all others because of his exercise of zeal. There was in him a burning flame of devotion. He wanted to do the most he could, the best he could. He had been deathly sick but he had been spared. God had kept him. Paul felt that was a favor from God. His words about Epaphroditus seem to say that he might have died if God had not interfered. He was sick enough. Things were bad enough. He could have died. But God was in it, and God did not let him die. God actually helped him to endure so that he could help other people. "Indeed he was sick nigh unto death: but God had mercy on him." It would seem that God actually wanted to help Epaphroditus so that he could accomplish what he really wanted to do. Paul felt that God had not only blessed Epaphroditus with this privilege to serve, but that God had done him a favor by sparing Epaphroditus because this young man was such a help in his work. It is a tribute to the young man's devotion to see the concern that he had for the folks back home when they heard he was sick. He was sorry that they were burdened by that. This interest in wanting other people not to be unnecessarily disturbed is from the Lord. Epaphroditus was a good man, a spiritually minded man, and thus he was led to be concerned about the state of mind and heart of the other people who believed. He did not want them to be unnecessarily troubled because he himself had been kept by the Lord and was being blessed.

## Chapter 36

## THAT YOU MAY REJOICE

### (Philippians 2:28)

*Can you see how the personal visit of an old friend can be a cause for rejoicing and relief?*

Paul is writing to these Philippians a very personal letter. He is like a pastor and he is concerned for them. As new converts they are going to face hard times. Paul wants them to meet trouble in a strong way. He wants them to feel strong and ready to give their witness and testimony. For that there was something they could do. He wanted these Philippians to have the joy of the Lord. He knew from personal experience that the joy of the Lord would be their strength. One factor that would inspire them and make them strong would be the joy they would have in renewing personal fellowship with a beloved brother, Epaphroditus, who had been sent with Paul to be his companion and helper in his ministry. Paul knew that these people would be strengthened by his return, because when Epaphroditus came back, after having been with Paul, he would be able to give them a great lift by telling them about Paul's triumphant attitude. He knew that the day of renewing personal fellowship and communion with this beloved brother, Epaphroditus, would be good for them.

Epaphroditus had been sent from the city of Philippi to help Paul in his missionary services. He was a sort of servant, a handyman. He was so diligent and so faithful in his service to Paul that he became ill. When the people at home heard he was sick they were troubled. They were worried about him. When Epaphroditus heard that, it bothered him and he was downhearted because of it. It was a long, tedious process in those days to communicate a message anywhere in the world. Paul had in mind that those believers in

134

Philippi who were facing trouble that would come to them, would be helped if they knew that Epaphroditus was all right, that he had recovered from his sickness, that he was strong again. He could have written this to them and he did. He could have sent someone to tell it but he knew that nothing would take the place of a personal appearance. So he wanted Epaphroditus to go back there in person and be seen by them.

> I sent him therefore the more carefully, that, when ye see him again, ye may rejoice, and that I may be the less sorrowful (2:28).

Although Epaphroditus had been "sick nigh unto death," Paul nevertheless sent him on this long journey back to Macedonia to the city of Philippi that the believers there might see him. When Paul wrote that he sent him "the more carefully" he does not mean that he was more cautious about exposing him to any trouble, in the sense of protecting him. That word "care" means: "I had it in mind to do it." Paul was saying, "I was all the more eager to send him back to you so that you might have the benefit of the fellowship of his company." Paul sent him on this long journey that he should go back there to boost their morale.

We can see here the unselfishness of Paul. He was in prison, in one of the old pagan prisons. It was a situation where to be left alone would be multiplying a person's distress. The prisoner needed someone to help him, to bring him food and drink, and to take care of him. The people in Philippi had sent Epaphroditus to do this, and Epaphroditus had been doing it. When Epaphroditus heard that the people back home were unhappy and worried because they had heard he was sick, he wanted to go and tell them he was all right. When Paul considered it and thought about it, he felt that was the thing to do. He himself was in danger and in need. Yet he sends the man home. Why? Because they were worried. If ever anyone needed a boost, it would have been Paul. He was standing, as it were, in the very presence of death, yet he sends this young man home so the people there will be strengthened.

This is a wonderful demonstration of a fact that was characteristic of Paul. He would think about the other fellow. He was thinking about the other believers. When he realized that the return of their beloved brother would encourage them and inspire them and gladden their hearts, Paul in his prison knew that he would rejoice in thinking that Epaphroditus had gone home and that the people there had been helped and blessed. The return of their beloved brother would encourage them and inspire them. This would give Paul joy and actually lift his own spirit. Here is a wonderful, profound truth. When a believer is depressed and fearful, would you know what would be the best cure? When a believer is depressed and fearful, and feels let down, he only needs to do something to help someone else, and he will be helped.

In the course of the Book of the Philippians, Paul had written various things to these people encouraging them not to worry about him. You remember how in the first chapter he said, "Don't worry about me. I can't lose. If they kill me everyone will talk about it and will explain why. If they don't kill me, I will talk about it. In any way my testimony will be talked about, the Gospel will be preached, and the name of Christ will be lifted up. I may die but for me to live is Christ and to die is gain. I will be ahead if I do. If they take my life, okay, I'll be ahead. If they leave me here, I'll preach and I'll teach and I'll tell you about the Lord." This is the way Paul understood his own situation. This is a way of saying, "Don't worry about me, I can't lose. I will win coming and going."

Toward the end of the first chapter he said to these young Christians, "Get yourselves together into one effort to stand together. Say the same thing. Be of one heart and of one mind." If a number of believers will aim to say the same thing, they cannot individually say everything each wants to say. They can get together and say the same things only in the Lord.

So Paul urged them, "Let this mind be in you, which was also in Christ Jesus." He pointed out how the Lord Jesus, though He was equal with God, did not think that was a thing to be kept, but gave Himself to be emptied, made Himself of no reputation, and, being found in fashion as a man, was obedient even unto death. Paul knew that as this mind of Christ, which was marked by humility, would be in them, each one in turn would have his or her experience of being rejected. Each one would have his or her experience of being actually put to death by the enemy, but he urged them to trust God. God can raise the dead.

Then Paul told them how he had sent Timothy to comfort them and to find out about them, that he might return and tell Paul how they were getting along. Then he told them he was going to send Epaphroditus back to them, so they would have the fellowship of his company. Paul wanted these young Philippian believers to stand strong. And one of the ways they could stand strong would be to fellowship one with another in the name of the Lord Jesus Christ.

## Chapter 37

## RECEIVE HIM

(Philippians 2:29)

*Can you see how it would help a congregation to honor its pastor?*

Any group of people would be greatly strengthened when their leader is honored. And as I have just intimated, that would be good for a congregation. Believe me, any congregation of people is strengthened when they honor their pastor. One of the most disastrous things that can happen is when a congregation gets the habit of criticizing, or downgrading the pastor or officers of that church. For anyone in a company of people to belittle the leaders is to hurt the whole company. It is true in any place where people work together. If you belittle the foreman you hurt the project, if you make fun of the teacher, you hurt the school, criticize or lampoon the president, and you hurt the country.

It is always a great thrill to see one of your own appreciated. If your own child is talked about and something big is made of it it lifts your heart. What a marvelous thing it is when your own friend is appreciated and praised! You personally are strengthened; and in the same way, by the same principle, if someone who belongs to you is disparaged it hurts you. If someone in whom you are putting your confidence is discredited it weakens you. I know it will not only irritate, it will annoy, and it will hurt your feelings; but it will do more than that. It will weaken your spirit. It will weaken your morale. Appreciating a leader strengthens each follower. Honoring the teacher improves the classroom. Respecting the pastor is good for the church.

There were steps these believers could take which would help them face the coming persecution. Just now we notice one of the things they could do was to treat Epaphroditus, whom·Paul was going to send, with a victory attitude. They were to treat him as something special.

> Receive him therefore in the Lord with all gladness; and hold such in reputation (2:29).

He was their servant and he had been serving them in the name of Christ by helping Paul. Paul wanted them, as we would say, to roll out the red carpet and give him the royal treatment, because this would be good for them. In the very way in which they would treat him, they would be strengthened. Paul wrote: "Receive him therefore in the Lord with all gladness." "Receiving him" was to treat him with respect, with special consideration. They were to receive him in the Lord. This is not to receive him because he was personally so strong. It was not a matter of receiving him because he was so attractive in appearance. It was not a matter of receiving him because he was so intellectually brilliant. He was to be received in the Lord. What would this mean?

They were to look upon this Epaphroditus as a believer. When they saw this man come back from Rome where Paul was, and come over to Macedonia where they were, they were to look on him as a confessed sinner, as a man who had turned to God in his sin and had believed on the Lord Jesus Christ and had been saved. This was a man who had received Christ Jesus as his Savior. This man was a fellow member of the body of Christ. He was a fellow believer and just as Christ was in them even so Christ was in him. This man was a witness before the world, and they were standing with him. He would tell the whole world the facts about Jesus Christ and they would support him. This man was a praying co-worker. He would be praying for them; they would pray for him. This is what it means to receive him in the Lord. As believers we need to realize that other believer is important. We should treat him that way, especially if he is a leader. We should receive him in the Lord with all gladness.

The Philippian believers could be glad about everything that involved Epaphroditus. They could be glad when they remembered what he went through to become a believer. They could be glad about what Christ Jesus went through to save him. They could be glad about how Almighty God watched over him to keep him, and they could be glad about his present service.

This Epaphroditus was a true believer. He could stand up before the world and talk for Christ. He would be persecuted. He might be mistreated but he was their fellow believer. They could know that they belonged to him and with him, and as far as the future was concerned, this was a man that would serve Christ all the days of his life and when this world was done, he would be finished here, but he would be seated with Him in glory.

"Receive him with all gladness; and hold such in reputation." This is the way we ought to feel about all other believers, other people whom we know who also profess Christ. Let us be careful we do not fall into the way the world does. Suppose a woman is expending herself in the name of the Lord. She teaches a Bible class or she works with young people. If there were any possible way to criticize her, it will be done. Paul would say, "Remember who she is and hold such in reputation, receiving her with gladness." It is so important to your Sunday school teacher that you stand by that person as well as with your preacher and your minister.

I am talking about someone who believes in Jesus Christ. I am talking about someone who believes in prayer. If you have in your company someone known to be an earnest believer, a hard-working Christian who is trying to win other people, calling on other people, visiting other people, handing out tracts, going to services and bringing other people to church, and someone criticizes that person, stand by him. Hold such in reputation. Why? For your sake. And for the sake of the church. Let me tell you right now you will be stronger if you honor the faithful servant of Christ. Stand by your pastor, support him inasmuch as he is a faithful minister of Christ. Hold up his hand and let him know that you are on his side. God will bless you for it.

*Chapter 38*

# FOR THE WORK OF CHRIST
## (Philippians 2:30)

*Did you know that there are believers so dedicated to the spread of the Gospel that they will risk their very lives in order to tell others about Christ?*

To be a witness for Jesus Christ in this world, to openly confess that one is a believer in the Lord Jesus Christ, has actually been the cause of sad treatment. In fact at times it has meant tragic death for many in the history of the Gospel. Many people living as believers today live rather comfortable lives. Yet, there are some who really suffer because they confess they are believers. Of this other believers are largely unaware.

Suffering believers do not often talk about their troubles. There are mothers who do not publish to the whole world how their children are disobedient and unruly when they are asked to attend church. To say "I believe in Jesus Christ" or to say "I confess that I hold that Jesus Christ is Lord" arouses in many places hostile opposition and in some places it involves real loss. A confessing believer can actually get hurt because of his witness.

> But call to remembrance the former days, in which, after ye were illuminated, ye endured a great fight of afflictions; partly, whilst ye were made a gazing-stock both by reproaches and afflictions; and partly, whilst ye became companions of them that were so used. For ye had compassion of me in my bonds, and took joyfully the spoiling of your goods, knowing in yourselves that ye have in heaven a better and an enduring substance (Heb. 10:32-34).

Paul told the Philippians that Epaphroditus was such a person and had actually exhausted himself for the sake of the Gospel. In the book of Philippians we read:

Because for the work of Christ he was nigh unto death, not regarding his life, to supply your lack of service toward me (2:30).

The history of the Christian church is marked by lurid examples of persecution unto physical death. And yet there is another form of witnessing at personal cost. I know it is one thing to stand up in a crisis and to say that you believe, at the risk of losing everything, but it is quite another thing to stand up and to live a long lifetime in which you suffer again and again, day by day, while your life is a living sacrifice offered to God. It is one thing to face one critical moment, as John the Baptist did in prison when he was beheaded. That is over quickly, but it is quite another thing to face a lifetime when the believer offers his body a living sacrifice. This is the harder task.

When I had the privilege several years ago of being in Brazil, I was taken in the city of Campinas to a cemetery where I was shown something that stirred my heart. In the center of the cemetery was a clean white marble shaft pointing up from the grave into the sky. When I drew near it, I saw there was scarcely any inscription upon it. It contained just the name of the man and this phrase taken from this verse: "Not regarding his life." It happened that several generations ago when that city was smitten with an attack of yellow fever that reached epidemic proportions, many people were sick and dying with scarcely anyone there to take care of them. A certain missionary who was serving in Campinas at that time was the grandfather of the man with whom I was staying in Brazil. This missionary was busy taking care of the sick and the dying, and with people dying all round about him, he personally expected that he would die. One day a young man got off the train in this city, and came over to this missionary. "Are you Dr. Lane?" "Yes." "I have come to work with you in taking care of these people." Dr. Lane said, "Listen, get back on that train right away. You can't stay here. This place is in epidemic situation. Yellow fever is everywhere. It is as much as your life is worth to be here. What in the world are you thinking about?"

And this young man looked at him and smiled, saying, "That is what I came for. I have one life. I want to use it." The story I heard was that that young man started to take care of the sick and the dying, until he himself contracted the disease. He died in the city of Campinas. The city was so moved by this action of this young man who had traveled hundreds of miles to come on purpose that he might help, even though it meant his own death, that they put that monument up for him. I stood in front of it and was deeply blessed in my own soul. I prayed Almighty God that something of that spirit might find its place in me: "Not regarding his life." One is reminded of Stephen who was stoned to death for his witness to Christ Jesus. It was this same kind of man that can be seen in Epaphroditus who worked himself sick.

> Because for the work of Christ he was nigh unto death, not regarding his life, to supply your lack of service toward me (2:30).

There are people today who suffer daily because they serve Christ. It is hard for anyone who wants to be a believer and who wants to be faithful. The believer will want to honor God's name. He will want to read the Bible and believe it. He will want to go to church and share in the fellowship of Christians. He will want to pray. He will want to give to missions, and he will want to bear witness to the Lord. He will wish his children would believe. He will wish his wife would believe. He will wish his brothers and sisters would believe. And so he will seek in any way he possibly can to bear witness and to hold a light up before them. He will want to tell them about it and they will mistreat him. They will criticize him. They will ignore him. They will neglect him. They will say "all manner of evil falsely" against him.

As you live your life there will be some of you reading this now who want to witness for Christ, and it would be true about you that so far as you are concerned, even though your life is being spent as if you were a hero or a heroine, you are actually suffering. You will remain unwept, unhonored, and unsung and I cannot promise you anything better. I cannot promise you any change in this world. Some of you will never see the day when things will be any different than they are on this earth; but oh, you have a future before you! You are one of those believers who in their own experience "fill up the sufferings of Christ." But it is gloriously true that "if we suffer with him, we shall also reign with him." If you yield yourself into His will, to do His will, and you suffer rejection and denial, and you suffer by being shut out and actually being resisted over and over again, I can assure you you have a place with Him. You will be with Him.

You may be a mother with your heart aching from long suffering on behalf of your children. You are praying for them. You are caring for them. You want to talk to them and they won't listen. You would do anything you can for them, and they mistreat you. God knows. You may be a wife and your life may be hard, with no prospect things will be any different, and you may die in the situation as it is, but He will raise you from the dead. You may be a parent, and the child of your own body, your own flesh and blood, may go out and bring shame upon you, and may mistreat you because you are a believer. God will be with you. It may be that you are concerned about a sister or a brother. It may be that you are concerned about a friend. You may remember how it was with Paul when he said, writing to Timothy:

> At my first answer no man stood with me, but all men forsook me: I pray God that it may not be laid to their charge. Notwithstanding the Lord stood with me, and strengthened me (2 Tim. 4:16, 17).

So I would say, don't forget this. Don't ever let it drop out of your sight. God sees you, when for the work of Christ you suffer nigh unto death, not regarding your life, in order that you might witness for Him. God won't miss that and He is "able to save to the uttermost" those who put their trust in Him. It may not be in this world but this world is not for long. It will be in eternity that God will surely exalt you into His presence beside the Lord Jesus Christ.

## Chapter 39

## REJOICE IN THE LORD

### (Philippians 3:1)

*Do you think that telling again and again what Christ has done for me would be any hindrance to me spiritually?*

Finally, my brethren, rejoice in the Lord. To write the same things to you, to me indeed is not grievous, but for you it is safe (3:1).

Paul is writing to prepare these young believers for the shock of possible persecution. They are going to be in trouble in days ahead, partly because they believe in the Lord Jesus Christ. Paul wants to prepare them for that, because to a young believer it is rather a shocking thing to think that because he believes in God the Almighty, and has put his trust in the Lord Jesus Christ as his Savior, the gracious and merciful Lord, that he will now have trouble. He could have expected that when he turned his heart to the Lord there would be an end to his troubles. When he put his trust in Christ, would God not take care of him? Then, too, Paul understood that because they are believers they would have in them the grace of God that is in Christ Jesus, and so they would be inclined to be humble and meek. They would be inclined to shrink in the face of opposition, and in the face of trouble. At the same time they were human and that would mean they could become discouraged.

Paul was a prisoner, and so in danger of execution. He was not assuredly expecting death, because he thought God might spare him, but Paul knew that when the Philippians heard that he was in prison they would be fearful. He knew that this would tend to depress them. It seems strange that whereas Paul was the one who was in danger of being put to death, they were the ones that were in danger of being discouraged. We see Paul standing in the face of death taking time out to build up their courage and their strength.

Paul assures them he is praying for them. He reminds them that he is thanking God for their fellowship in his sufferings: they stood by him when he was in prison. Paul appreciated this very much, and he gives thanks to God for their comradeship in his trouble and in his bonds. He wants them now to become increasingly filled with the inward disposition to lay themselves out on behalf of other people. He wants their love to abound. He yearns that they would have an open heart to concern themselves about other people. He wants them to be able to see all things clearly as they are, that they might be filled with all the fruits of righteousness.

Paul wrote to these believers in Philippi to take the pressure off their hearts. He urged them to close ranks in their common witness, and to be gracious to each other. This would be a source of comforting strength to them. Then he went on to tell them to let the mind of Christ prevail in them. "Let this mind be in you, which was also in Christ Jesus." He pointed out that they should have humility as Jesus of Nazareth had. He tells them that God will be working in them "to will and to do of his good pleasure." He also tells them how the mind of Christ showed up in Timothy with his consideration for others, and then how it showed up in Epaphroditus with his zeal for the work. After that he told them how he had been personally led to consecrate himself totally into the service of his Lord. He also told them to remember that their home was in heaven and that that was where they were going. In all of these things, the apostle was seeking to strengthen their faith.

After this he writes: "Finally, my brethren, rejoice in the Lord." Whenever you have that word "rejoice" you will remember that you cannot rejoice unless first you have joy. You cannot rewrite unless first you write. So you cannot rejoice unless first you joy. One can have joy in thinking about what the Lord has done. It is a joy to think about how you were reconciled to God. It is a joy to think about how God had sent His Son to help you. It is a joy to think that Christ Jesus came to die for you, and a joy to think that when He was buried, your sins were buried with Him. He rose again that you might rise from the dead. He ascended into heaven where you will be going, and while up there He sent down on the Day of Pentecost His Spirit to be in the believer's heart. All of these things fill the believer with joy. Paul says, "I am repeating myself. For me that is not grievous and for you it is good. It is a good thing to keep these things in mind." Paul emphasizes to them, no matter how ominous the situation, no matter how much it looks as though the whole world is going to crowd in on them and they will have trouble, as believers they should look up. When the believer looks up into the presence of God, he can have joy. So Paul says to them, "Always keep this in mind. Look up and rejoice in the Lord." Look into His face. There is not a single blot in that picture. That is as clear and plain as sunlight. Look into His face and let His presence be your blessing.

## Chapter 40

## THE CIRCUMCISION

(Philippians 3:2, 3)

*Can you see that the biggest trouble for any group of people will always come from inside?*

Opposition to the Gospel from unbelievers can be expected. Such opposition is easier to withstand than the opposition that arises from those who profess faith, but whose hearts are natural. Part of the sufferings of Christ was: "He came unto his own, and his own received him not." That the world should have rejected Him would not be so strange, since the world did not know Him. But when His own people, who knew about His coming, refused to recognize Him, this was part of His great distress. Along with this was the fact that one of His own betrayed Him. "He that eateth bread with me hath lifted up his heel against me."

We will find that some of the most stubborn opposition will come from groups inside the church. So it was in the early days of the church. There were those in the church who were not willing to follow closely with the Lord. They wanted the name and the benefits, but they did not want the discipline. You will remember that Isaac had two sons, Esau and Jacob. They were quite different and there was war between their descendants always. You will remember that there was strife even in the family of Noah. It was Ham as over against Shem and Japheth; and again in the family of Abraham, Isaac truly was the son of promise, but Ishmael was also a son of Abraham, though he did not receive the promise.

Paul warns in the time of the Philippian believers there would be people among them who would distract and distress them by bringing in contrary ideas. He has this to say:

148

> Beware of dogs, beware of evil workers, beware of the con-
> cision. For we are the circumcision, which worship God in
> the spirit, and rejoice in Christ Jesus, and have no con-
> fidence in the flesh (3:2, 3).

Look at this first phrase: "Beware of dogs." That may
seem rather harsh, when one realizes that he was referring to
people who were bringing in ideas that were not true to the
Gospel. It was not uncommon in that culture to call anyone
who differed with preferred views a "dog." Among the
Jewish people it was customary to call the Gentiles "dogs"
because they had views about God that did not agree with
the Jewish revelation. Paul wrote "Beware of dogs. Beware
of those people in the community spreading ideas that are
contrary to your Gospel. Beware of evil workers." They are
mischief makers. It is somewhat obscure when he writes
"Beware of the concision." We do not use that word often
today. It refers to people who felt that to get right with
God they had to mutilate their flesh. Paul is saying to his
followers: "Keep away from that." Sometimes men will walk
among the believers as proud as the devil. They claim to be
very spiritual because they do not do this and they do not do
that, and they do not go here and they do not go there.
Paul says, "Avoid them." Three times over he gives this
warning: "Beware of dogs, beware of evil workers, beware
of the concision." But how in the world would a person know
who these are? The believer should go to the Bible. "To
the law and to the testimony: if they speak not according to
this word, it is because there is no light in them" (Is. 8:20).

Paul goes on to say more positively:

> For we are the circumcision, which worship God in the
> spirit, and rejoice in Christ Jesus, and have no confidence
> in the flesh (3:3).

This is the classic utterance. You will not find anything
better stated as far as the Gospel is concerned. "We are the
circumcision." By this term he is referring to the whole idea
that was back of this ceremony as practiced by the Jews,
a ceremony which gave notice that the flesh was not to be
considered. The flesh was not to be trusted. The flesh was

not to be depended upon. To belong to "the circumcision" means that such a person is ready to set the flesh aside, and will in due time be led to follow the Lord Jesus Christ: he will take up his cross, crucify the flesh and follow the Lord. When the flesh is set aside the believer will be standing in the presence of God not on the basis of what he does.

Anything the believer may do, good or bad, does not depend upon him at all. He is not trusting in himself. He is trusting in the Lord. He trusts in God because of who He is. So he rejoices in Christ Jesus. This is his joy. He can rejoice in Christ Jesus. He can rejoice in His grace. He can rejoice in Christ's self-denial on his behalf. He can rejoice in His power by which He can raise the dead. He can rejoice in Christ's plan to present him faultless in the presence of God. The believer finds his joy in Christ Jesus and has no confidence in the flesh: not in anything that is human, not in himself, not in others, not in any future promises. The believer worships God in the spirit. He rejoices in Christ Jesus, and in all that He has done and will do for him. This is the way in which we can understand the whole outlook of the believer in Christ Jesus.

## Chapter 41

## NO CONFIDENCE IN THE FLESH

### (Philippians 3:4)

*Have you ever noticed how often it is the really capable person who is humble?*

It belongs to the glory of the Gospel that God is no respecter of persons. Anyone can come to Him. He sees all men as sinners. They are as sheep scattered having no shepherd. Everyone of them is doomed to destruction. The soul that sins shall die and there is no man that does not sin. "All have sinned and come short of the glory of God." Because of His mercy God has sent His Son into the world to seek and to save the lost. Christ Jesus came to give His life a ransom for many.

Among human beings it is a natural thing to compare ourselves with ourselves. However, when I get to be a believer in Christ Jesus, and am born again in Him, I come to understand something of the goodness and the grace of God. It is then I understand that flesh and blood cannot inherit the kingdom of God. Receiving the blessing of God will not be by human effort. One can wonder why God in His wisdom arranged that man should be born in the flesh. One can wonder if the plan was that man was to begin his relationship with God by exercise of his own will and judgment. Must a man condemn himself, so that he can repent? This is the first step the believer takes. He must repent and believe in the Lord Jesus Christ. Repentance is a matter of looking into one's own heart and evaluating one's own conduct, and just seeing that one is not what he ought to be. A man can turn from his own being so that he may depend entirely on the grace of God in Christ Jesus.

This is undoubtedly what Jesus of Nazareth had in mind when He told Nicodemus, "Ye must be born again." Here

151

is the basic issue for all men everywhere. The Savior comes to seek and to save the lost. His grace is available for those who in themselves can feel themselves to be lost: like Isaiah:

> Woe is me! for I am undone; because I am a man of unclean lips, and I dwell in the midst of a people of unclean lips: for mine eyes have seen the King, the LORD of hosts (Isa. 6:5).

Or Job:

> I have heard of thee by the hearing of the ear: but now mine eye seeth thee. Wherefore I abhor myself, and repent in dust and ashes (Job 42:5, 6).

The Apostle Paul calls himself "the chief of sinners." It is of basic importance that one should understand one's self, and honestly answer the question, "What think ye of Christ?" If I say, "He was a good man," that is true, but there is more. He died for me, I now am reconciled to God. Because He gave Himself for me, I am taken into the family of God as a child of God. That is the important thing. The believer may have no confidence in himself, but can rejoice in the conviction that his own blessing comes as a gift from God through Jesus Christ.

> Though I might also have confidence in the flesh. If any other man thinketh that he hath whereof he might trust in the flesh, I more (3:4).

Paul was a very fortunate person. He was a gifted person, but he saw he needed more. Some of us can think back on our heredity, and be aware that our family has been known down through the years. This is a great snare actually. Some folks are strong. Some folks are smart. Some folks are clever. Some folks are wise. Some folks are able. But any of these traits can be a snare. The great danger is in the possibility they will begin to trust in themselves. Some people have a good reputation. They even work and struggle for it. If a witness were to come to one of them and ask, "Will you accept the Lord Jesus Christ?" he might ask, "Why?" And if he were told that he is a lost sinner, he might well reply: "Wait a minute. People around here think I am a great man. In the church I am considered a great worker, and you are telling me I must be born again?" This is exactly what the witness wants to tell him, but it is very difficult to make this seem true because he is taken in a snare of his own self-esteem. Others can be snared by their own zeal. They work hard at good things. They are active whenever there is anything to be done. They are right in the forefront, and may be about to work themselves to death. They can then get to where they have big confidence in their own work. They think they do so much, that they easily have the feeling that if there is a God in heaven at all, He will certainly appreciate what they have done. But Paul reminds us he has "no confidence in the flesh." As important as his personal gifts and achievements may have been, they could not save the soul. Gamaliel, that great teacher among the Jews at the time of the New Testament, spoke plainly about all of the capacity of any man when he said, "If this thing be of men, it will come to naught." For anyone to put his confidence in man is to make a big mistake. "Cursed be the man that trusteth in man, and maketh flesh his arm, and whose heart departeth from the LORD" (Jer. 17:5). Paul plainly stated, We "have no confidence in the flesh." You know he knew the Lord. And so we are encouraged to put our confidence in Him.

## Chapter 42

## A HEBREW OF THE HEBREWS

### (Philippians 3:4, 5)

*Can you see why it is that it is so hard for a good person, one who is religious and moral and respectable, to become a real believer in Christ?*

Jesus of Nazareth taught His disciples that it is hard for a rich man to enter into the kingdom of God. It is hard for a strong man to enter the kingdom of God. It is hard for a beautiful woman to enter the kingdom of God. It is hard for a successful business man who has made money to enter into the kingdom of God. It is hard for a good woman who is clean and honest and respectable and decent and kind to enter into the kingdom of God. Why? Because no one gets there by what he does. Because Christ came to save sinners, not the righteous, but sinners. If a person establishes himself as a righteous person he is out of the picture. Christ came to save sinners, to redeem failures, to save losers. And it is hard for a rich man to see himself as needing help.

You will remember the rich young ruler; when he heard what it would take to enter into the kingdom of God, he went away sorrowful. He had great possessions. The first thing he would need to do would be to give them up. That he did not want to do. The first essential step in living in Christ Jesus, belonging to God and living in the Spirit viz. the first essential step toward being saved is this: "If any man will be my disciple, let him deny himself." In all honesty this is a difficult thing for any person to do. Men are so sensitive about being considered lacking in anything. It is natural for them to develop an attitude of alibiing. They get into a defensive frame of mind. Whenever they see anything at all where they seem to be better than someone

154

else, they immediately ascribe to themselves a superior position. Every such action on their part makes it that much harder for them to come into the kingdom of God.

There are men who are strong just as there are women who are beautiful. There are young people who are outstanding. Do you realize that for such there is a special problem about coming into the kingdom of God? And do you realize why? It is because the first step they have to take is to repent. And how can you repent when you are good? How can you repent when you are strong? What that person needs to understand, needs to read and see and enter into and believe, is "there is none good." I can tell you that means you. There is nothing about you so good that God will give you salvation because of that. Now Paul could have had this difficulty. He realized it, and he said about himself:

> Though I might also have confidence in the flesh. If any other man thinketh that he hath whereof he might trust in the flesh, I more: circumcised the eighth day, of the stock of Israel, of the tribe of Benjamin, an Hebrew of the Hebrews; as touching the law, a Pharisee (3:4, 5).

"Circumcised the eighth day" means that his family believed in God, and they dedicated him as an infant to God. He came out of a believing home. Now not many persons have that privilege.

In Paul's case, his parents were people who believed in God. They dedicated this infant to God, and when he was eight days old, they circumcised him. This marked him for life as belonging to God. That would be a great advantage for any man. "Of the stock of Israel." Israel had the promises of God and Paul was one of them. Thus he was an heir of all the traditions that belong to Israel. "Of the tribe of Benjamin." When the nation of Israel was split into two parts, the northern part was made up of ten tribes, and the southern part constituted the two tribes that were orthodox. They were the people who had the Temple. Those two tribes were Judah and Benjamin. So Paul was a man who had an orthodox heritage. Paul came from a community of people who were faithful to God: "A Hebrew of the

Hebrews." He was one who shared in the covenant of Abraham and he rested on it all the way through his life.

"As touching the law, a Pharisee." I am sure that many people should have their concept of the Pharisees corrected. No doubt many have gained the wrong impression because of the fact that the Pharisees were often criticized by Jesus of Nazareth and their views were actually rejectèd. Some might think that perhaps they were an ugly people. This is by no means true. Do you know what the normal pattern of a Pharisee was? A Pharisee believed the Scriptures to be the Word of God. He was faithful in all his religious exercises. He attended all of the worship services. He made his sacrifices to God and he fasted twice a week and he gave tithes of all the income that he had. Even amongst ourselves it is true that if there were someone in the church of whom it could be said that he believed the Bible was absolutely the Word of God, that he tried to keep everything in the Bible strictly the way in which it was written and that that man actually fasted twice a week for religious reasons, and that he actually gave one tenth of his income to the church, you would be inclined to think you had a pretty good man, and you would be right. Paul was this sort of a man but he knew none of that would count. It belonged to his Jewish upbringing that he felt that these religious items that he had listed here were his greatest assets.

Now I cannot help but think that some of us might say, "My uncle was a great financier, or one of my family was one of the original signers of the Declaration of Independence, or one of my family was one of the great generals in an important war that we fought," and so on. We might find some human reason for thinking that we were better than other people. But I note that Paul showed his Jewish upbringing in that when he reviewed all the things that could make him exceptional, he stressed those which belonged to his relationship with God. The Jews considered a man's relationship to God more important than anything else.

If I were to come to God, I must confess myself to be

unfit. The Gospel requires that a man repent, acknowledge himself as unfit before God.

It is a hard thing to repent, to consider myself unfit, when I know that compared to other people I am good, I am moral, I am respectable and I am even religious. It is natural that I would want to justify myself so far as I had any real virtue.

When a man comes from a godly family, and belongs to a historic persuasion such as Protestant or Catholic, or if he belongs to an honored denomination such as Episcopalian, or Presbyterian, or Baptist, or Methodist, it could be expected that it would be said about him, "There is a Christian if I ever saw one. He goes to church and does all the right things. In the matter of handling the Bible, he is a fundamentalist, a conservative, and you mean to tell that man that he must repent?" Exactly. It is no wonder that many cannot do this. But Paul did, and by the way, we should not forget Paul's whole feeling about this. It is expressed clearly in his own words:

> Brethren, my heart's desire and prayer to God for Israel is, that they might be saved. For I bear them record that they have a zeal of God, but not according to knowledge. For they being ignorant of God's righteousness, and going about to establish their own righteousness, have not submitted themselves unto the righteousness of God (Rom. 10:1-3).

And how many there are like that, who think that because they belong to the church and are active in the church and are trying to live a good life, that that will qualify them before God. Paul would definitely deny this conclusion.

## Chapter 43

## ZEAL — BLAMELESS
### (Philippians 3:4-6)

*Do you realize that it is especially difficult for an active church worker to become a real believer in Christ?*

Paul wrote to encourage these young believers because of the trouble they were sure to face. They would face persecution. His major emphasis was to urge them to let the mind of Christ prevail in their hearts. For a frame of mind and attitude that they were to maintain, he described the mind of Christ in chapters 2 and 3. He pointed out that the primary aspect of the mind of Christ was seen in Jesus of Nazareth. Christ's humility is basic in all His conduct. Paul also brought Timothy to their minds and showed them how in Timothy there was to be seen consideration for others. After this he brought Epaphroditus to their attention and pointed out that he was distinguished by one thing, his zeal in service. This dedicated man worked himself sick helping Paul with the Gospel. Throughout his presentation Paul was admonishing these young believers in Philippi to let the Holy Spirit activate such behavior in them.

In chapter 3 Paul brought in himself as an example. He did not hesitate to set forth his own consecration to God. In telling of himself, Paul dwelt upon the course of his experience. He said:

> If any other man thinketh that he hath whereof he might trust in the flesh, I more: circumcised the eighth day, of the stock of Israel, of the tribe of Benjamin, a Hebrew of the Hebrews; as touching the law, a Pharisee; concerning zeal, persecuting the church; touching the righteousness which is in the law, blameless (3:4-6).

This description helps us to see what a person might have in the flesh. Not all human beings have their backs turned to God. Some actually seek God. Not all discredit God. Some

158

actually want to honor Him. Some folks are more fortunate in themselves than others, and Paul has outlined here how he was more fortunate than others because of his background.

Paul had been "circumcised the eighth day." This showed that he was reared in that kind of family, "of the stock of Israel." He had that kind of heritage "of the tribe of Benjamin." That showed where he came from. "Hebrew of the Hebrews" was his cultural relationship. "As touching the law, a Pharisee" was a reference to his own attitude toward the Scriptures. Paul belonged to people who believed the Bible to be the Word of God. Now he mentions two other things. "Concerning zeal, persecuting the church" showed his personal attitude. Saul the Pharisee had been in dead earnest. He put himself into his convictions. "Touching the righteousness which is in the law, blameless," showed that his personal conduct was concerned with doing what was right. Saul the Pharisee had been blameless. He pointed out that if anyone could get anywhere because of natural assets, he had them. Not only had he been fortunate in his heritage but he had been diligent in his personal conduct. Saul was in dead earnest but, we can note very humbly, he was dead wrong. He learned this later.

In Saul's case, he had been persecuting the believers. He was so zealous for the truth that he thought the Jewish doctrines, the truth that he believed, which was included in the Jewish religious beliefs, should be maintained. When Christians believed something else and talked to others, he brought them into court and accused them of being subversive. He thought they were wrong, and that he was right. All the time it was he who was wrong, and they were right. Paul realized that his zeal as he persecuted these good people because he thought they were wrong, would have qualified him as being a good man. Many people would have said, "He is a good man. He is trying hard. He is really putting himself into it. You have to say one thing for him, he is in dead earnest." But being in dead earnest does not make a person right. Going in the right way and knowing the truth makes a person right.

Concerning his personal conduct Paul could say this: "As touching the righteousness which is in the law, whether I do right or wrong, whether I steal, whether I lie, whether I hate anyone, whether I am unkind to other people, whether I covet other people, whether I am disrespectful to God, all those things would break the law. But as touching the righteousness which is in the law ('whatsoever a man soweth that shall he also reap'), judging by the way in which I act, I am blameless." This does not necessarily mean that Paul said he never made a mistake, but Paul knew according to the law what to do if he did make a mistake. Every person who knew the law knew what to do if he sinned. If he sinned he would bring in a sacrifice. His sin would be forgiven. And then what would be the situation? He would be blameless. This was what Paul meant. He honored and accepted the Ten Commandments as the law of God. He tried to obey them, but if he failed in anything, he would bring in his sacrifice before God and confess his sin; this would keep him blameless before God.

A person could do all this in the flesh. A person could go to church, be active in church, read the Bible, listen to the preacher, sing the hymns, accept all things that are said about God, and even feel that he believed all things as he understood them, and still be thinking and acting as a human being in his own wisdom and strength.

Are you trusting Him for your salvation? Or are you trusting your own righteousness? Are you depending upon Jesus Christ or are you depending on your record? Paul was now, at the time he wrote this letter, able to see that all that was true about him as a privileged human being, which is described in verses 4, 5 and 6, was by the flesh; and because it was by the flesh, good flesh, religious flesh, moral flesh, zealous flesh, orthodox flesh, and yet only flesh, it was inadequate. It would not do. Paul rejoiced in the fact that while the flesh could never qualify as acceptable before God, the soul through faith in Christ Jesus could come with confidence into God's presence "acceptable in the beloved."

## Chapter 44

## LOSS FOR CHRIST

(Philippians 3:7)

*Do you think that if a person became a believer in Christ, he would ever have to give up any good thing?*

But what things were gain to me, those I counted loss for Christ (3:7).

Each person has certain personal assets that give him an advantage over other people. Each of us can ask himself, "What is it that I have that I wish I had more of?" And such assets can become very precious to any natural person. Paul, after he understood about Jesus Christ, would say that accepting Christ Jesus as Savior means taking Him as my confidence in place of anything else. The basic issue in the Gospel is a proposal from God to me that I should agree to an exchange. He offers to exchange the Lord Jesus Christ for all that I have in me in which I might put my confidence.

It works something like this. If a boy came with a pail to get some honey, and his pail was full of water, how could he get his pail full of honey? He would have to pour out the water so that he could put in the honey. Exactly. First, he must empty the pail before it can be filled. In this simple procedure, can be understood the most profound truth in the Gospel of Jesus Christ.

Let me speak of myself as a believer. I am naturally full of myself, whether I am conceited or have an inferiority complex. Now, if I am going to come to Christ Jesus as my Savior, I must empty out all of me in self-denial. His own Son, Jesus of Nazareth, demonstrated how this is done: He emptied Himself. He made Himself of no reputation. This is the pattern I must follow. The fact that I am a sinner does not disqualify me. Christ Jesus said, "I came into the world to save sinners. I did not come for the righteous but for the sinners." So it would appear Christ Jesus did not come for the good people. Many persons think they are good, but they are mistaken. Many think they are righteous, but "there is none righteous, no, not one." "I came not for the righteous but for sinners."

This idea used to bother me. Of course, it was a wonderful thing if it could be true, because I was a sinner. If it were true it would mean that I would have a direct entrance into the very presence of God through Christ Jesus. Another statement in the Bible that always startled me said that publicans and harlots would enter into kingdom of heaven before many righteous people. This bothered me at first because it sounded so unlikely, but in time I could see that it was so much easier for a scoundrel to feel that he actually was a sinner. It would be so much easier for a wrong-doer to admit he was wrong. It is an easy thing to give up as a failure. On the other hand, it is a hard thing to give up when I feel that I am something worthwhile. Consider the rich young ruler. When he came to the Lord Jesus Christ, he asked, "What must I do that I might have eternal life?" The Lord told him to keep the rules according to the regulations. The young man was able to say, "I have done this since I was a child, all my life. What do I lack yet?" Then the Lord looking on him, loved him and said, "Now, if you really want what I have, you can start by taking everything you have, and giving it to the poor." In other words, I should transfer the ownership of all that I have, sell what I have and give to the poor. Then I should take up my cross, which is self-denial, and follow Him. Then I would have eternal life.

That is what Paul did. In Philippians 3:7 it is recorded that he said, "But what things were gain to me, those I counted loss for Christ." In these words he is saying, "I counted all my assets as no good. I put them aside. I had them, but I put them aside." It reminds me of a strong young man who wants to become a saved person. One of the first things he must have in mind is that he will not put any confidence in his own strength. He will still be strong even after he is a believer, but he is not counting on that. Perhaps the man has brains, in this case after he becomes a believer he will still be smart; but he will not count on his brains. He will not trust in his cleverness. He will trust in Christ. Paul said, "What things were gain to me," and by these words he means that although he was circumcised in the prescribed manner by his family on the eighth day he did not trust that any more. It was true, and even after he became a believer he was still a circumcised man, but that is not what he was depending upon.

In the matter of his heredity, he was of the stock of Israel and that was very fortunate. Not many people were, and he was one of the fortunate persons, but he would not count on that. He was of the tribe of Benjamin — which meant he had the right tradition. Benjamin had, all through the tribal history, been faithful to God. Paul was one of these people but he would not count on that. He was a Hebrew of the Hebrews, which meant this was his culture and he belonged to that group of people, blessed of God, followers of Abraham, but he would not count on that. As touching the law, he was a Pharisee, which meant he really believed in the Scriptures as the Word of God. Insofar as his record was concerned, he had zeal, he put himself into what he was doing and worked at it in dead earnest. But he was not trusting in that. As far as his character was concerned, it was above reproach. He was blameless but he was not trusting in that. "Those things which were gain to me" he counted as loss for Christ.

Believers do not depend upon heritage or family or church. Paul put no confidence in any of those good things. This is the crux of the whole Gospel call. This is a hard truth. Christ Jesus went to the cross of Calvary. He wants to save my soul from hell. He does it by shedding His blood. I thank God I was given the insight to see that I must put my trust in His blood. I do not need anything else. Paul counted all other things but loss that he might win Christ.

## Chapter 45

## SUFFERED THE LOSS

### (Philippians 3:8)

*Can you understand that the most important experience anyone can have is to become personally acquainted with the living Christ Jesus?*

The issue, "self or Christ," is to many persons drastic indeed. Some would say this leaves a person no ground upon which to stand. And that is a fact. The whole aim in the Gospel is for the believer to be none of self and all of Christ. The Apostle Paul used himself as an example and showed how he personally had no confidence in the flesh. For a believer who receives Christ Jesus as Savior and Lord, the issue boils down to this: that this person, this sinner needs to empty himself. This naturally seems hard, but it is essential and necessary. In coming to God, the believer must have no confidence in the flesh, not even when the flesh is strong or able. Paul speaks about himself as an example of one who has come to believe, and his testimony is clear:

> Yea doubtless, and I count all things but loss for the excellency of the knowledge of Christ Jesus my Lord: for whom I have suffered the loss of all things, and do count them but dung, that I may win Christ (3:8).

All things, past, present and future that he might have attained as a person, Paul would count but loss. He would get rid of them, "For the excellency of the knowledge of Christ Jesus my Lord." Above all else he wanted this superior excellent knowledge of Christ Jesus his Lord.

I grew up into manhood as an unbeliever. I was an agnostic skeptic. I came to believe in the reality of God, the reality of the Gospel that Christ Jesus died for me, and was gloriously, wonderfully blessed when I realized that

164

God had forgiven me my sin and made me His own. It was several years later when I faced the call that was coming into my soul that I should give up my chosen profession, which was law, and devote myself in my lifetime to telling other people about Jesus Christ. As I faced this call, I remember the final critical moment when one Sunday night, kneeling beside my bed, I asked God to let me know definitely whether He really wanted me to leave the law office and to go to the foreign fields. It was then that I realized something I had been unconscious about: I wanted a law office. I wanted my name up before people as a lawyer, and I wanted all the benefits and the privileges and the income that would come from being a lawyer. Now, in considering the possibility of the call to the mission field, I was faced with the fact that I would have to give up my personal hopes in order that I might obey the Lord.

I was reminded of my own experience when I was thinking about Paul's testimony. Paul says, "I count all things but loss for the excellency of the knowledge of Christ Jesus my Lord." When he wrote of "the knowledge of Christ Jesus," he was not referring to such knowledge *about* Christ which anyone could get by reading some history book. Paul meant the actual personal experience of Christ by meeting Him face to face. "For whom I have suffered the loss of all things." The only prospect Paul ever had was that of dying for the faith. He was made a martyr. He accepted this with all of its suffering gladly. Paul suffered the loss of all things and did "count them but dung." There are various translations of this passage, and various translators try to use a more elegant word than the word "dung." A person would need to be familiar with a farm-yard to know what that word actually means, but Paul knew what it meant. It has been suggested that one could use the word "refuse," and some people will say "dregs," "rubbish." One has translated this term to mean "less than nothing." One could almost say "like dirt under your feet." These various translations all convey much the same idea. As far as Paul was concerned, anything past, present, or future in which he could have found any personal satisfaction or could have felt any kind of personal pride in having, was thrown out. He counted such things but dung. Of course, in one sense, they were not dung. They were actually good things in themselves, but he treated them like that, and Paul meant exactly what he wrote. He would throw out all of that, that he might win Christ. This was not to win Christ as Savior, for he already had Him. And he did not mean Christ only as his atoning sacrifice. Christ had done that on the cross. But Paul wanted to win Christ as his living Advocate. He wanted to have a personal fellowship with the living Lord Jesus Christ to whom he could look as his living Intercessor in the presence of God, and as his personal Companion here by reason of the Holy Spirit being within him. This passage makes one think of what John wrote in his epistle: "to know Christ is life eternal."

## Chapter 46

## BE FOUND IN HIM!

## (Philippians 3:8, 9)

*Can you see that the greatest desire a believer can have is to be altogether involved in Christ Jesus?*

It is tomorrow that gives special meaning to what I do today. Whatever I do today, it is tomorrow when I am going to reap the consequences. This is true in spiritual things. When we think of Paul accepting Christ Jesus as his Savior and Lord at the total loss of everything personal that he had, what did he think he was getting? If I invite anyone to accept Christ, what can I promise him? Money? You say, no. Position? Can I promise him he will be president of a company, chairman of the board? No. Pleasure? Can I promise him that every day will be a delight? No. Profit? Can I promise him that he will get rich? No. Then what can I promise him? Let us listen to Paul.

Paul had just said that he suffered the loss of everything:

> That I may win Christ, and be found in him, not having mine own righteousness, which is of the law, but that which is through the faith of Christ, the righteousness which is of God by faith (3:8, 9).

That is exactly what Paul wanted. He wanted to have the righteousness which is of God by faith. What is meant by this word "righteousness"? Righteousness is the general quality of being right, of being in the will of God. When a person is right he is straight up and down before God. So when Paul is saying that he wanted to be found in Christ "not having my own righteousness," Paul was not particularly aiming to arrive at a spot where he was beyond fault in himself, so that he could act and live in such a way that he could expect blessing, protection, help, satisfaction from God, all because of what he did — "which is of the law." If

167

Paul had tried to achieve this kind of righteousness, he would have tried it by doing what was right. Then, in that effort, it would be true that if he failed in any one point, he would be guilty of the whole thing; he would fail all together. Trying to measure up to the standard of the law is something like a man who is trying to join a certain group of people when the requirement is that he should be 6 feet tall. So, any other measure would not do. A person 6 feet 1 inch or 5 feet 11 inches would not be admitted. If a person wants to be right in the sight of the law by what he does, it will have to be perfect. Paul is admitting that he did not want to try that. He knew he could not. "There is none righteous, no, not one." He wanted to be found in Christ so that he would have that righteousness which is through the faith of Christ. The Gospel provides a righteousness to be received by faith, and this is what Paul wanted.

Abraham believed God and it was counted to him for righteousness. Receiving righteousness from God because God would work in him to will and to do of His good pleasure. Such righteousness would be real and it would show up as righteous. It will not be produced by human effort but it will be produced by the grace of God within the believer. James speaks of achieving righteousness in this manner:

> But wilt thou know, O vain man, that faith without works is dead? Was not Abraham our father justified by works, when he had offered Isaac his son upon the altar? Seest thou how faith wrought with his works, and by works was faith made perfect? And the scripture was fulfilled which saith, Abraham believed God, and it was imputed unto him for righteousness: and he was called the Friend of God (James 2:20-23).

Abraham believed God, and because he did, in God's plan, God imputed to him the grace that he needed. God gave him, without his working for it, what he needed to do the right thing. His faith was imputed to him for righteousness. "You see then how that by works a man is justified, and not by faith only." By faith to be sure, but not faith cut off.

Not just faith. It would be a faith that works. It is not faith and works. It is faith that works.

> Likewise also was not Rahab the harlot justified by works, when she had received the messengers, and had sent them out another way? For as the body without the spirit is dead, so faith without works is dead also (James 2:25, 26).

This faith that produces this righteousness is the faith of Christ. That is to say, it is faith that follows through in Christ Jesus. Let us see it simply this way: everything that Christ does is appropriated, taken over by the believing person, who commits himself to Christ. God shares the life of Christ with him and so we read of the righteousness which is of God by faith.

The Bible speaks of a believer being just. That is the way the Bible refers to God's judgment about a man who is in every way right in the sight of God. He is "just," i.e., he is "just right." He is exactly what God wants him to be, and this righteousness can be seen this way, but the word "righteousness" refers more directly to conduct, and it is essentially right being and right doing. This rightness was demonstrated in Christ Jesus as Jesus of Nazareth. He was right in the sight of God. He did right in the sight of God, and His whole manner, His whole way of living, was righteous in the sight of His Father. Now this can be shared by His grace with anyone who will believe in Him. The Bible speaks of this righteousness which is of God by faith. When the Bible says "of God" it means that God is the origin of the right being and the right doing, which can be seen in the life and conduct of the believer. God is personally responsible for the right living of the believer. The believer yields himself to God and lets God work in him to will and to do of His good pleasure. It is absolutely true so far as a believing Christian is concerned, that Christ is the answer to the problem of becoming and being "righteous."

## Chapter 47

## THAT I MAY KNOW HIM

### (Philippians 3:10)

*Can you understand that to truly know Jesus Christ one must have fellowship with the living Lord in his own daily life?*

And this is life eternal, that they might know thee the only true God, and Jesus Christ, whom thou hast sent (John 17:3).

These words were spoken by the Lord Jesus as He was praying to His Father in heaven. The Greek word "know" implies much more than "knowing about." We are so often inclined to say we know something, when we mean we have some information. But in our usage we actually make a difference in the use of the word "know." For instance, someone will say, "Do you know John Smith?" The answer may be, "I know about him. I know who he is and I know where he lives but I do not know him." We understand this. If I had said this I would have meant that I could identify him on the street, but I do not know what kind of a man he is. I could not be sure how he would act in a deal. Or if I could trust him. I could not say that he is dependable. Suppose you hear this sort of question? "Do you know Henry Brown? He is a member of your church; is he a real Christian?" You might hear an answer like this: "Yes, I know Henry Brown; he is a member of our church. But frankly I don't think he knows the Lord." Such a statement could be valid.

Paul was confronted by the risen Lord on the Damascus road. After meeting the Lord, Paul went about witnessing and showing by the Scriptures that Jesus was the Christ. By the time he wrote this letter to the Philippians, Paul had spent a lifetime as an apostle, as a missionary, and as an evangelist. Then what could Paul mean when he writes thus?

170

That I may know him, and the power of his resurrection, and the fellowship of his sufferings, being made conformable unto his death" (3:10).

We could ask ourselves, did not Paul know Jesus Christ? Had he not met Him on the Damascus road? Had he not proven to other people that Jesus of Nazareth really was the Christ, and had he not personally preached in His name for years in various places? Apparently this is not so much a matter of Paul wanting to be sure that he would be saved, as perhaps that he wanted to be sure that he would be sanctified.

Paul wanted personally to enter into the fullness of the blessing that was available in Christ. He had accepted Christ, and he had committed himself to him. He had served Him but there were things that Paul wanted to experience by the grace of God in Christ Jesus, that go further and deeper than he had ever experienced until now. There were four aspects in the Gospel of Jesus Christ as Paul preached it. For instance, Paul states the Gospel in 1 Corinthians 15:1-5: Christ died for our sins, that was one thing; He was buried, that is the second thing; He rose again on the third day, that is the third thing; and He was seen, that is the fourth. Here are four events in what happened to Jesus Christ and on the basis of these four things, the believer is blessed. Christ died for our sins: we can be forgiven; He was buried: we can bury our sins with Him. He rose again on the third day; we can be regenerated. He was seen during the space of forty days; we can be indwelt by the living Lord Jesus Christ day after day.

Paul in writing to the Colossians could say: "If you then be risen with Christ," because that is the way it is with every believer. In Paul's own writings it is plainly stated that the believer is risen with Christ, and Paul is one of the believers. He was risen with Christ. Then what else is there for him to have? Now look at the fourth aspect. Christ was seen. The living Lord Jesus Christ continues daily in the believer as long as the believer is here on earth. This was what Paul wanted to have happen to him in the fullest extent. Paul wanted this to be fully realized in himself.

When Paul says "that I may know him and the power of his resurrection" it should be remembered that he knew the facts, the data, of Christ's resurrection. Paul went about preaching, and actually was being stoned, because he affirmed that Jesus Christ was alive. But Paul wanted to realize this living Christ in himself. He wanted personally to be raised from the dead inside himself. In what sense would Paul be raised from the dead? He would ultimately be raised from the dead after this world was over. But he wanted to know what it was to live in newness of life here and now. Paul had an understanding that in the Christian person there is "the old man" which is natural, and "the new man" which is spiritual. Paul wanted to realize in himself that the spiritual is over the natural. He wanted to feel the power of the spiritual man, of the new man that was in Christ Jesus.

When Paul writes of the fellowship of his sufferings: "that I may know him, and the power of his resurrection, and the fellowship of his sufferings," Paul wanted to share the rejection of Christ. If people would reject Christ Jesus, they would have to reject the Apostle Paul. Paul had in his mind to do something like what is written in the Book of Hebrews to the believer: "Let us go forth therefore unto him without the camp, bearing his reproach" (Heb. 13:13). In these words the Scripture is admonishing all believing people: "Let us identify ourselves with the name of Jesus Christ, so that if they turn Him down, they must turn us down. If they do not want to think about the Lord Jesus Christ, let them turn their backs on us. We belong to Him." Paul wanted to share His rejection.

There is one more thing in this statement:

> That I may know him, and the power of his resurrection, and the fellowship of his sufferings, being made conformable unto his death (3:10).

Paul wanted to share in the crucifixion of the Lord Jesus Christ. He wanted his own flesh to be crucified, in a real spiritual sense. This is what he said had happened to him.

I am crucified with Christ: nevertheless I live; yet not I, but Christ liveth in me: and the life which I now live in the flesh I live by the faith of the Son of God, who loved me, and gave himself for me (Gal. 2:20).

Paul wanted this spiritual condition to be fully, one hundred percent, developed in his life. He wanted to enter into the fullness of the blessing of the Gospel in Jesus Christ that he might be completely delivered from the flesh, which was the dead thing. As far as he was concerned, his flesh was to be reckoned dead, because Paul knew that "if we suffer with him, we shall also reign with him."

## Chapter 48

## IF I MIGHT ATTAIN

### (Philippians 3:11)

*Does one who has accepted Christ Jesus as Savior and Lord need anything further to be fully blessed?*

> If by any means I might attain unto the resurrection of the dead (3:11).

It is a wonderful truth that all one needs to do to be saved is to believe on the Lord Jesus Christ. Do you remember what happened with the Philippian jailer when he came to Paul and Silas and, falling at their feet said, "Sirs, what must I do to be saved?" The answer was simple and direct. "Believe on the Lord Jesus Christ, and thou shalt be saved, and thy house." That very night he believed and was blessed.

The New Testament is filled with examples of how people have believed and have been blessed. One is reminded of the coming of the leper. "Lord, if thou wilt, thou canst make me clean." "I will. Be thou clean." And immediately he was cleansed. We have no hesitation to proclaim "Believe on the Lord Jesus Christ, and thou shalt be saved." "Whosoever believeth in him shall not perish, but have everlasting life." We mean really, totally, altogether, and forever. In that salvation there is forgiveness and deliverance from the power of sin. There is regeneration by the grace of God. There is receiving the Holy Spirit in the will of God. There is being kept in the love of God. There is resurrection promised by the power of God when the Lord Jesus Christ returns. That is all included in the initial promise "Believe on the Lord Jesus Christ, and thou shalt be saved."

What can Paul possibly mean then when he writes, "If by any means I might attain unto the resurrection of the dead" (Phil. 3:11)? Do you think he had any doubt about the resurrection? Do you think Paul had any doubt about himself being raised from the dead? If you have any question about that, read 1 Corinthians 15. There Paul wrote a lengthy discussion to show that Jesus Christ actually did rise from the dead, and because He rose from the dead, we shall rise too. Then what does he mean by these words? "If by any means I might attain unto the resurrection of the dead"? Remember what Paul teaches about believers. He says that each believer has in him the flesh and the spirit. He was born first in the flesh. This is called human nature. Man comes into this world born of father and mother, as he is born of the flesh. He is brought up in the flesh. He goes to school in the flesh. He lives in the flesh. Then there is such a thing as being born in the spirit. When he is born again, there is in him the Spirit of God. Now he has in him both the flesh with which he was born from his earthly parents and the spirit with which he was born by the power of God. This creates a problem because the flesh hangs on.

This is taught in Scripture in various ways, such as in the Old Testament when Israel moved into the land of Canaan. The record is that when they moved into Canaan under Joshua they conquered the whole land, but the Canaanites remained. Through those Canaanites, Israel had miserable experiences. Or we may note when David was crowned king in Judah. It happened then that the house of Saul, led by the man Ishbosheth, was opposed to David, and engaged him in seven years of ugly, miserable civil war. This resulted from the fact that there were two opposing leaders in the country at the same time.

Paul describes this situation in the individual believer's experience in Galatians:

> For the flesh lusteth against the Spirit, and the Spirit against the flesh: and these are contrary the one to the other: so that ye cannot do the things that ye would (Gal. 5:17).

This shows a battle going on inside the believer: the flesh as over against the spirit. That is the way it is in the individual believer. Paul describes this again in Romans 7:14-24.

Read it and let it speak to you. It will tell you that in Paul himself there were these two opposing forces. There was in him the flesh and the spirit. Sin will be in you as long as you have the flesh, but if you have the Spirit in you, greater is He that is in you than he that is in the world. You can, through the Spirit, have the victory over the sin that is in your own body.

Evidently Paul is referring to this conflict, and he is testifying to his own battle in himself where he is exercising his faith in Christ Jesus that he might gain the victory over his flesh, and that he might attain to the resurrection of the dead. He wants actually to be living in spiritual power rather than to be in carnal interests and carnal ideas. Notice that in 1 Corinthians 9:27 Paul writes: "But I keep under my body, and bring it unto subjection." He was a Christian, he was an apostle, but he had the flesh that had been the flesh of Saul, the Pharisee. He did not want his flesh to ever gain control as far as his conduct was concerned.

In Romans we read:

> But if the Spirit of him that raised up Jesus from the dead dwell in you, he that raised up Christ from the dead shall also quicken your mortal bodies by his Spirit that dwelleth in you (Rom. 8:11).

This is what Paul wanted to have happen in him. He wanted the Holy Spirit to quicken his mortal body to make it alive. His mortal body was involved in death and in chapter 7 he says: "Who shall deliver me from the body of this death?" That is that natural, human body that he had — his natural, human desires. They were with him as long as he lived in this world. He had to maintain an attitude toward them of constant vigilance, and he kept them under in any way that he possibly could, struggling, wrestling with principalities and powers outside himself. One of the things he had to do with his own flesh was to bring it under subjection to the Spirit of God, that the power of God through the Spirit of God might quicken his mortal body and lift him up by the grace of God to obedience in Christ Jesus. Paul strove to control his flesh to obedience. This is the significance of this sentence: "If by any means I might attain unto the resurrection of the dead."

The natural human interest in any person would be to preserve himself. Someone will tell you that self-preservation is the first law of nature. There is no objection to that. It is the first law of nature, but do you realize that self-denial is the first step of the spiritual life. In the Spirit there will be self-denial. In nature, there is self-preservation. Paul wants to deny himself to death in order that Almighty God might raise him in Himself, in his daily experience, from the power of the flesh into the life of the Spirit by the grace of God.

## Chapter 49

## I FOLLOW AFTER

(Philippians 3:12)

*Do you think that if I still have not realized all that is available in being saved, this is any sign of something wrong in me?*

Paul is encouraging these young Christians and attempting to guide them into the fullness of blessing. He has used a number of examples. He first of all drew attention to the outstanding characteristic in the life of Jesus of Nazareth — His humility. Then he referred to Timothy with his consideration for others. Then he referred to Epaphroditus with his zeal, who worked himself almost to death in order that he might help to spread the Gospel.

Now in chapter 3 Paul uses himself as an example. There have been those who have questioned Paul's judgment in speaking about himself. One reason why he would use himself as an example would be to let them know how the grace of God works inside a believer's heart. Living as a believer involves more than outward conformity. There is an inner response to the call of God. There is something that is done inside, and Paul could talk about that. He drew the attention of his readers to certain things that were true about him in his own personal experience. Paul put special emphasis on how he renounced all the advantages he had in his fortunate personal career; his own family upbringing, because he had been circumcised on the eighth day; his own heritage, in that he was one of the people of Israel; his own tradition, since he was one of the tribe of Benjamin; his own culture, "a Hebrew of the Hebrews." Paul had been a Pharisee of the Pharisees and, in addition, there had been his own personal record of zeal. He had been much in earnest, and had maintained his character, so that he was blameless in the way he lived. Now in all these different ways Paul had much to give him advantage, yet he had told these people in his letter that he counted all those things simply refuse. He treated them as if they were rubbish. In our language of today he treated all those things as if they were just dirt. They were in fact very worthwhile, but he treated them as if they were nothing, in order that he might win Christ and be found in Him and know Him. This is what he could tell, and did.

He went on to tell them something about his inner attitude.

> Not as though I had already attained, either were already perfect: but I follow after, if that I may apprehend that for which also I am apprehended of Christ Jesus (3:12).

Paul did not rest on his laurels. He did not take for granted that everything was as it could be as far as he personally was concerned. As far as the past was concerned, as far as his attitude toward Christ was concerned, he felt he had done all he could, but in his daily conduct he did not think he had it made. He did not assume that he had reached his goal.

Here is a common snare for a new convert. Some feel the matter of actually accepting Christ is quite an issue. If you were a child, it wouldn't be much of an issue. If your father and your mother believed in the Lord Jesus Christ, they could put your baby hand in the hand of the Lord, and you would walk with Him as if that were the only thing to do. But if you grew up without that, so that you were living by yourself in the world, then the matter of turning to Christ would be a real problem. It could involve a real crisis and perhaps even a real emotional experience. Often the word "conversion" means a real emotional experience in spiritual matters, as it often is. It is not necessarily so but it can be. For people who have had a vivid experience of conversion, there is a great snare. It is customary that after you have once stood up in front of the congregation, have been examined and accepted, you will now be counted as a member. That can be a real snare. You could be tempted to think all was settled, but actually there is more. You can now grow.

I remember how it was when I graduated from high school. I did not understand why they called all those exercises "commencement." As far as I was concerned, I was through. They should be "celebration" exercises. But in using the word "commencement" they were preparing me for the idea that when you have reached that point of preparation, you are ready to start to grow.

Paul did not assume he had already attained. As far as he was concerned, when he had accepted Christ on the Damascus road and came to know Him, his relationship with the Lord started with him then. But Paul did not consider himself to be "already perfect." The Greek word "perfect" means complete, mature. Paul did not think he was finished. What Paul meant can be seen by looking at a garden. Getting the ground ready and getting the seed ready is all preparatory. Then comes the day when the seed is planted. But putting the beans into the ground is just the beginning. Cultivation, irrigation and personal attention throughout the growth period is essential. Paul says, "Not as though I had already attained, either were already perfect: but I follow after." This expression means "I chase, I run after." "If that I may apprehend that for which also I am apprehended." Paul wanted to "catch on" to that very thing for which Christ had "caught on" to him, namely, that he should belong to Christ and He belong to Paul. This was what the Apostle Paul kept as his regular, daily attitude. He was forever trying to get closer, closer, that he might have more, more of Christ. He never did esteem that he had it made. He never did think it was all done. Paul did not think of himself as if he could take anything for granted. He continued to strive in every possible way that he might appropriate to himself as much as possible what was available to him in the grace of God.

## Chapter 50

## THIS ONE THING I DO

(Philippians 3:13)

*Can you understand that if I want to make progress, I must look ahead?*

"This one thing I do." This is the way the apostle describes his own inner attitude in living. There is an aspect in believing in Christ that is very much like living or breathing. A person never finishes breathing as long as he lives. When one thinks about spiritual experience, living the life of the believer is somewhat like this. It is a continuous process. In becoming a believer, there is an aspect of accepting Christ. If this happens when you are a little child, you may not be conscious of it. Your parents can put your baby hand in the hand of the Lord Jesus Christ and you can start walking with Him then.

If, however, you wait until you are older, the matter of accepting Christ can be a very real problem. You attend services and listen to preaching. You read pamphlets, books and the Bible. Then the day comes when you accept Christ. This is the beginning. But there is more to follow, there is growth. There is first this matter of accepting Christ, committing yourself to Him. This can happen in various ways. With the Apostle Paul, it happened in a very dramatic fashion on the Damascus road. You will remember Saul's responses: "Who art thou, Lord?" "What will thou have me to do?" It happened so quickly, and right then and there the whole life of Saul the Pharisee was transformed. However, it was what happened after that that made him the Apostle Paul.

Paul made this clear when he wrote:

> Brethren, I count not myself to have apprehended: but this one thing I do, forgetting those things which are behind,

181

and reaching forth unto those things which are before
(3:13).

It is as if Paul were saying: "I just do not figure that I am
finished. I am not done. Not only is it true that I am still
believing, going on; but I am continuing to seek Him with
purpose." When Paul affirms "this one thing I do," he implies on his part a disciplined intention. He is seeking a
close relationship with Christ and he intends to get there.
By the way, looking at what he says after that is even more
revealing. "But this one thing I do, forgetting those things
which are behind, and reaching forth unto those things
which are before." One of the first thoughts that will come
to us might be: "Well, that is really wonderful. I will now
be able to forget all my failures." And this is true. "I will be
able to forget all those times when I neglected." That is
right. "I will be able to forget all those times when I
doubted." That is also true. But we should not stop there.
You may have had great victories, but you should now
forget them. You may have accomplished great things.
Now is the time to forget them. People thought very well
of you. This was good but you should now forget it. You
should not depend on this. You should not try to live in
your past.

The past is very important and often the past is a real
inspiration. I know that I have again and again in my lifetime been greatly blessed by remembering the wonderful
way in which God worked with me to bring me to faith,
because when I was born, as I have often said, I wasn't
born a Christian; I was born a Canadian. I had to grow up
first as a Canadian and then when I grew up that way, I
found myself an agnostic skeptic. I was really skeptical of
everything there was in the Bible, but then by the ministry
of various persons and the ministry of the Holy Spirit, all
working together in a way that is far beyond what I even
now understand, God worked it around to where I came to
believe in Him.

But now if I stop there, it would be just too bad for me.
"Forgetting those things which are behind." There have

been times in the past when God heard me and answered my prayer. There have been times in the past when God blessed me and made my efforts fruitful. There have been times in the past when God blessed the open proclamation of His Word, my preaching and teaching of His Word, with souls that were actually turned to God and were blessed in the Lord. All this is wonderful and I remember with appreciation, but I must not stay there.

So let us turn our back on the things that are behind us, the failures, yes, but the successes too. Let us remember no matter what happened yesterday; today is here and tomorrow is lying before us. This was the attitude of the Apostle Paul. He not only gave up all that he ever had, whether good or bad, but he also, as he went forward in obedience, avoided anything else. You will find instances of people who start out to serve the Lord and become interested in His affairs and become active in so many other things. The Apostle Paul made it a point to limit himself to one thing. He wanted to get to know the Lord. "This one thing I do." He wanted to win Christ above everything else. And he sacrificed everything else. He set aside all that was in the past, and he set aside everything else in the present, but that which would contribute to this one end: that he would get to know the Lord. So the apostle could give his testimony to the whole world. It was as if he were working under a motto. Over the life of the Apostle Paul you could put this one word: "This one thing I do."

## Chapter 51

## I PRESS TOWARD THE MARK

(Philippians 3:14)

*Do you see how important it is to have an objective, or a goal in view?*

Paul lived his life believing in Christ, as a man running a race. Several times in talking about his own personal experience, Paul has used figures of speech that referred to physical activity. In one place he speaks of himself as a boxer and he says about himself: "So fight I, not as beating the air." He is under control. Then again he speaks of himself as a wrestler: "We wrestle not against flesh and blood, but against principalities, against powers." Then there are times when he would speak of himself as a pilgrim, walking with the Lord. Here in Philippians he speaks of himself as a man running a race. He points out that in his running a race, he is not just running to be running, but he is running to win. Paul says:

> I press toward the mark for the prize of the high calling of
> God in Christ Jesus (3:14).

This is a picture of a man running down the home stretch. It is the sprint at the close of the whole race when he is running as hard as he can to the goal line. "I press toward the mark." The language implies, "I strain, I push on, I try hard." And here again someone might say, "Does the Christian life involve this or require this?" And I could say to you in a gentle way, "Yes, it does." Paul is saying words like this: "As I live, as long as I live, I press, I strain, I push on, I try to get to the goal." In other words, "I take myself in hand and I keep myself at it." If you wanted to speak a little more formally you could say, Paul means: "I lead a disciplined life, I apply all my energy toward this one thing."

Paul was thinking day in and day out, devoting all his thoughts to the service of Christ. If he had had any money to give he would have given all to this end, with the purpose that he might please Christ. He gave all his time and effort to this one goal, that he might be pleasing in the sight of Christ. This was a very practical matter, and it was important for him to have this goal.

The spiritual things of God, the invisible things of God, are clearly seen by the things that are made; so let us take such a practical matter as planting beans. "Whatsoever a man soweth, that shall he also reap." This is true in the spiritual world. If I want to have faith in God, I will have to sow the seed to get that faith in God. How can I do that? "Faith cometh by hearing, and hearing by the word of God." I will need to read my Bible. I will need to think about the things of God. I will need to pray. I will need to take time to be holy and speak oft with my Lord.

The spiritual career of many a person is marked by a good beginning and then nothing more. That is one of the great tragedies of all spiritual experiences. Getting a good start is very important, a good beginning is half the battle; but to win, you must continue. It is a bit like baseball. Getting to first base or second base is good. But a player could get as far as third base and still not score. In the game of baseball, so much like life as it is, the only one who scores is the one who gets across home plate. In spiritual things it is exactly the same way. The good beginning is very important but you must carry on through to the end. You must stay with it. You must persist until you get home. There is an old proverb, "One thing at a time and that done well." This is good common sense. If you will apply this in the spiritual world you will be blessed. Pathetically, so many of us are like the man who "jumped on his horse and rode furiously in all directions." How many times I have dreaded that I would spend my days like that: get on my horse and ride furiously in all directions, but of course to no avail.

So in living, Paul would have us concentrate. He says, "I press toward the mark. I have a goal in mind, a reward in mind, an end in view." "For the high calling of God in Christ Jesus." That word "high calling" is well translated as "upward." The "upward" calling of God. The believer does not just get up, he keeps going up. He goes up, up, on and on, and this is the way in which he lives in Christ. Paul's goal was to establish such a relationship in Christ, that he could feel the lifting power of God in his own soul; because that lifting, raising up, resurrecting power of God is available at all times for those who put their trust in Christ.

## Chapter 52

## BE THUS MINDED

(Philippians 3:15)

*Do you ever have the feeling when Paul describes his own experience that he is setting forth something exceptional that was intended only for him?*

These Philippian believers were new believers and they were moving forward into a time of persecution. Paul knew this and presented all that he wrote to them for their benefit. He showed them how they might be inspired to live in the will of God, if they would let the mind of Christ be in them — a mind that was revealed in Timothy in his consideration for others, and in Epaphroditus in his zeal. It was also shown in Paul's own description of himself in consecration. Here is a very important truth: not all believers are equally ready to enter into all that is possible. I remember a. conversation I once had with my stepmother about spiritual things. I was trying to explain the Gospel to her, and I was pointing out how Paul lived in his humble, self-denying way; and sadly she said to me, "Oh, but that was Paul, he was an apostle. Nothing like that could ever be for me." Then I had the problem of showing her that Paul was just a sinner as any of the rest of us. She was right in saying that she would never be able to achieve it in her own strength. But, she was wrong when she thought she never could receive it. She may not have been spiritually prepared, but she could become that way, because God is no respecter of persons. Paul wrote:

> Let us therefore, as many as be perfect, be thus minded: and if in any thing ye be otherwise minded, God shall reveal even this unto you (3:15).

Paul wanted all to share what he had in the assurance that he had in Christ, and the dedication that he had in his own soul to Christ. He knew that not all who heard him would be ready to follow his advice at that moment, so he put it that way: "as many as be perfect, be thus minded." This word "perfect" does not refer to something flawless. This means to say "full grown." You can speak about an apple tree being perfect when it is bearing apples. As far as Christians are concerned, their spiritual life is much like the natural life. You can think of a certain boy being born into the world, and being named John Brown. As an infant, he is helpless. He must grow and mature. The same sort of development takes place in a believer. He starts out as a babe in Christ, then he grows through the sincere milk of the Word until he becomes mature, full grown, complete; and that means fruit bearing, like that apple tree. Now here is an astonishing fact about the heart that lives in faith.

The more a believer understands God, the more answers to prayer that he gets, the more powerful and effective that his witness is, the humbler he will be.

> But whosoever will be great among you, let him be your minister; and whosoever will be chief among you, let him be your servant (Matt. 20:26, 27).

> But he that is greatest among you shall be your servant. And whosoever shall exalt himself shall be abased; and he that shall humble himself shall be exalted (Matt. 23:11, 12).

Here is a remarkable principle that is true for all Christian people. For one to go up in the communion of the Lord means that he must go down in self-esteem. At this point Paul wrote to the mature, which meant that they had set everything else aside that they might win Christ. The epistle to the Hebrews had this same spiritual experience in mind.

> Wherefore seeing we also are compassed about with so great a cloud of witnesses, let us lay aside every weight, and the sin which doth so easily beset us, and let us run with patience the race that is set before us, looking unto Jesus the author and finisher of our faith; who for the joy that was set before him endured the cross, despising the shame, and is set down at the right hand of the throne of God (Heb. 12:1, 2).

What should be said to the immature, to the imperfect? Paul gave them no admonition. He did not put any pressure upon them. They are not grown. There was a word of assurance for them however. Paul wrote: "And if in any thing ye be otherwise minded, God shall reveal even this unto you." God might lead them through trouble, distress and sorrow, but they should trust in God's providence and grace. God would show them by His Holy Spirit what He wanted them to do. Believers can always expect that at times when they are alone Scripture passages will come to their minds which will teach them. God teaches the believer who is not yet mature, who is not yet fully yielded to God, so that He can lead them.

## Chapter 53

## BY THE SAME RULE

(Philippians 3:16)

*Do you realize that I am not so much responsible for what I may think, as I am responsible for what I do?*

Believers are not alike, even in their dedication. Some are more dedicated and others less. It would be good if all believers would agree on a certain way of acting and doing. This could be the norm. Paul had forsaken all that was important to him that he might be in Christ Jesus. He reminded the Philippians that he was of the nation of Israel, of the tribe of Benjamin, and concerning the law, a Pharisee. So far as his own personal record was concerned, he had been zealous; and so far as his personal character and conduct was concerned, he had been blameless. All these were good things. But Paul had forsaken all that he might win Christ. This pattern of Paul's conduct should be the norm for other believers. They all should aim at this, so that each could be lowly and humble, and easy to be entreated, and small in comparison with others; but with one outstanding characteristic: trusting God.

> Nevertheless, whereto we have already attained, let us walk by the same rule, let us mind the same thing (3:16).

However, in spite of this admonition, there would be some who would do differently, to whom Paul referred when he wrote: "If in any thing ye be otherwise minded." Some could not go along with Paul as they were not as far advanced in spiritual dedication as Paul. Even so, he said God would reveal to them what they ought to do. Paul did not accept the idea that they belonged to another group. In spite of individual differences, in spite of the fact that some were closer and some were further away, in spite of the fact that some had stronger faith and some had weaker faith, in spite of the fact that some were more self-denying and others were less self-denying, in spite of the fact that some had the mind of Christ but some did not, yet they all believed in Him. Paul included himself with them. He did not claim that he had reached the end. He was on the way walking with the Lord. This was part of his blessing. He appreciated that the Lord had done certain work in him and in them.

What Paul wrote applies to us today. We may not be grown, finished; but we should be growing in the things of the Spirit. We should confess our sins. We should draw nigh to Him. If we would live lives of humility with Him, and would confess our sins to Him and would walk softly in His sight, we would learn, because God would teach us. We are not honoring God if we have to tell the world we have not grown spiritually in the last ten years.

Paul and the Philippian believers had made some progress, as he said, "Whereto we have already attained, let us walk by the same rule, let us mind the same thing." Now that they had reached this level of humility, of dedication to God, they should keep growing. Had they been taking the mind of Christ as their pattern? Had they tried to be humble? Had they tried to be considerate of others? Had they been dedicated to God so that they really wanted Him to be honored in their lives? Then they should thank the Lord. It had not always been that way. They should give God the praise and give Him the glory. They should keep on!

If other believers in our community are witnessing for Christ, we should join them. If the believing persons in our community are in favor of certain things that are good for the poor, we should join them. If they are against certain things that are worldly, we should join these folks. If we join others in walking with the Lord, in trusting God, in serving Him, in trying to honor Him, this will be impressive to the unbelieving who see us. And if any of us should have trouble, if we endure persecution, if someone is against us, it will mean a great deal if we have some companions, if we have some folks who stand with us. This is what Paul wanted them to have. If he could get those Philippian Christians to come together, to stand together, he knew they would be stronger in the day of stress and strain, in the time of trouble and persecution, than they would otherwise have been. There is great strength in united testimony, in joining with others in saying the things of the Lord. This would be a great help to anyone of us in the day of trouble, persecution and distress.

## Chapter 54

## FOLLOWERS TOGETHER

### (Philippians 3:17)

*Can you see there is nothing really unhealthy about church members who think of their pastor as being a model Christian?*

Every now and again I hear the complaint, "In that church they just worship their pastor. Anything he says or does is just right." Then I ask myself, "Is that really bad?" Actually members of a congregation are influenced by the preacher, as children are influenced by their parents. It is normal for a little child to walk with his parents, as it is for a pupil to follow his teacher. This is both good and bad, depending on the parents. If the parents are walking in a good way, the child is fortunate.

Church members live in a congregation which is their spiritual home. Here they are under the leadership of the man who is their preacher, their pastor. Paul had this in mind when he wrote: "Be ye followers together of me and of the Lord." The important thing here is that the pastor should walk in the right way. At the present time there is great emphasis in our country on the campuses of our universities where young believers are being urged to witness for Christ; and this is stirring. A very important aspect of their witnessing will be the way in which they personally walk. Witnesses for Christ, whether pastors, preachers, teachers, parents, friends, crusade workers, or personal workers, need to be very careful how they walk. People are looking at them. If parents do not read the Bible in their home in the presence of their children, this has an unhealthy influence. If parents read the Bible in the presence of their children, this will be registered deep down in each child's consciousness. If preachers do not talk about the Lord in personal conversation, they will actually influence their members to become cold in their attitude toward the Lord.

When I find myself for any great length of time, in any prolonged conversation, when I have not been talking about the Lord, I feel somewhat smitten by that; and I should perhaps be more so. People get the impression I have other interests than Christ who gave Himself for me. People see me as a pastor, a Bible teacher, and a minister of some years of service. If I should be with a group of people and do not find an opportunity of talking about some spiritual aspect of the Lord's work, what impression would I leave? To reflect on this will make a man stop and think. If teachers in Bible classes do not pray openly in connection with their teaching, all their pupils will lose. If I were discussing matters in a church meeting, there would be something inadequate and missing if that group did not hear me lead in prayer. The same is true as far as meetings of church officers are concerned. I happen to belong to a communion that is organized into Presbyteries. In these Presbyteries ministers and elders meet periodically for the purpose of doing the business of the church. When I was an active member of a Presbytery in Texas I urged upon my fellow Presbyters the idea that just to hear each other debate the issues of the church and never hear each other pray was very inadequate. I am glad to say that in the course of my fellowship in that Presbytery there came a time when it was our practice to spend the whole day preceding the meeting of Presbytery in prayer. We ministers spent the day praying over those items that we knew would be discussed in Presbytery.

A believer's example is important. If parents do not go to church, this will certainly have an influence on their children. Some may say, "But we send them to church." Now what do you think will happen when those children grow older? Should you not expect those children to drop out of going to church? If parents do not profess their faith, it will be easy for the children to avoid open confession of Jesus Christ. After all, this is what they learned from their parents.

Paul wrote:

> Brethren, be followers together of me, and mark them which walk so as ye have us for an ensample (3:17).

When we note his use of the word "brethren" we could say this is certainly for Christians only. When Paul wrote, "Be followers together," he surely meant that members of a congregation should expect to share with each other. The tendency to be independent of the other members is not wholesome. Mutual encouragement is good. Each should be helping the other. When he wrote, "Mark them which walk," Paul was saying there is nothing wrong about seeing how other people walk. We all need to realize that our walk is in public. And anything that is in public is up for examination. I may criticize and condemn what I see. I need not be condemning the man's soul: he may have a heart of gold in the sight of God, but his example is not good. It is a wholesome thing to compare the way people act toward the Lord. It will be helpful for any one of us to get to know some true witness for Christ, and then seek to be like that person.

Chapter 55

## ENEMIES OF THE CROSS

(Philippians 3:18)

*Do you realize that when a believer acts selfishly or indulgently, he is actually an enemy of the Gospel?*

Church members are often criticized publicly today. People have noticed that in the church there is worldliness, selfishness, pride and arrogance. We are sorry about it but ever since men professed to believe, there have been poor examples in the church of what a believer ought to be. Selfishness does not have to be learned, I can begin as a baby. I can be selfish before I can ever talk. It is as natural as breathing. I come by it naturally because I am human and sinful. Many people who indicate that they are uncertain about the original sin of mankind just haven't looked closely at babies. Sinfulness of mankind is everywhere. There is selfishness, pride and indulgence. Oh, there will be variety in men's tastes. Some people will be very self-controlled, others will be more impulsive. This is just as true in the church as it is anywhere else. People do not join the church because they are good. They are sinners, and the church is made up of a group of sinners who have turned to the Lord.

When I say men are sinners I am not using such a term politely to refer to all men whether it is true or not. What I say is true, and all men are sinners. Someone may say to me, "I have seen some people in church who didn't sin." Does that mean they didn't get drunk, they didn't use profanity? That is quite possible. Does that mean all are not crude? That may well be, but it is possible to be as refined and cultured and suave and sweet as anything in the world, and yet be as proud as the devil. Persons may not all be crude, they may not all be vulgar, and yet they are sinful. If a person has been brought up in a faithful godly home,

he is very fortunate. Such a child could become a person
whose character and whose pattern of living is good, and
that person would actually be very fortunate. Such a person
would not be inclined to be self-indulgent, nor inclined to
be extreme about anything. But at the same time deep down
inside that human heart there would be the roots of all
temptations which beset men. Actually sin is there. Everyone
has it. Any notion anyone may have that people will join the
church because now they are rid of sin is simply not true.
John says that if any man says he has not sinned he makes
of God a liar.

Just so the notion of any church being above sin is not
valid. I think often that one of the worst aspects of this error
is that people get the idea they should be or would be above
sin. No! Anyone who has ever been present in a church
officer's meeting will know perfectly well that selfishness,
pride, personal interest will be seen on every side. In 'all
church history, the whole testimony of all believers everywhere has been blotted and blotched and smeared again
and again by sin from within. This is all because there is
always one weak element in any church, and that is man
himself. The trouble of the church is in this fact that it is
made up of men. Anything man puts his hand to will be
spoiled.

One problem in any personal situation is myself, the other
problem is the other person. I am sorry to say that only in
the Lord can I ever be hopeful of peace. Only in the Lord
can I ever be safe. That is the reason why I try to stay as
close as I can to Scripture when I teach. Scripture is from
the Lord Jesus Christ and He is without sin. As far as people
are concerned, as long as men are involved, the truth can
be summarized in this word of Jeremiah: "Cursed be the
man that trusteth in man." This does not mean that man is
"cursed" in the sense that God will do him harm or slap
something on him. This means that man just is that way. It
is just too bad for anyone who puts his trust in any man and
who "makes not the Lord God his stay." Someone may say,
"But look, you must go along with your work and you must

deal with people." That is true and I should pray daily that God will keep me. I put my trust in God to forgive me. I trust in God to cleanse me. I trust in God to lead me in all the work that I do. Everything that I undertake I should do in the name of the Lord. Whatever is not of Him I should cast out. This is the privilege even as it is the responsibility of the believer.

> For many walk, of whom I have told you often, and now tell you even weeping, that they are the enemies of the cross of Christ (3:18).

Paul admitted sadly that many among the believers did not walk with the Lord. We have great respect for the early church. We have great respect for a pioneer church anywhere. If we were to go to the foreign field and see some group of Christians gathered together, we would see a replica of the early church. That would be a congregation of people just out of paganism. We should have great appreciation of such persons who have risked their lives and their property and their personal relationships because of their faith in the Lord Jesus Christ. But even among such it will occur that some live in a way that is contrary to the truth as it is in Christ. Paul actually talked about these wrongdoers. He did this to warn others. It might be said "That sounds judgmental, critical." Actually Paul commended them to the Lord. He left them with God, knowing that God would judge them. But Paul judged their conduct. The way they were doing wasn't right and that was obvious. Paul criticized that. He found no pleasure in doing this. "Of whom I have told you often, and now tell you even weeping." Actually he was sad about it. Then why did he do it? He did it to warn them of their danger. Paul had no pleasure in noting these things but he recognized them for what they revealed; and he cared about the souls of the believers. Any parent would like their children to be healthy and well. They would not particularly find any pleasure in pointing out that one of their family had measles or scarlet fever. But if that child had measles the parents would want to know about it, because they would not want him to be infecting others. If any person had smallpox we all would want to know about that. We would not want that sick person to spread the disease. "They are the enemies of the cross of Christ." How could such believers be the enemies of the cross of Christ? They were enemies of the cross of Christ because the cross of Christ is primarily a matter of self-denial and they were influencing other believers not to deny themselves. They were influencing others to be proud, to be selfish, to be self-indulgent; and none of that was good. Paul just called it by its right name, "the enemies of the cross of Christ." May God help each one of us humbly to yield ourselves to Him, that we may be kept from such unfortunate wandering away, falling away, from the Lord, and so become "enemies of the cross of Christ."

## Chapter 56

## WHOSE END IS DESTRUCTION
(Philippians 3:18, 19)

*Do you realize that a person could be doomed to destruction who had never been accused of doing anything harmful to anyone?*

So often we readily accept the view that it is the criminal who will one day be punished. And he will be. We are not wrong about that. But the alarming truth is that a person could face destruction who has never actually harmed anyone else. This comes out of the Book of Philippians. Paul is instructing the believers in that city about their own personal living. He has been sharing with them how they could live well in the Lord and could be victorious in Him.

Paul warns these young Christians against certain enemies of the cross. He speaks of the enemies of the cross of Christ as those who are against self-denial. You will remember how the Lord Jesus said, "If any man will come after me, let him deny himself, and take up his cross daily, and follow me." The significance of what we mean when we talk about "the cross of Christ" is self-denial. This is rather definitely pointed out for us in the record of an incident in the life of Jesus of Nazareth:

> Then Peter took him, and began to rebuke him, saying, Be it far from thee, Lord: this shall not be unto thee. But he turned, and said unto Peter, Get thee behind me, Satan: thou art an offence unto me: for thou savourest not the things that be of God, but those that be of men. Then said Jesus unto his disciples, If any man will come after me, let him deny himself, and take up his cross, and follow me. For whosoever will save his life shall lose it: and whosoever will lose his life for my sake shall find it. For what is a man profited, if he shall gain the whole world, and lose his own soul? or what shall a man give in exchange for his soul (Matt. 16:22-26)?

200

Paul writing of these "enemies of the cross" says:

> For many walk, of whom I have told you often, and now tell you even weeping, that they are the enemies of the cross of Christ: whose end is destruction, whose God is their belly, and whose glory is in their shame, who mind earthly things (3:18, 19).

That is rather a definite description: "whose end is destruction." This ruin, this destruction, will not be forced on them arbitrarily, but will come upon them as a consequence of the way they have been living.

Their end was implicit in the course they followed. By way of illustration, let us say that a man receives a certain amount of money, and then he spends this money recklessly until his bank account is empty. Is the emptiness of that bank account a punishment? Or is that empty bank account the consequence of his spending his money? Again when a child plays with another child who has measles, and the first child becomes sick, is that punishment? Is that arbitrary action? Not at all, but it is actually a natural consequence.

When Paul said about these "enemies of the cross" that their end is destruction, he meant to say that the very way in which they have lived has ended in ruin, "whose God is their belly." I admit that this is not a very elegant expression. We might say, "whose God is their appetite." If we say that God is their appetite, what do we mean? We mean their appetite has first call upon their resources. But this is what God wants. If I am going to make the Lord my God, I bow down my heart and myself before Him saying, "Lord, I want Thee to rule." On the other hand, when a man makes his own appetite, his own body, his God, he gives his appetite full sway. "Whose glory is in their shame" means that what they actually love to do is really a shameful thing. They actually are scheming and planning and spending money on doing things which are sinful.

When is a person actually ashamed of anything? It is when he wants to do it out of sight. Then one can tell he is ashamed, whatever else he may be. But these people, of which Paul wrote, were the kind of people who actually enjoyed, spent money on, took time out for, such things which they wanted to do in the dark. They wanted to do them unseen from other people. "Whose glory is in their shame, who mind earthly things."

This statement touches us where we live. Who am I going to marry? Who is my child going to marry? What good job can I get? These things are in this world. Someone may say, "Those things aren't bad." That is why I chose them as examples. I could have described vulgar, coarse and obscene things. I am mentioning these good things to you because the characteristic, to which Paul is referring, is that they are the things of this earth. When Paul writes of minding earthly things, his attention is focused upon the things of this world. Suppose I spend time thinking about how I can get a lot of money. Why do I want the money, to get to heaven? Am I going to use it when I am in heaven? I need money for this world. I am aware that money has its place in this world, and we use money in this world. Believers are not going to get along without money, but believers ought not to put money first. They should trust God for that. Money is an earthly thing.

Perhaps some girl will say, "I wonder what I would have to do to get clothes like that to wear?" Such thoughts may be entirely innocent, but such a problem belongs in this world. On the other hand a person might say, "What would I have to do to look right in the sight of God?" Paul indicated that people should be counted enemies of the cross "whose God is their belly," who live by their appetites, whose "glory is in their shame." Such persons want to do things which belong in the dark; they mind earthly things; they are involved in and completely absorbed by the things of this world. The sad, grim, sober truth is that for these the end is destruction. Should we not rejoice that we have a Savior? Should we not be glad we have Someone we can turn to who will take care of us. We certainly need Him.

Chapter 57

## OUR CITIZENSHIP

(Philippians 3:20)

*Can you understand that it is the believer's confidence about heaven that makes his manner of life reasonable?*

We have been noting Paul's ideas about living as a believer in this world. He has been preparing these young believers in Philippi to face the times of persecution that will surely come to them. He has been urging them to live obediently in the Spirit, having the mind of Christ in them in all humility as we see it in Jesus of Nazareth. He desires them to be considerate of others as was Timothy, and be filled with zeal as was Epaphroditus, and now he speaks of consecration, using himself as an example. Paul is calling on them to deny themselves entirely. He warns them not to be influenced by worldly fellow believers, and he spells out sober warning of the dire consequences that will follow for .those who yield to worldly influences. Having done this Paul reminds these young believers of their spiritual relationship with God. Thus he writes:

> For our conversation is in heaven; from whence also we look for the Saviour, the Lord Jesus Christ (3:20).

This is the ground upon which Paul expects these believers to be able to move into the life of self-denial to which he is calling them. They are to walk in the presence of God, yielded to Him, denying the flesh, denying the influences of the world. "Conversation" means citizenship. "Our citizenship is in heaven." For the believer heaven is his homeland. Although he lives in this world, he does not belong here. Scripture tells him he is here as a stranger and a pilgrim. He is journeying through this world to his eternal home.

I was born in Canada, and I have always appreciated the poet who could say, "Breathes there a man with soul so dead

203

who never to himself has said, This is my own, my native land." It is a very normal thing for one to appreciate the land of his birth. To this day when anything good is said about Canada or the Canadians, I rejoice privately. When anything evil is said of Canada, I grieve. Since my citizenship is in heaven, and heaven is really my home, everything about heaven matters to me. That being the case, when I see someone who ignores God, I feel he is ignoring the very center of my whole existence; if someone speaks lightly of spiritual things, he is casting a reflection upon where my soul is resting. If some person makes some aspersion against the Gospel of the Lord Jesus Christ, he is actually talking against me as far as I am concerned. If words are spoken which are unkind, as well as untrue, to the name of the Lord Jesus Christ, that hurts me; even as when anyone takes His name in profanity, that hurts me. My citizenship is in heaven.

"From whence also we look for the Saviour." That is where He is: He is in heaven right now. I mean Jesus of Nazareth, raised from the dead, has been made both Lord and Christ by the power of Almighty God. Even now in heaven at the right hand of God the Father, as seen in the Book of Revelation, He is sitting upon the throne. He is the Almighty God, the everlasting Father, the Prince of Peace: He is in heaven. That is where I belong. I should be very humble about it, but I certainly am not going to retreat from it. That is my privilege. My Lord Jesus Christ is right now alive in the presence of God at the right hand of God. He is right now active on my behalf. This is very real. I am, day in and day out, to have in mind that my living Lord Jesus Christ is praying for me. He is not praying for me only for something exceptionally good. When I walk along in this world and I falter or stumble in any ordinary way on any ordinary day, He prays for me. If I get into wrong doings, He prays for me.

If I am actually, in the very presence of God, involved in sinful things, He is praying for me. Any number of people might say as they see me, "He ought not to be praying for you. He ought to just let you go as you are going." They might feel that is what I deserve. And I would agree with them, but I have news for you. He is not going to leave me to my own mistakes, because He will not give me what I deserve. He will treat me in His grace and in His mercy. He is the Savior, and He is in heaven. Now let me tell you something else, He is coming back. "This same Jesus, which is taken up from you into heaven, shall so come in like manner as ye have seen him go into heaven" (Acts 1:11). When He returns He will be the Lord Jesus Christ.

There are many references made in public to the Lord these days. Many people are talking about "Jesus." I expect people will think that such talk would be good, but I want to point out to you just now that it is not nearly as good as it sounds. When people are talking about "Jesus," they are referring to His earthly life. They are referring to the career He had down here in the flesh, when He took upon Him the form of a man and was found in fashion as a man. When He lived and died on Calvary's cross His name was "Jesus" all the way through. When you read the gospels you will note the name "Jesus" occurs over and over again. But the Bible teaches you that "the Lord hath made that same Jesus, whom you crucified, both Lord and Christ."

The great truth is that Jesus of Nazareth was the One who came for me, and was born in this world as the Babe of Bethlehem, lived in this world as a perfect person, always did the things that were pleasing to His Father. "The Son can do nothing of himself." "My Father worketh hitherto, and I work." He did all things pleasing to His Father while He was here on earth. Continuing in the will of His Father He went to the Garden of Gethsemane and faced the prospect and the possibility of dying on Calvary's cross. Being separated from His Father in that moment, He went forward and said, "Not my will, but thine, be done." He humbled Himself and became obedient unto death, even the death of the cross. "Wherefore God hath also highly exalted him, and given him a name which is above every name, that at the name of Jesus every knee should bow . . . and that every tongue should confess that Jesus Christ is Lord to the glory of God the Father." All that is gloriously true. But now let me say very earnestly and soberly that we have not really heard "the Lord" referred to, unless we have in mind that we are referring to "the Lord Jesus Christ." Christ Jesus is in heaven, right now, alive, God's chosen One, the fulfillment of the Old Testament promises. He is the One who is right now interceding on our behalf. He is our Savior and Lord. His present function is to be Lord of all. Paul would mean that when he calls the believers to walking softly before God, humbly before God, denying themselves on every side, in everything looking toward heaven, he is reminding them that it is the looking for the return of the Lord Jesus Christ that makes sense.

## Chapter 58

## SHALL CHANGE OUR WAY

(Philippians 3:21)

*Did you know that the believer expects to be completely
transformed?*

Christian convictions, Christian ideas, are so commonly
thought to be idealistic. People usually consider what the believers talk about and what they believe, to be visionary,
and by that they mean hopeful and nice, but not necessarily true. Such things are not taken to be actually true.
And so believers are often criticized for being impractical
because they think of heavenly things. For this reason it is
intimated that ideas of believers are invalid in this world.
Sometimes on the other hand, people will undertake to take
the good aspects of the believer's ideas and restate them
in such a way as to imply that what believers really should
be doing is seeking to achieve an improvement of this
world's affairs. Both such views are wrong because of the
basic unbelief in each. Neither of them is grounded in the
Scriptures. Such criticism is grounded in viewing the ideas
of believers from a natural point of view.

The believer does not think that this world is everything.
When a believer looks ahead he sees beyond this world. He
looks into the presence of God. He is looking out into
eternity. When any person is evaluating life in this world,
the believer will rise up and tell him he is not finished,
heaven is real. Jesus Christ is alive and He is the Lord of
all. The believer has in mind and heart that the Lord Jesus
Christ will return to this world. The frame of mind of a believer has been described by Paul:

> And to you who are troubled rest with us, when the Lord
> Jesus shall be revealed from heaven with his mighty angels,
> in flaming fire taking vengeance on them that know not

God, and that obey·not the gospel of our Lord Jesus Christ:
who shall be punished with everlasting' destruction from
the presence of the Lord, and from the glory of his power;
when he shall come to be glorified in his saints, and to be
admired in all them that believe (because our testimony
among you was believed) in that day (2 Thess. 1:7-10).

This is what the believer actually expects. Paul points out
that the Lord Jesus Christ will change the bodies of
believers:

Who shall change our vile body, that it may be fashioned
like unto his glorious body, according to the working where-
by he is able even to subdue all things unto himself (3:21).

The expression "who shall change our vile body" has been
translated by some scholars as "the body of our humiliation."
This is the origin of the word "vile" and is to be understood
in contrast to the next statement "that it may be fashioned
like unto his glorious body." The word "vile" may be misleading, because it could be taken to imply there is something intrinsically evil about the body, but that is not true.
If we use the word "our lowly bodies," we are referring to
the fact that we are limited. How far can we reach? Two
feet? Four feet? How far can we see? Several miles? How
far can we walk in a day? How fast can we run? How much
can we lift? We are so limited and so we speak of the
"body of our humiliation," because we are humbled in this.
But this is to be fashioned like His glorious body. Some
translations call it "the body of his glory."

Actually the body of His glory, the glorious body in which
Jesus Christ was raised from the dead, was different in its
essence and its nature than the body that died on Calvary's
cross. His resurrection body was different than the body in
which He lived as Jesus of Nazareth upon the earth. You
will remember that after He was raised from the dead He
was able to appear and disappear at will. He did not do that
before. Then, too, He could enter into a room when the door
was shut. You will remember after He had spent forty days
appearing and disappearing with His disciples, there came a
day, when in full view of them all, His body left this world.

He ascended into heaven. He was taken up in a cloud and taken away. He had a body of glory. Paul is saying, "Our vile body, our lowly body, this body we have here is so limited in time and space, so limited in strength and ability, is actually to be changed into a body like His glorious body."

Paul had this in mind when he wrote:

> Behold, I shew you a mystery; We shall not all sleep, but we shall all be changed, in a moment, in the twinkling of an eye, at the last trump" (1 Cor. 15:51, 52).

When Paul wrote "we shall all be changed," he meant that the changing that will take place for all believers at the time of the return of the Lord Jesus Christ will be like the changing that took place in the resurrection of Jesus Christ from the dead. This truth can also be seen in these words from John:

> Beloved, now are we the sons of God, and it doth not yet appear what we shall be: but we know that, when he shall appear, we shall be like him; for we shall see him as he is (1 John 3:2).

We shall be "like him."

In other words Paul has been saying to these Philippians, "I have been setting out for you the way to live. I have been laying out for you the challenge that there is for you to walk with the Lord. Walking with the Lord will involve on your part self-denial. It will involve on your part the forsaking of everything as far as this world is concerned, but this makes sense when you stop to think what is ahead of you. Your citizenship is in heaven. The Lord Jesus Christ is going to come back for you, and when He comes, you are going to be changed and this glorious prospect of being changed into the likeness of the living Lord Jesus Christ in glory should strengthen your commitment to Him while you are down here. You could walk along down here with more confidence because you know God has great things in mind for you in His plan for you."

## Chapter 59

## SO STAND FAST

(Philippians 4:1)

*Do you realize there are times when the important thing to do is to stand steady under pressure?*

As you read Scripture do you notice that the line of thought is not always all on the same level of emphasis or of urgency? Sometimes the theme deals with the things of the Lord, and that in my estimation is highest. Sometimes the admonition or the Word that is given deals with things that are very practical.

It is natural to have the impression that a believer should be doing something. It is easier to maintain a good testimony when there is action or movement involved. However, there are times when the thing to do is to stand steadfast, and in some ways that is the hardest to accomplish. It seems most difficult to hold steady when things are going contrary. It would be easier to attack.

In a worship service, for example, there are moments of testimony which may be the brightest parts of the service. When the Gospel is preached with power, so that the minister brings some truth that stirs the heart, there may be a moment when interest is aroused and everything seems to be so bright and clear. Sometimes in a revival service, the people are brought face to face with the call to surrender, so that they must decide whether or not they will commit themselves to the Lord. This becomes significant because others who are witnessing for Christ will join in their action. And there may be times when others are falling away, then one must stand! And this is as it comes naturally. Life is not moving in quiet, neutral circumstances. I am not paddling my canoe in a quiet, still lake. Things do not simply stay where I put them. Life is a moving stream. Sometimes the current is strong, actually rushing to sweep me off my feet.

Paul set forth a number of constructive ideas to bolster the morale of the Philippians. He wanted to help them, urging them to let the mind of Christ prevail in them. He ended that whole passage by saying: "be followers together of me." That seems to be a strong admonition to urge them to follow him, and he walked a very straight line in the presence of God.

Sometimes the wind may blow in my direction, and when that happens I may feel like putting up a sail and letting it blow me along. Sometimes the current flows toward blessing and that is fortunate. But there are times when the wind is contrary and the waves are against me. Paul gives this admonition over and over again: stand fast in the Lord. I should hold the position I have reached, as far as I have gone; I should stand there steady. Peter speaks of an adversary, the devil, who is active with malignant purpose, "as a roaring lion, walketh about, seeking whom he may devour." It is also true that any person has in himself the tendency to ebb. Life is not easy and steady; it ebbs and flows. The course of fortune rises and falls. The Scripture records facts about people who were following the Lord. It is written about them at one point, "from that time many of his disciples went back, and walked no more with him." Old habits can pull back at unexpected moments. Old customs that were formerly practiced may come up again. There may be popular procedures, as whenever every one else is going off for a picnic. It would be so easy to pack my lunch and go with them, and thereby neglect some duty in my service to the Lord.

Paul is referring to such peril when he writes:

> Therefore, my brethren dearly beloved and longed for, my joy and crown, so stand fast in the Lord, my dearly beloved (4:1).

There is a great deal in that word "so." The reading of this Scripture presents an overwhelming description that Paul has given of wholehearted dedication to the Lord. He urged

"Walk as I walk that you might have the blessing." They will be strengthened when they remember that God is going to change them. The Lord will change their bodies into bodies like the body of the Lord Jesus Christ. He is going to take them to Himself. With all that in mind, Paul now says, "My brethren dearly beloved and longed for, my joy and crown, so stand fast in the Lord, my dearly beloved." When he called them "my brethren dearly beloved," he said to these people, "I am very much concerned for you. I want the best for you and I want to see you very much. I wish I could be with you because you really mean much to me." When they came to believe it was a victory for Paul. They represented his trophy of achievement. He had been blessed when he was among them telling them the Gospel, and they had come to believe. They were very precious and special to him. They were one of his achievements in His service. He wanted them to stand fast in the Lord. He urged them to move up to this way of being and doing that he has been describing. They were to be humble as Jesus of Nazareth, considerate of others as Timothy, have zeal in service as did Epaphroditus.

Paul knew that if they took this position the enemy would be active, and would be pulling on them from all directions. So he urged them to stand fast in the Lord for herein they would be safe. In writing to the Ephesians Paul spoke of the devil as "cunning and active and malicious, an enemy." It is interesting to note that in this epistle to the Philippians he doesn't mention the devil. I am not so sure that you and I ought to mention the devil so much. We should be aware of him but I wonder about the wisdom of giving him excessive publicity. If he came after us with split hoofs, tail and horns, we wouldn't have any trouble. He doesn't come that way. He will come in just the way we would approve. He will tempt us to drop short, to turn back, to let go, to say "That was all right to do on Sunday but we do not have to do that on Thursday." We should not let that happen. Safety is in the Lord and when Paul writes, "stand fast in the Lord, my dearly beloved," he means the Lord will hold those who turn to Him. We cannot make it ourselves. Peter says, "Lord, to whom shall we go? thou hast the words of eternal life." We should turn to Him. Let us remind ourselves simply, plainly and gently that we haven't got it in us, and then remember the Lord has what it takes to keep us. Let us turn ourselves over to Him. He is able to keep that which we commit to Him, so let us trust in Him.

## Chapter 60

## OF THE SAME MIND

(Philippians 4:2)

*Can you feel how important it is to be conscious of the Lord at all times?*

Do you realize there are persons with whom it is just natural to disagree? There are human differences which are just so real, and human ideas which are so contrary to each other, that conflict between human beings is unavoidable. What happened at Babel continues to disturb the peace of men everywhere. When men gather themselves together, their tendency is to split apart. That there were differences of opinion among the believers in the early church, there is no doubt. There were differences in purpose. There were differences in values. This does not mean that there is any confusion in the universe with God, but among men. Tom is different from Dick, and he is different from Harry and he is just different from Jim, and they are all different from Mary and she is different from Jane. Such differences arising out of their human natures are altogether natural.

Believers in Christ Jesus are born again in the Lord. This is a very important truth. Paul will tell you that if any man be in Christ he is a new creation. Old things are passed away, behold all things have become new. Paul described his own experience in this way, when he said: "I am crucified with Christ." By the way, in that "I" is included all his personal ideas, his personal opinions, his personal judgments, his personal values, his personal attitudes, in fact, everything about him. All that was his was crucified with Christ. "Yet nevertheless I live, yet not I, but Christ liveth in me." Since Christ lives in each believer, and Christ is always One, then any believer, all believers, are one in Christ Jesus.

This makes Paul's admonition here in the Book of Philippians possible:

> I beseech Euodias, and beseech Syntyche, that they be of the same mind in the Lord (4:2).

What does this imply to us? This actually is admitting that in the early church there was controversy, argument, difference of opinion, between two women, one named Euodias, and the other Syntyche. Paul names them specifically, calls them, as it were, to the attention of everyone in the church. Who was at fault? We cannot tell. He urges each one to act. "I beseech Euodias," which meant to say, "I have something for you to do, Euodias." "I beseech Syntyche," which meant, "I have something for you to do, Syntyche. I want you, each one, to be of the same mind in the Lord." Why name these two individuals so specifically? If any change in that congregation, and between those two specifically, was ever to occur, it must originate in the heart of either one or both personally. Paul speaks clearly to each: "Now listen, you two, I want to tell you something. You have a job to do. You have to get yourself in line so that you can think together the same things in the Lord."

There was evidently some tension in that church. There was evidently some contention between those two women. A condition like that could spread through the whole church, so Paul puts his finger on the spot where it started. This quarrel is between these two, and he names them. He doesn't make a general statement. He doesn't say, "I want all of you people to quit fussing." As a matter of fact all the people were not quarreling and that would have made any such statement needless. By such comments Paul would not affect the people's hearts and minds. They would say that the preacher did not know what he was talking about. But when he put his finger on these two names, everyone would understand what he meant. These women were both Christians, they both believed in the Lord. He wanted them to accept the responsibility of saying the same thing in the Lord, so that this quarrel would not spread. When these two women would show that they were of the same mind in the Lord, all the others around them would be released from any kind of mistaken loyalty they have to one or the other.

If Bill Brown would stand up, and Jim Turner would stand up, so that these two men who have been opposed to each other and argued against each other and talked against each other, would now stand up and say the same thing, so that they could walk arm in arm and stand shoulder to shoulder and work elbow to elbow, there would be a quietness spread through the whole congregation. We should notice the "same mind" will be "in the Lord." Euodias doesn't have to take Syntyche's view, and Syntyche doesn't have to say Euodias was right and she was wrong, but each of them is to say the Lord was right. We must want His will to be done, because the Lord Himself has His own mind about any issue that may exist in the church, and Paul would ask each one of us to find out the mind of the Lord, and say that and be done.

# Chapter 61

## HELP THOSE WOMEN

### (Philippians 4:3)

*Do you know what the Bible teaches about women being active in the spreading of the Gospel?*

From time to time in the history of God's people there has been much interest as to the part that women play in the spreading of the Gospel. No one questions the function of believers in God's plan to spread the Gospel. We all have in mind the Great Commission that was given to His followers, "Go ye into all the world, and preach the gospel to every creature," and we realize that the spreading of the Gospel is not the responsibility of any one person. All believers should share in witnessing to the truth of Jesus Christ.

Witnessing is done by personal contact, person to person. Witnessing is by preaching, and by expounding the promises of God as seen in Scripture, and showing how they are carried out in and through the Lord Jesus Christ. Witnessing is done by praying openly in the presence of other people, calling upon Almighty God to show His favor and His grace, by giving thanks and asking Him for help. Witnessing is done by teaching and explaining Scripture; and again, it is done by the manner of life, the very way in which we live — that of humble obedience to God, of honoring Him, of being respectful toward other people, considerate of others and kind to the poor. All such activities are aspects of witnessing to the whole world that we believe in the Lord Jesus Christ, and we want His will to be done. We want people to know about Him. Nowhere in the Bible does it describe specifically what kind of person is to witness. The only requirement apparently is that they should be believers.

In the course of history some questions have arisen about the mode and manner of witnessing, the personnel of witnessing — who ought to do it. There has been much discussion among Christian people as to which way, and who, and how, witnessing for Christ should be done. Some have thought that testimony for the Lord Jesus Christ should be limited only to authorized persons, such as an ordained minister. This has given rise to the concept of a class of people called the "clergy." Some people have high respect for the clergy, just as some people frankly do not believe there should be any.

The same differences have developed about administration. Wherever there is a group of Christians together, so that they belong in a group like a church, or in a larger group like a presbytery or synod, or in a convention or conference of any kind, there needs to be administration of common affairs. Some people have thought that administration should be limited only to authorized persons such as ordained clergy, probably calling them priests, and having the conviction that such persons get their authority from Someone else to do what they are doing. But others have thought just as earnestly and sincerely that there should be no clergy at all, that the whole concept of the clergy is a mistake, that such procedure interrupts things and that this ministry should be carried on by saved persons, whoever they might be. In the same way, with reference to leadership, some people have felt that the leadership of believers should be limited to men only and, generally speaking, authorized men, ordained officers. So some churches have deacons and some have elders, some have bishops, and at least one large group of people look up to a Pope. They think the leadership should be limited to some certain persons or person, and that instruction about the Gospel should be given only by certain persons, ordained teachers, so that if any person is not ordained, he should not be teaching the Bible. Thus the leaders should be all men, and only men who lead and instruct; no women should be involved.

Some time ago I was appointed to a committee by our General Assembly to study and report on this question: what is the place of women in the work of the church? We first of all reviewed what we understood about the whole matter. We were aware of the historic procedures in the history of the church and the responsibility of elders for the order of the church. We could see that in Scripture, and we saw it in history, but we also noticed that there were certain changes in procedure from what had been set up in the Scriptural history. We were also mindful of mission work because when you go out to the mission field you will find it is not limited to men.

It was amazing that denominations that were very strong on the idea that the teaching and preaching should be done only by men, nevertheless used women for their Bible classes, even women teaching mixed classes. We saw that and we recognized that God blessed such work. We were mindful of the early church in Acts 15 when it met to discuss procedures, when Paul and Barnabas came in and told what happened when they preached the Gospel to the Gentiles. That was not what others thought should be done, but when Paul and Barnabas preached the Gospel to the Gentiles, the Gentiles believed and were saved. We considered the Sunday school teachers who were women, and the mission work where women are both teaching and preaching, and we recognized that this has been blessed of God and souls have been saved.

The Scriptures do not disqualify any soul from serving the Lord because that soul happens to be a woman, as a matter of fact, it does not even disqualify that soul because it happens to be a nun. It does not require that all these servants should be angels; it only requires they should be sinners. There is nothing in the Bible that says a six-year-old boy could not be an elder; no one is going to be elected an elder unless some people are led to elect him. We felt that the Holy Spirit could have something to do about the election. Nothing in the Bible indicates that anyone is to be disqualified because he is a man or a woman just as nothing in the Bible indicates that a person should be disqualified because he is educated or uneducated. That Paul expected women to pray in public was indicated by his instructions very carefully outlined in 1 Corinthians, as to how they should dress when they prayed and prophesied in public.

All this can be felt when Paul wrote:

> And I entreat thee also, true yoke-fellow, help those women which laboured with me in the gospel, with Clement also, and with other my fellow-labourers, whose names are in the book of life (4:3).

He named Clement and then he indicated that it did not make any difference whether he named them or not. Their names were in the book of life and God knew who they were. There were women, therefore, who labored with Paul in the Gospel, and he wanted them to be helped by such persons as were ministering to the church of Philippi. All of this is being done to strengthen the church, to encourage them. This is being done to prepare them for trouble.

One of the best ways for believers to prepare for trouble is to be on good terms among themselves; they should get together. They should remember that when God has used someone and has blessed someone, it is not any human being's prerogative to disqualify that person whom God has used. If God has used a person, other believers should acknowledge it and be humble about it and help him in his personal fellowship with the Lord. May the Lord grant to each one of us an understanding heart that in all of these difficult matters we may humbly seek His mind and His will and go with Him.

# Chapter 62

## REJOICE

### (Philippians 4:4)

*Have you ever realized how very important and encouraging a personal smile can be?*

Rejoice in the Lord alway: and again I say, Rejoice (4:4).

These are well-know words which Paul writes for guidance. He makes it seem almost an order in his effort to strengthen these Philippian believers. Remember, he is writing to prepare them for trouble, for persecution. You will also remember that in this letter he began by telling them of his gratitude to God for them. He thanked God for them and for their support as they ministered to him. He told them also of his praying for them that their love might abound in knowledge and all judgment, that they might see things clearly, distinguishing the things that differed; and that they might be filled with the fruits of righteousness so that their lives might be fruitful.

These were the things that he prayed for and they could have this in mind in everything that would ever come up. As the days went by they could always remember that Paul was praying for them to this end. Then he urged them not to worry about him; he was in prison and was facing possible death, but he puts it in so many words that he had it made, so to speak. If it should happen that they would take his life everyone would talk about it and speak of the Gospel that he died for; if they did not kill him he would talk about it and tell them what he had in mind. Either way the Lord would be talked about and people would hear about Christ, and that is what he wanted.

He then admonished them with his first advice as they were facing the future: "Get together. All of you believers get together. Deny yourself and live in the Lord." He went on to urge them to promote among themselves a mutual concern one for the other. Each was to be thoughtful about the other, and in dealing and working together they were to do so humbly and meekly, with forbearance. Also he urged upon these believers that they should let the mind of Christ be in them.

Paul outlined four characteristics that would show up as they let the mind of Christ prevail in them. Humility, as seen outstandingly in the case of Jesus of Nazareth who emptied Himself and was obedient unto death; consideration of others, as in the case of Timothy who would naturally care for other people; and zeal in service as in the case of Epaphroditus (that young man almost worked himself to death that he might help to spread the Gospel) and finally, as in Paul himself, consecration. He had put all these things before them: setting up for them things that were true in their background, his praying for them, and Almighty God's power. All these things were brought to mind. He then set forth the attitudes they should have, indicating how they should stand, as it were, the way they should look, and the approach they should make. Now, when all of this had been done, in the closing part of his letter he urges them to practice their faith. He wanted them to rejoice in the Lord. This would be what they were to do: they were to practice "rejoicing in the Lord."

Understanding the word "rejoice" will be easier if we take it apart a bit. Look at those first letters "re." When you "re-write" something, this means you have already written it. When Paul says "rejoice" he means his readers already had joy. And here is one reason why so few people find this word of Paul meaningful to them. We should be careful that we do not think this means believers are supposed to be happy. The word "happy" is a human word; it has to do with human experience. But that is not the word here. When Paul wrote "Rejoice in the Lord" he was not saying "be happy." "Joy" is the basic element in the idea "rejoice." A believer can "joy" in the Lord; it is like feeling good all over, and it is real. The believer can look into the face of Jesus Christ —

that will give him joy. He can hear Christ saying to him "Come." "Come unto me, all ye that labour and are heavy laden." "Let the wicked forsake his way, and the unrighteous man his thoughts: and let him return unto the LORD, and he will have mercy upon him." Such Scriptures will warm the believer's heart.

We should remember that gracious promise: "Whosoever will may come." That is as broad as the whole world and all time and for everyone. Anyone can be sure of a gracious reception.

> But as many as received him, to them gave he power to become the sons of God, even to them that believe on his name (John 1:12).

We joyfully sing, "There is life for a look at the Crucified One. There is life at this moment for thee." That is true, and one look at the Lord Jesus Christ is enough to save the soul; and it is gloriously true that gazing into the face of Jesus Christ will sanctify the believer. Such worship will lift up the heart of the believer, and as he thinks about His Savior, he has that first wonderful experience of realizing that the Lord Jesus Christ offers full salvation without reservation, and with no condition attached: whoever believes will not perish, but have everlasting life.

When all of this comes into the heart and mind of the believer his experience of the grace of God will be wonderful. In some cases, and with some people, they will shout. Some people will sing. Some people will cry out of sheer joy. Recalling this gracious truth will bring joy every time the believer thinks about it; and in this joy of the Lord the believer will find his strength. Recalling what brings joy to the soul begets strength in the spirit.

Paul says "rejoice in the Lord always." The believer can rejoice in the Lord at any time. I do not fully understand what joy is until I realize that I can have joy even when my heart is breaking. I can have joy even when I have lost my dearest friend. I can have joy in the face of any calamity, because the things of the Lord do not change. The Lord

Jesus Christ is always my Savior. It is for this reason that Paul not only could urge them to rejoice alway, but he could write: "and again I say, Rejoice." Strength in the Lord comes not so much by understanding what is happening now, but by remembering what has been done.

## Chapter 63

## YOUR MODERATION

### (Philippians 4:5)

*Have you ever considered what great blessings and advantages will come to anyone who does not expect too much from another?*

> Let your moderation be known unto all men. The Lord is at hand (4:5).

This statement remains vague to many of us since we do not normally use the word "moderation." Let us look at several other translations which are English expressions of the same Greek word but put in other phrases. For example, "Let all men know *and* perceive *and* recognize your unselfishness — your considerateness, your forebearing spirit. The Lord is near — He is coming soon" (*Amplified Bible*). Or here is another one: "Let everyone see that you are unselfish and considerate in all that you do. Remember that the Lord is coming soon" (*Living Bible*).

You will notice that in each version the idea is brought out clearly that the word "moderation" implies a certain self-control in the interest of working things out agreeably and acceptably with other people. The natural man is, first of all, interested in himself. He evaluates everything that happens to him in terms of what it will do for himself. This is a normal procedure. The natural man feels that he has all the issues of his life in his own hand, or at least he should have; he feels as if it is up to him, and so if things go against him he gets nervous, upset, prone to despair. If things are going for him, this same person can be exalted, excited, inclined to be proud. It is natural for a person either to blame himself too much, or to praise himself too much.

The believer holds that all is in the hands of God; he has an understanding about things that if he yields himself to the indwelling Holy Spirit of God and has the Scriptures in his hand and in his heart and mind, the Holy Spirit will give him to see and to understand all things are in the hands of Almighty God. When things are bad an intelligent believer trusts God; when things are good an intelligent believer thanks God. All is God's business. It is possible for the believer to think this way because he has yielded himself into the hands of God. The believer sees clearly how things are and rests himself in the will of God. This insight on the part of the believer enables him to act with yieldedness and forebearance.

The believer is yielded as to the Lord. One outstanding Old Testament example is that of Job when he lost every bit of property he had, and then lost all his family. They were all taken away. But the words of Job are classic: "The LORD gave, the LORD hath taken away; blessed be the name of the LORD." This did not mean that as far as Job was concerned what happened was all right. Job trusted God: if things were coming his way, he thanked God; if things were going against him, he trusted God. This is the way Job thought.

Paul expressed almost the same frame of mind when he wrote: "I have learned, in whatsoever state I am, therewith to be content" (Phil. 4:11). Sometimes he was fortunate: then he thanked God. Sometimes he was unfortunate: then he trusted God. He was never too highly elated by victory, and never too deeply dejected by defeat. He kept an even keel as things went along.

This reminds us of Jesus of Nazareth: on the occasion when Jesus of Nazareth was arrested on the night of His betrayal and when the Roman soldiers gathered around to take Him in, Peter wanted to defend Him, and drew his sword to attack the soldiers. But the Lord told Peter to put up his sword, saying, "Don't you know that even now, if I wanted to, I could ask my Father, and He would give Me twelve legions of angels?" No doubt the American version of that would be something like: "Don't you know that if I didn't let them, they couldn't lay a hand on me? The only reason in the world that they can arrest me is that I let them do it." This was the attitude of the Lord Jesus Christ. He had yielded Himself into the will of God His Father. Why did He do that? Because He was afraid of the Romans? No! Because He could not have controlled them? No! Why then? He came for our sakes to die for us, and this was in the plan of God; so He meekly yielded Himself in the arrest, as He yielded Himself later to death.

In the affairs of a believer this may result in the loss of goods. A believer may lose his property, and in the case of some he may lose a nice order in business. He may suffer the loss of goods because of his faith or he may suffer the loss of health. But Paul would urge the believer to be yielded to the Lord, and the Scriptures would promise him, "in confidence shall be your strength." This whole outlook that I have been discussing strengthens the believer in forbearance. Yieldedness is as unto the Lord; forbearance is as unto other persons. For a demonstration we can turn to Jesus of Nazareth and see Him on the cross: "Father, forgive them; for they know not what they do." They were not doing right, and what they did the Lord did not like. He did not approve it, but He did not want judgment to come upon them because of this.

Paul in writing to these Philippians emphasizes that in the affairs of a believer it is important that he should live with meekness and longsuffering: the Lord is at hand. Suffering will not go on forever, because the Lord Jesus is standing in the wings, as it were, of the world's stage. When His turn comes He will move on the stage and He will bring to an end this present confusion that the believers are in. The Lord is at hand, and we can close our meditation by reflecting on the idea that the believer resting in God, trusting in God, is invincible.

## Chapter 64

## BE CAREFUL FOR NOTHING
### (Philippians 4:6)

*Do you realize that a believer need not be personally concerned about what is going to happen tomorrow?*

Let us note the first words in this famous Scripture:

Be careful for nothing (4:6).

Common usage has blurred the original meaning of this phrase. The words actually mean "be full of care about nothing": do not be completely overwhelmed with care about anything. Another translation reads: "Do not fret, or have any anxiety about anything." Still another reads more simply: "Don't worry about anything"; while another is put in the words: "Have no anxiety about anything." Perhaps "Do not worry about anything" may be the best statement of what Paul had in mind. This does not mean, however, that a person should pay no attention to the future.

The words of Jesus of Nazareth are really quite clear:

For which of you, intending to build a tower, sitteth not down first, and counteth the cost, whether he have sufficient to finish it? Lest haply, after he hath laid the foundation, and is not able to finish it, all that behold it begin to mock him, saying, This man began to build, and was not able to finish. Or what king, going to make war against another king, sitteth not down first, and consulteth whether he be able with ten thousand to meet him that cometh against him with twenty thousand? Or else, while the other is yet a great way off, he sendeth an ambassage, and desireth conditions of peace (Luke 14:28-32).

Here the Lord points out clearly that any person who has a project of any kind which he intends to complete should estimate that project, that he might know what it will take to complete it. Any person confronted with a crisis should

228

study the possibilities. He should learn what to expect if he looks ahead. Such fore-thought is not a matter of worrying. There is in this no fearsome dread of disaster, no foreboding of evil. When the dire possibilities of danger, of possible defeat, loom in the mind the believer can recall instruction from his Lord:

> Take therefore no thought for the morrow: for the morrow shall take thought for the things of itself. Sufficient unto the day is the evil thereof (Matt. 6:34).

Actually in this guidance the mind of the believer is directed to consider the possibility of the evil involved. This whole idea is developed more fully in the Sermon on the Mount. I can remember how one sentence in that passage often troubled me as a new believer:

> Behold the fowls of the air: for they sow not, neither do they reap, nor gather into barns; yet your heavenly Father feedeth them. Are ye not much better than they? (Matt. 6:26).

That bothered me because it seemed to discount the responsibility to work. It seemed almost as though those words would make you feel that if you really put your trust in the Lord, all you had to do was to sit and wait. I grew up on a farm and I knew that if you were going to get any kind of results, you would have to work. If you wanted beans you would have to plant and hoe beans; I knew that. As time went on and I became more responsible in my interpretation, and continued to study the Scripture, it suddenly dawned on me how much I had missed. No doubt you have heard the expression "getting up with the birds"? Matthew 6:26 does not mean that the birds sit on fence posts waiting for Almighty God to drop worms into their mouths. Birds are industrious: they get up early. And they are hopeful. When you see a robin going across your lawn looking to find a worm, he is expecting it to be there. This, it now seems to me, is what the Lord meant when He taught: "Do not worry." The believer should go out and look with confident expectation that what he needs will be there. The basic principle in all of this attitude toward the future seems to be expressed in these words, "Seek first the kingdom of God and all other things will be added to you."

To have the mind and heart free from concern about things is not a matter of will power. It is an exercise of faith. Such faith is not a matter of having certain expectation of the outcome of events. Someone may say, "I just have faith." Perhaps what they mean by that is they think everything will turn out all right. But the Bible means more when it tells the believer to be anxious about nothing. The kind of faith involved is to be a certain confidence in Almighty God. Actually all things are in the hands of God, and He is Almighty: He is able to overrule. That being the case, what can give the believer his confidence? His confidence can be grounded in the conviction that God is kind and He is gracious; God is good and the goodness of the Lord endures forever. The believer can know this because of Calvary. He can look into the face of the Lord Jesus on Calvary's cross and know that He died for him. Then he can remember the words of Paul, "He that spared not his own Son, but delivered him up for us all, how shall he not with him also freely give us all things?"

The believer can be confident simply by looking up into the face of God, as seen in the person of Jesus Christ. He will not need to be worried or depressed; he will not need to be fearful about what the future holds in store. He can look up into the face of God who did not spare His own Son. If God gave His Son for the believer, need he think God will now stop caring for him? To some this line of argument will not matter much, since they are not now in trouble. Everything may be going along fine. They may feel fairly well physically; they may have good meals to eat. Their clothing may be adequate, they may have a job, so that for the present they are getting along all right.

Actually, as far as I am concerned I can read this and be comfortable, "Do not be anxious about anything." But the fact is, I may not be anxious because I may feel that I have everything in hand. However, if I were to have trouble, if I were to have sorrow or grief, if I were in danger, and I were face to face with something that would make me troubled because I did not know how I was going to face it, then I would need these words in a special way: "Do not be overly anxious about that. Do not let it get you down with anxiety. Look up. Look into the face of God. God is and God is Almighty; and God is good and God is gracious; and God is on your side."

Let me keep in mind the fact that this world is not going to last forever. It may be rough now, it may be hard and mean at present, but it is not going to last. But I will! And God is! He has everything in hand for me. I should look up into His face and trust Him; then I would be worried about nothing.

# Chapter 65

## LET YOUR REQUESTS BE MADE KNOWN

### (Philippians 4:6)

*If a person were not sure as to what would be the best thing that could happen, how should he pray about it?*

But in every thing by prayer and supplication with thanksgiving let your requests be made known unto God (4:6).

Since all this is true, why don't we pray more? Is it that we do not know what to ask for? I am reminded of a person who may be sick and may not want to go to the doctor, because he says, "I don't know what is wrong with me. I would not know what to tell him or what medicine to ask for." I might smile and think to myself, "No one would be that foolish." But any one could wisely tell me, "Don't kid yourself."

Compare this Scripture, "In everything by prayer and supplication with thanksgiving let your requests be made known unto God," with Romans 8:26, "Likewise the Spirit also helpeth our infirmities: for we know not what we should pray for as we ought: but the Spirit itself maketh intercession for us with groanings which cannot be uttered." It seems clear that Paul recognized his own personal infirmities as such that he was hindered in knowing what he should pray for. And we know that Paul would have wanted to ask for what would be acceptable to God.

So let us examine these words more closely. "In everything" means that nothing is too small. Someone may say, "I don't know whether I should pray about that. It is too small." But is it bothering you? If so, it is big enough. The first time I ever realized clearly that nothing is ever too small was when I had a cinder in my eye. That speck of dust really hurt! I knew then that a thing does not have to be big to hurt. Paul says "in everything": he means nothing is too small.

When Paul wrote "by prayer" he meant my prayer. What is prayer? Prayer begins as communion with God. I lift up my face and look into heaven. God knows every thought of my heart. But I need to express it. If I want to think about God, and I ask: "I wonder what God is like"; I should think about Jesus Christ. "He that hath seen me hath seen the Father." Christ is the express image of God. So I say to myself, pray according to the revelation of God that I find in the Bible, and as I am led by the Spirit of God; for, after all, the Spirit of God is all about me.

If I have a burden, if I have a problem, if I have something that is troubling me, I should lift up my eyes. I should lift up my face to God and tell Him what is on my heart. "By prayer and supplication." I need to ask for something. What if I have nothing to give? I need not worry for all the cattle on a thousand hills are His. All of the silver and gold belong to God. But there is one thing I can give to God, because if I do not give it, He will never get it. *That is my thanks and my praise.* Apart from that He already has everything. So "in everything by prayer and supplication with thanksgiving," I need to recall what He has done for me. I need to review today, yesterday, then go back over the past week, the past month, the past years. I need to look up, and I need to remember I have something for which to be thankful. Whatever He has done in the past, He will not quit doing today. He will not cancel future activity, so "with thanksgiving let your requests be made known unto God."

Let us look at the word "request." I will not be telling God what to do. I will be asking Him for something. That will be my request. I will bring that before God. It may be that a cleansing operation will take place. It may be that something will be screened out. I need only tell the Lord about it, and then see what will happen. My own thoughts would probably just die in my own mind and heart. It is a marvelous thing to talk to God. Remember, it is *my* requests, not those of anyone else. Here is the wonderful benefit of united praying. The Scripture says, "If two of you shall agree on earth, I will do it." Have you ever wondered why "two"? Because this fellowship is part of the screening process. If John and Jim are going to pray, and John has something so selfish he will not mention it in the presence of Jim and if Jim has something so self-indulgent he will not mention it before John, those were not good things anyway. Then what John and Jim can agree on, that will be good.

But in everything by prayer and supplication with thanksgiving let your requests be made known unto God.

## Chapter 66

## PEACE OF GOD

## (Philippians 4:6, 7)

*Do you realize there is a wonderful blessing guaranteed for any person who will ask God for what he really wants?*

We are just now considering one of the most wonderful prayer promises in the Bible.

> Be careful for nothing; but in every thing by prayer and supplication with thanksgiving let your requests be made known unto God. And the peace of God, which passeth all understanding, shall keep your hearts and minds through Christ Jesus (4:6, 7).

Those words are so sweeping they say almost more than one can grasp. They seem to cover all the concerns anyone could ever have. "Do not let anything worry you overmuch." No doubt there will be disturbing and annoying situations. There will be troublesome times. These things will come, but it is written: "Do not let them overwhelm you." This applies to any believer in the Lord Jesus Christ.

We need to remember the grace of God is open and free for everyone — anyone can come. This is particularly significant and will clearly be felt in heart and mind when I have committed myself to the Lord. Then here is the word to me. "Do not let anything worry you overmuch. In everything by prayer and supplication let your requests with thanksgiving be made known to God. Ask for what you want, praying to God, communing with Him, asking Him (actually supplicating), thanking Him for what He has done. "And the peace of God, which passeth all understanding, shall keep your hearts and mind through Christ Jesus."

When I look at this in all honesty and straightforward integrity, I see this is no unconditional guarantee that I am going to get everything I ask for. I am promised: "And the peace of God, which passeth all understanding, shall keep your hearts and minds through Christ Jesus." I can be sure that when I ask Him I will be heard: whatever I may ask, my request will be considered. But I can be quite sure that God will act according to His wise and holy and just will. He is not going to do anything for me that would not be good for me.

Consider the teaching of Jesus of Nazareth about prayer, and notice how a father will consider the request of his child:

> Ask, and it shall be given you; seek, and ye shall find; knock, and it shall be opened unto you: for every one that asketh receiveth; and he that seeketh findeth; and to him that knocketh it shall be opened. Or what man is there of you, whom if his son ask bread, will he give him a stone (Matt. 7:7-9)?

When the son asks for bread which is good, shall I think the father will give him anything that is evil? But now let me turn that around. Suppose this child foolishly asks for something that is evil. Shall I think the father will give it to him? For example, suppose there is a three-year-old child who asks for a razor blade, would his father give it to him? I could see the father getting something else and giving it to the child but I would not expect the father to give him the razor blade, just because the child asked for it. Now if I would do like that or you would do like that, we can be quite sure God would do like that.

> Or what man is there of you, whom if his son ask bread, will he give him a stone? Or if he ask a fish, will he give him a serpent? If ye then, being evil, know how to give good gifts unto your children, how much more shall your Father which is in heaven give good things to them that ask him? (Matt. 7:9-11)

We may notice that the father will give good things. When are things good? When they are helpful. And who would know? The father would know. We should always remember that in any earnest believing prayer, the last aspect of that prayer will be: "nevertheless not my will, but thine, be done." That is how the Lord Jesus prayed in Gethsemane and that is how His Spirit will pray in me and in you. "Not my will, but thine, be done."

We need always to remember Romans 8:26, "Likewise the Spirit also helpeth our infirmities: for we know not what we should pray for as we ought." We do not know what to ask for; we are not that smart nor that good. We are not that wise, but the promise is clear. "The peace of God, which passeth all understanding, shall keep your hearts and minds through Christ Jesus." The peace of God means that my heart will be comforted. My mind will be at rest. I can quietly and really trust in God. If I have turned things over to Him, I should take my hands off. When I ask Him, when I put my request before God, I should leave it there. God will take care of all things.

God will give me His peace which will guard my heart and mind. The English word "keep" is hardly rich enough in its meaning. The Greek word can be understood something like this: "will garrison your hearts and minds." This is as if the commander of the city were to send a garrison of soldiers to this particular castle or home to protect it. The peace of God will protect, will guard, will surround; and it passes understanding. God will guard my heart and mind through Christ Jesus, Please notice "through Christ Jesus." I will not have this peace of God because I got what I asked for. I will have this peace of God which passes all understanding "through Christ Jesus."

Recently I had a phone call from a woman who was in great need. She felt she wanted to know something more about God and the peace of God, because deep down in her heart she was frightened. She was facing surgery, and she felt very apprehensive. She sought some reason not to fear. I asked her if she believed in God, and she said, "Yes." I asked her did she believe God had her in His hands, and again she said, "Yes." I then asked her, "How long do you think God would keep you? Would He keep you to the end of your life?" She thought so. "Would He keep you through death?" "Yes." "Would He keep you after death?" "Yes."

"How long?" And when it came out of her heart: "Into eternity." Then I asked: "Is that true right now?" She said, "Yes." Then I said, "Don't you see that God has you in hand and in mind? Remember, God has never promised to me or to you that we are going to stay here forever. God knows what He is doing and we are in His hands. In Christ Jesus we can look up into the presence of God and be comforted to remember God will take care of us. That is the comfort we have in Christ Jesus. Christ Jesus stands both in this world and in the world to come. He has bridged the gap. He has taken away the idea of a barrier between this world and the world to come, and we say when we think about Him, 'O grave, where is thy victory? O death, where is thy sting?' Because Christ Jesus has taken away the sting of death and the victory of the grave. Whatever the problem or request, even of life or death, we are in His hands." I am happy that this helped her.

Because I am in Christ Jesus, God will let His peace garrison me. He will surround me with His love, mercy and power, and I can remember the words we find in the New Testament, "nothing shall by any means hurt you." If I can bring this into my heart, my heart will be comforted in facing anything. People do pass from this world into the world to come, and if they are Christians they will not drop off the edge. They go straight to the arms of Jesus, straight to His gentle breast. This is a marvelous thing: "The peace of God, which passeth all understanding, shall keep your hearts and minds through Christ Jesus."

Chapter 67

## WHATSOEVER THINGS ARE TRUE

### (Philippians 4:8)

*Do you realize that God is concerned about what any person believing in Him thinks about?*

The Apostle Paul was writing to the believers in the city of Philippi, and he laid out for them certain considerations which he intended should help them to be strong in their faith.

> Finally, brethren, whatsoever things are true, whatsoever things are honest, whatsoever things are just, whatsoever things are pure, whatsoever things are lovely, whatsoever things are of good report; if there be any virtue, and if there be any praise, think on these things (4:8).

Here he gave them an agenda. There would be many other ideas that might come into their minds, but these were to be preferred.

How can I control my thinking? Have you ever considered that when you are thinking you are talking to yourself? Or perhaps you imagine yourself talking to someone else. And so you think things out while you are so talking. If I were to ask, "How could I start thinking about the poor?" I only need to start talking to myself about the poor. How could I stop thinking about something that is evil, or thinking about some wrong thing I would like to do? I only need to stop talking about that to myself; I need to stop thinking about it.

If something affects me, so that I want to think about it by sharing it with someone else, but I have the feeling it is not the right thing, what can I do? I should not say anything about it. Can you think what would happen? If I never mentioned it to anyone or to myself, soon that would drop out of my memory. No matter what I hear, even if someone else comes and tells me, if I will not say it, if I will not repeat it, that thing will fade out of my mind.

Paul's agenda in this passage indicates the things that the believer should talk about and think about. "Whatsoever things are true." There are many things we hear about that are not true. We should let them go unrepeated.

"Whatsoever things are honest." Some things could be true enough in themselves, but if I were to tell them, it would not be honest. Suppose I were to see a certain man, a local pastor, come out of a beer parlor. I actually saw him step through the door and come out into the street. This would be true. But do I know why he was there? Do I know why he went into that place? Do I have any idea what he did when he was in that place? Then if I tell people that I saw James Smith coming out of a beer parlor and thus leave the impression that that was his way of living, my statement would not be honest.

"Whatsoever things are just." The English word "just" means that my statement is exactly as the event it is supposed to name. Another good word would be "whatsoever things are fair," meaning fair and square. There are things that could be true, and that could be honest enough, but they would not be fair. For instance, if I stopped a person on the street and asked him to help the poor, and he said, "No," that man might be very active in helping the poor in another situation. Then if I reported that in this case he did not help the poor I would not be making a fair statement; I would be leaving the impression that he does not help the poor at all.

"Whatsoever things are pure." This is simple. It does not make any difference whether the statement was true and even honest; it could just be plain dirty. In that case what I am about to say would be true, and might even be fair, but it would be dirty. I should hush my mouth. If I am a believer in the Lord Jesus Christ, I should simply "shut up." I should not repeat anything that is unclean. Someone might say, "But it is true." Even so, I should not say it. "But it is honest." Even if it is, I should not say it. "But it is a fair thing to say it" — I would not need to deny that. The statement could be fair, but if it is unclean, I should not say it. I should let it go.

There could be some things that might even meet all these criteria, so that they could be true and honest and fair, and even clean, but they are not lovely. It might be an ugly thing. I should not talk about it. Perhaps some concerned person may say, "But something should be done about it." Maybe so, but you are not going to do it. That would be in God's hands. Remember, in all this, I am talking to believers.

The Apostle Paul would say to you, "If it is not lovely, don't say it." In this world there are lovely things — roses, lilies, etc. In this world there are also dirty things — sewers, slime, muck. In every house there are pictures on the wall that are lovely, and there is furniture that is lovely. In that same home there may be a bathroom that has a commode in it, with a sewer going out from it. Decency will guide anyone as to what to display. I use the word "decency": this belongs to anything that is clean. We put our roses in the front yard for everyone to see; we put our sewers underground and hide them. We do this because we are civilized, we are decent. If I am a believer in the Lord Jesus Christ I will make this the rule of my life. Jesus of Nazareth knew all that was in the hearts of men; wouldn't He know some dirt? Some unclean things? But did He ever speak of these things?

One more thing, "Whatsoever things are of good report." Good report means a good reputation. The believer, the person who believes in the Lord Jesus Christ and witnesses for Him, will be careful to edit everything he says and thinks. Again, "If there be any virtue, and if there be any praise, think on these things." Choose the things that are true and fair and lovely, and the Lord will bless you.

Chapter 68

## THOSE THINGS DO

(Philippians 4:9)

*Can you understand how it is that living the life of a believer in God in this world is really not hard to do?*

Becoming a believer in Jesus Christ is not a complicated affair. Explaining it to people can be complicated, and of course that is because no human being can understand all of the things of the Spirit. A human being is out of his depth trying to explain what God is going to do, and such an attempt can lead him into all kinds of trouble. As far as the believer is concerned, the Gospel is simple: a wayfaring man need not err therein. Children can accept Christ and old people can accept Christ. No one needs to fear that he might be confused by what it means; it is not that difficult.

Everything we preach and teach in the Gospel is based upon the reality of God and man. God is in heaven! Man is on earth. God is holy and of purer eyes than to behold evil. Man is sinful — "in sin did my mother conceive me." Because of sin man is condemned to destruction and is lost. But because of the grace of God, the condemned sinner can be saved to the glory of God. Some people would say "Hallelujah!" He can be saved! And we tell the whole wide world "Whosoever believeth in him should not perish, but have everlasting life." We make it a matter of record, that "as many as received him, to them gave he the power to become the sons of God, even to them that believe on his name."

Then what shall a sinner do? What is involved? This also is simple: believe the Gospel that he hears, accept Jesus Christ about whom he is told. When a man accepts the Lord Jesus Christ and commits himself to Him, it does not follow that he knows everything; it doesn't even mean that

242

he knows always just what he should do next. It does mean that now he has the disposition so that he wants to do the will of God. But what would this actually be? The Apostle Paul knew that these believers in the city of Philippi were the same as any other believers and humanly speaking they would not know what to do. So he gives them very simple instructions and a wonderful promise:

> Those things, which ye have both learned, and received, and heard, and seen in me, do: and the God of peace shall be with you (4:9).

The Philippian believers would never have known about Jesus Christ if Paul had not told them. Nowhere in the world has any human being ever known the truth about Jesus Christ, unless some missionary, some apostle, some preacher, some witness told them. Perhaps they read about it, but in that case what they read was written by a witness.

If someone were to say to me, "But I don't know how to become a Christian," I would say to such a person very simply, "You should learn. It isn't difficult." Even a young child in the primary department of Sunday school could tell him. "Believe on the Lord Jesus Christ, and thou shalt be saved." He could not get it any simpler than that. The person might say, "But I don't know about Jesus Christ." I would ask, "Can you read? Then read the Bible. Can you listen? Then listen to someone who teaches. Can you talk? Then talk with someone who believes it." A person does not need to know about all the religions in the world, but he can learn about Jesus Christ. Someone will tell him the Gospel. When a person learns that God has offered to save him and he feels there is offered to him the possibility of his actually becoming a child of God — he knows all he needs to know.

The Bible will tell any person that God offers to make him His child. Is he willing to receive this? Will he take this promise to himself and actually rest in it? It is there in the Scriptures. Surely he knows a preacher who believes it, or a layman or a business man. Perhaps he knows a woman who believes it; maybe he knows some young people who believe it. I am sure there is someone in any community who can tell anyone what to do. A person does not have to run the fastest mile, climb the highest mountain or swim the widest river. He needs only to open his heart to receive. All in the world he needs to do is to humble himself and be willing to take what is offered to him. God will save his soul. Now if any person has any trouble with what I have been saying, he should not rest until he finds someone who does believe and can tell him about it. Just let him tell such a person: "I'd like to become a Christian and I don't know how." Then let him see what will happen. There are willing persons who would go anywhere and do anything to help another soul come to faith.

Whatsoever "things ye have both learned, and received, and heard." When the Bible uses the word "hear" it always includes the idea of understanding. When a person says he has listened and has "heard" the Word, this always means that he has understood what was said. If a person has listened and learned, received and heard, this means he now understands the Gospel; and he now knows out of the Bible that if he believes in the Lord Jesus Christ God will make him His child. The Bible will make clear to any believer that the Holy Spirit is given to him. He will not be able to see it on the outside. There will be nothing happening in the air, and nothing will happen in the room he is in when he receives the Holy Spirit. But will he open his heart and believe? If he will open his heart he will understand when God has given the Holy Spirit. By the time he has learned the Gospel, has received it and has understood it, he will see it in other people. He will see the effect the Spirit has on mature believers, how they read the Bible, attend church, have family worship, and so on.

In all this that I have written I have intended to bring the reader to an understanding of what is involved in becoming a believer. Anyone can learn it, can receive it, and can understand it. Now Paul has one further word to say: "Do it." The person now sees how it is done, so he should put it into actual practice. He should give himself over to God; trust in Him. Then he can claim the wonderful end of this sentence: "And the God of peace shall be with you."

The believer will have Almighty God, and this particular aspect of Him. There will be quietness and peace in his own soul. There will not be any confusion or any conflict. His whole soul and spirit can be at rest. It is wonderful to believe in God, to believe in the Lord Jesus Christ, to trust and give oneself over to Him. This will happen to anyone who will simply respond to the things that he has learned and the things he has received, the things he now understands, and the things he can see in other believers, that have given themselves over to the Lord Jesus Christ.

I hope all my readers have a church to go to. I hope that in that church they can recognize real believers and that they will join with them and pray for their pastor. If the minister is a genuine believer in the Lord Jesus Christ, the believers should let him know that they want the same faith and blessing he has. And believe me, the God of peace shall be with all such and their hearts will be happy in the Lord.

## Chapter 69

## YOUR CARE OF ME

(Philippians 4:10)

*Do you realize that the way a congregation takes care of its pastor is very important in his ministry?*

Paul has been writing to the believers in Philippi to help them in their living and we have noticed how he has tried to guide these believers that they might have a strong, clear testimony to their faith, because he felt this would glorify the name of Christ. It was known, of course, that he was the preacher, the apostle who had taught these people. Paul generally even today is esteemed as being perhaps the greatest, and certainly perhaps the most famous, of the believers in the New Testament. It is so easy for us even now to assume that he would be so strong and so self-contained that it is almost a shock to realize he was only a human being, and he shared life in this world just as others do.

I suspect his own people would be tempted to think from time to time that the apostle would not need anything. I can't help but think that today in many congregations there are members of the church who do not go out of their way to show their pastor how they feel about him, because they probably assume that he doesn't need them. They think that he is a great man and everyone is looking up to him. But we get a different impression as we read Paul's own words:

> But I rejoiced in the Lord greatly, that now at the last your care of me hath flourished again; wherein ye were also careful, but ye lacked opportunity (4:10).

There was apparently a time in Paul's ministry when these believers in Philippi could not send him any help; he may have been a great distance away or perhaps he was in prison somewhere. He knew that they cared and he knew that they had no opportunity to show their care for him,

246

but in this situation they now had the chance and they took it. We will remember how they sent Epaphroditus to help take care of him. Epaphroditus was the servant or the delegate, so to speak, from the church at Philippi to Paul, and Paul was greatly blessed and rejoiced in the Lord greatly because of the ministry of Epaphroditus. It is important to notice how he expressed himself: he "rejoiced in the Lord."

What they had done was to send Epaphroditus to help him. Today we would be more inclined to send some money which would enable the missionary to live in a certain place, or have certain comforts that he could use in his life. I suspect that a good many times there would be those of us who would have the feeling that if we sent money to that preacher he would certainly be glad. Yes, I am sure he would be, but we would need to be careful not to misunderstand: Paul did not rejoice in the service of Epaphroditus. Of course, he was glad to have it and he could use it, but that is not what he was saying. He rejoiced "in the Lord greatly." He thanked the Lord and when that help came he appreciated their thinking of him. He appreciated the help, but he appreciated all these things because it showed him the faithfulness of the Lord. The Lord prompted those people in Philippi to send the help.

I hope for each reader that his family shares in caring for his pastor. A minister deals with spiritual matters and generally speaking these are strange to people. He always seems to be dealing with things that are far above them and out of their reach, and it is easy to get the impression that naturally he is closer to God. He may well be, but we could get the impression that since he is depending on God and God is taking care of him, he would not need anything that we might do to help him. For just such reason the preacher may often be neglected. People do not really mean him any harm; they really would be ready to help, but they often do not. I would like to urge you that you do not fall into this error. Do not make the mistake of supposing that your help does not count. We all should remember what Paul says,

"I rejoiced in the Lord greatly, that now at the last your care of me hath flourished again."

How can a person care for his pastor? I can imagine some of you thinking that you seldom see him, perhaps only on Sunday. If you want to show that you care for him, greet him with a smile, and tell him you are glad to see him. Extend to him a warm handshake. That will mean a lot. Some of you can do better than that: if you have a garden, take him some vegetables, or a dozen eggs. This is a big thing. Some who have orchards could take a bushel of apples; he would appreciate it. These are things you might think are too small to be noticed, but any gift would be appreciated. I was twice a pastor: once in Winnipeg, Canada, and once in Dallas, Texas. I remember very well how good it was to have some people from time to time make it a point to let the pastor know that they thought about him. For thirty years I was a professor — three years in college as a professor of Bible and twenty-seven years in seminary as professor of Bible and I can tell you it was a lonely life. I did not have a congregation. In recent years I have been a radio speaker, and I certainly do appreciate letters, cards, and special contributions to the work, which show the personal regard with which some listeners think of me. And you can help the cause of the Gospel if you will show your care for the man who is preaching the Gospel: God will bless you.

# Chapter 70

## TO BE CONTENT

### (Philippians 4:11)

*Can you understand how blessed it is to be content at all times in all situations?*

After Paul expressed his joy in the Lord when the believers in Philippi began to take care of him, he went on to say something further. In our last study Paul expressed a great joy because the Philippians were showing their care of him by sending gifts to him, but now he has something further to say:

> Not that I speak in respect of want: for I have learned, in whatsoever state I am, therewith to be content (4:11).

This is a wonderful blessing. In writing to Timothy, Paul told him "godliness with contentment is great gain." This is truly a wonderful thing.

But we need to be careful that we do not misunderstand the whole situation. Paul writes this because he does not want them to misunderstand his joy in their gift: he does not want to leave the wrong impression with them, as though he were longing for more gifts personally. He wants them to know that in his spiritual experience he had gained a certain mastery over his natural wants and desires.

Paul did not allow himself to be wishing for things he could not have. This is an example we all need to observe for ourselves. This verse reveals that such contentment is something to learn, because it does not come naturally. Naturally speaking, a person is not always contented with what he has. It is true a believer is just as aware of needing things as anyone else would be: a Christian feels the lack of things. Believers know what it is to be happy when they have plenty, but the believer knows more than that. Jesus of Nazareth on one occasion used these words in teaching

His disciples, "A man's life consisteth not in the abundance of the things which he possesseth." It is true, of course, that the things that a person possesses do matter. If he has more of certain things he feels better, and if he has less things, he does not feel so well. And if a person does not have enough to live amply he will not feel well, but the believer in the course of experience learns not to be disturbed or disquieted when he has less. There may be times when he has less than he could use. He may not have what he could actually make use of, but he learns how to get along with what he does have. He understands all things are from God and God does all things well. The truth about Paul was not that he had no interest in things, but that he had learned to be content with what he had.

The word "content" does not mean delighted or pleased. "Content" is a descriptive word which describes the condition in which a person has contained himself. He holds himself in and does not reach out from where he is. He is not reaching for that which belongs to others. Paul was personally as much aware of his need as anyone else would be.

> For though I would desire to glory, I shall not be a fool; for I will say the truth: but now I forbear, lest any man should think of me above that which he seeth me to be, or that he heareth of me. And lest I should be exalted above measure through the abundance of the revelations, there was given to me a thorn in the flesh, the messenger of Satan to buffet me, lest I should be exalted above measure (2 Cor. 12:6, 7).

No one has ever known for sure what that thorn in the flesh was.

It seems a remarkable providence of God that it was never described. Any number of people who have personal difficulty have been inclined to think Paul must have had something like their own problem. We can be quite certain that "a thorn in the flesh" was something in his human situation that hurt him, that actually disturbed Paul. He had this ". . . a messenger of Satan to buffet me" — which pushed him around, which bumped him — ". . . lest I should be exalted above measure. Paul wrote about it:

For this thing I besought the Lord thrice, that it might depart from me. And he said unto me, My grace is sufficient for thee: for my strength is made perfect in weakness. Most gladly therefore will I rather glory in my infirmities, that the power of Christ may rest upon me. Therefore I take: pleasure in infirmities, in reproaches, in necessities, in persecutions, in distresses for Christ's sake (2 Cor. 12:8-10).

Such things hurt and we are not to assume that Paul was callous or indifferent. When the Scripture says "infirmity" we think it might be a personal weakness, whatever that may have been — bad eyesight or a weakness in body. He asked Almighty God for relief, for he knew that God could heal him if He wanted to. He had asked God to take this away three different times, but the Lord said "No, I am leaving it there for a purpose." Paul could be hurt when people said or did things that were unkind. He was hurt when they reproached or criticized him, when they gave him a bad name in public, but he states that if it took these things to glorify the Lord, he would take pleasure in them all. There were occasions when he did not have things he needed. He suffered in those times, but he took pleasure in them. Now when they persecuted Paul — beat him, threw stones at him and cast him out, he was hurt just like anyone else. But when he had occasion to endure these sufferings "for Christ's sake" he rejoiced. "I take pleasure, for when I am weak, then am I strong." It was when he was personally weak — meaning when he was actually at the very limit of his strength — that he said, "when I am weak then I am strong." He meant that then the Lord was with him and the Lord would give him strength.

For many of us who believe, this testimony of Paul continues to be a beacon light to guide us. And we will pray that Almighty God will give us the strength so that as far as we are concerned, when troubles come, and we may ask the Lord to be delivered but if He does not deliver, we can remember how it was with the Apostle Paul. "I have learned, in whatsoever state I am, therewith to be content."

Never let us misunderstand or think that such commitment was any mark of indifference. Paul had feelings just like everyone else, but he had learned to contain himself and he did not allow himself to be upset or disturbed. Others had things he could not have. If that was the way the Lord wanted it, that was fine with Paul. "All things come from God" and "God doeth all things well."

Chapter 71

## TO BE ABASED

### (Philippians 4:12)

*Can you realize that a believer in Christ Jesus is delivered from concern about this world by being instructed how to live with things and without things?*

We continue our study in the last chapter of Philippians. The Apostle Paul has been talking to and writing to believers in the city of Philippi, helping them to understand how they can live successfully as believers in Christ. He is now in the latter part of the fourth chapter, talking about himself as an illustration of this living in the will of God. And here he makes a very important statement.

> I know both how to be abased, and I know how to abound: every where and in all things I am instructed both to be full and to be hungry, both to abound and to suffer need (4:12).

Paul is seeking to say to these believers that which will help them live triumphantly, and we have noted that the first part of the letter was directly addressed to the believers themselves. A great deal of the latter part was his personal testimony.

After Paul had expressed his joy in the fact that their care for him had flourished again he made it clear that this joy was not because of the things that they brought him, or the things that they gave him, saying that he had learned in whatsoever state he was, therewith to be content. Now he wants to explain this further; he wants to expand it somewhat because this is such an important principle. We may wonder how he had learned this marvelous truth, that he could be so content no matter what his circumstances were. The fact was that he had been through so much, as he now reminds them:

253

I know both how to be abased, and I know how to abound:
every where and in all things I am instructed both to be full
and to be hungry, both to abound and to suffer need (4:12).

The truth in this passage can be felt as we note in another
version:

I know how to be abased *and* live humbly in stricken
circumstances, and I know also how to enjoy plenty *and* live
in abundance. I have learned in any and all circumstances
the secret of facing every situation, whether well-fed or
going hungry, having a sufficiency *and* to spare or going
without *and* being in want (*Amplified Bible*).

We can check this line of thought again in still another
translation:

I know how to live on almost nothing or with everything. I
have learned the secret of contentment in every situation,
whether it be a full stomach or hunger, plenty or want
(*The Living Bible*).

When Paul says "I know" he is indicating that this has been
the result of his experience. This is a case of experimental
knowledge.

In other words, the Apostle Paul had been through a lot
and he had learned a great deal. Because of what he had
experienced he said, "I know how to be abased" (he had
been treated like a prisoner) and "how to abound" (he had
been treated like a prince, standing in the presence of the
governor). Then he goes on to say "everywhere," meaning
that no part of his career was in vain. Everything that ever
happened to him counted everywhere. When he says "in all
things" he means that physically he found this to be true,
personally he found this to be true, socially, as far as people
were concerned, "in all things I am instructed both to be
full and to be hungry." Not only in one phase but in everything this experience of having life come either with or
without was all about him. He knew how to abound and how
to suffer need, both to be favored and to be abused.

An illustration of such varied experience is recorded in
the fourteenth chapter of Acts, where the account tells how
the Apostle Paul was actually handled in both ways by the

same group of people. First there was what happened at Lystra:

> And there sat a certain man at Lystra, impotent in his feet, being a cripple from his mother's womb, who never had walked: the same heard Paul speak: who stedfastly beholding him, and perceiving that he had faith to be healed, said with a loud voice, Stand upright on thy feet. And he leaped and walked. And when the people saw what Paul had done, they lifted up their voices, saying in the speech of Lycaonia, The gods are come down to us in the likeness of men (Acts 14:8-11).

There Paul was hailed as being a god. But now look at what followed:

> And there came thither certain Jews from Antioch and Iconium, who persuaded the people, and, having stoned Paul, drew him out of the city, supposing he had been dead (Acts 14:19).

The same people who at one time were ready to look upon him as if he were a god, at another time stoned him and left him for dead. How many times such treatments actually happened to Paul is not recorded, but we do have the record of some. There was the occasion when Paul was taken as a prisoner on a ship going to Rome. The ship was shipwrecked on the island of Melita, which is the island of Malta, and while there these things happened:

> And when Paul had gathered a bundle of sticks, and laid them on the fire, there came a viper out of the heat, and fastened on his hand. And when the barbarians saw the venomous beast hang on his hand, they said among themselves, No doubt this man is a murderer, whom, though he hath escaped the sea, yet vengeance suffereth not to live (Acts 28:3, 4).

These people were ready to think that he was a murderer because the snake bit him. But the account goes on to say:

> And he shook off the beast into the fire, and felt no harm. Howbeit they looked when he should have swollen, or fallen down dead suddenly: but after they had looked a great while, and saw no harm come to him, they changed their minds, and said that he was a god (Acts 28:5, 6).

This was the account of what was done by the same men, the same people. In other words, Paul had all kinds of fortune coming and going. It seems obvious that you cannot depend on people. The believer may be depreciated at any time, and people may make little of him, talk him down, so the only thing he can do is trust God. Or the believer may be exalted and treated as if he were actually like God Himself; then he must thank God. But whatever may be the case, the believer should keep in mind that when things are going against him, while he is being depreciated and abased, he should not be too depressed; whereas, on the other hand, when he is being exalted and treated as though he were something extra, he should thank God but be careful that he be not too much elated. He must school himself to be not too much depressed in defeat, and not too much elated in victory, because these conditions do not make that much difference.

We might well note in passing that as far as the treatment of believers is concerned, even as the treatment of pastors is concerned, one thing should be kept in mind: the people will not be completely right either way. If they make a god out of him, this is not right; and if they make a slave out of him, that is not right. If they say everything he does is wonderful, that is too much; and if they say nothing he does is any good, that is too little. The people are seldom right about these things. But God is, always, and He is the One in whom the believer should put his trust.

Chapter 72

## DO ALL THINGS

(Philippians 4:13)

*Can you understand how a believer in Christ Jesus can be confident that he can endure any test in this world?*

> I can do all things through Christ which strengtheneth me (4:13).

No doubt many professed believers shrink from their own experiences. I suspect many people who are living in faith in God, and professing faith in the Lord Jesus Christ, are actually fearful about what may happen tomorrow. Some may lament that they are not able to force the unfair demands people may place upon them; and some will despair because of an honest appraisal of themselves. They know they are not strong enough to face what is coming up, and they are not wise enough to know how to manage. They are not good enough to choose the right thing. In all such judgment they are right. It may be a matter of degree in how they realize it, but basically they are right. Yet in their conclusion they are wrong. It is true they do not have strength enough in themselves, but it is not true that it cannot be done.

Paul testified in his letter to the Philippians that he could do all things through Christ who strengthened him. This is brought out in the latter part of this letter. He testified to the people that he could live with abundance and he could live without having enough of what he needed; that he could live with success and he could live without any victory in this world. He could live as a prisoner and he could live as a free man. Because he wants them to understand how this is possible, he writes: "I can do all things through Christ which strengtheneth me" (4:13).

This is a wonderful statement and it is popular among be-

257

lievers because it is easy to memorize and easy to say. I am afraid it is often used carelessly, or defiantly. Sometimes it is quoted exultantly, and again it may be stated confidently, as one might say: "You can depend upon me. I am a believer in the Lord Jesus Christ and He is going to help me and so I can do it." It may be that all the way through it is implied that the individual has now some personal power, perhaps because of his own virtue, or perhaps because he has committed himself to Christ. We are reminded of the line the poet used years ago, which often has been quoted as a reference, "My strength is as the strength of ten because my heart is pure." All this sounds good, but a statement like that misses the whole point of what Paul is saying.

Whatever may have been Paul's estimate of himself as a man we do not know, and that has no bearing here. To understand what he says here is to let it have this meaning: "I through Christ which strengtheneth me." This is what Paul is speaking about. This can apply to any one of us, no matter who we are or what we face. For instance, there may be some who are facing the thought of death, perhaps they are suffering from illness that may be terminal, or they may have some sickness that they are afraid they will never be free from. Their faith in the Lord Jesus Christ will prepare them for death.

Perhaps your own problem is sickness; right now your body is weak and you are suffering. You have a fear that some day you may be crippled or an invalid. Now is the time for you to put your trust in the Lord. He bore your sickness and carried away your infirmities. He took them to the grave. "It is appointed unto man once to die," but God can raise the dead.

With some it may not be a problem of illness or the fear of death, but it may be trouble in finances. As far as that is concerned, I did not bring anything with me into this world, and I am not going to take anything away with me. I will leave behind every single thing, whether it is a dime or a million dollars. In other words, if trouble of such nature comes I need not be afraid of that: all my money is going to stay here. If I should have trouble with people, I should look up to God and put my heart as it were into His hands. I should trust in Him; He can take care of me. People may do me harm; they did Him harm. "The servant is not greater than his Master." They could not do any worse than kill me, and God can raise the dead. If they were to take away everything I have, they would not really have anything when all is done. They will have to leave it when their time comes.

Some may be troubled with uncertainty; they do not know what will happen. But God does know, and He cares for them. He has said "Take no thought for tomorrow . . . sufficient unto the day is the evil thereof." He will share all of the hurt and He will never leave anyone alone. He will come and be with His believers, and underneath will be the everlasting arms. Some may be troubled with sin. Such persons should bring their sin to the Lord and confess it. "Though your sins be as scarlet, they shall be as white as snow; though they be red like crimson, they shall be as wool" (Isa. 1:18).

Man cannot perform any kind of wrongdoing, or do any such evil in this world, that the blood of the Lord Jesus Christ cannot cleanse. "The blood of Jesus Christ his Son cleanseth us from all sin." There is only one sin that cannot be forgiven and that is the sin of turning away from Christ. As far as guilt is concerned, why not trust Him? He died for you. He will take your guilt away. As far as shame is concerned, remember that is just in the minds of other people, it is not in the mind of God. You should have fellowship with the Lord and turn to Him. You will not need to be ashamed. He knows all about you and loves you just the same, so it is in Him that you can have the victory. This is what Paul meant when he said: "I can do all things through Christ which strengtheneth me."

# Chapter 73

## YE HAVE DONE WELL

### (Philippians 3:14)

*Do you realize that it is a good thing to help someone else in trouble?*

> Notwithstanding ye have well done, that ye did communicate with my affliction (4:14).

As we continue our study of the Book of Philippians we notice in the last chapter how the apostle is talking to the Philippians about himself by way of illustration of certain truths. Some things had been demonstrated in his own life before them that should help them understand what is involved in living by faith in the Lord Jesus Christ. In telling about himself Paul emphasized that he was more than conqueror in Christ Jesus.

> Who shall separate us from the love of Christ? shall tribulation, or distress, or persecution, or famine, or nakedness, or peril, or sword? . . . Nay, in all these things we are more than conquerors through him that loved us (Rom. 8:35).

This is the way the apostle expressed it; to the believers in Philippi he testified his triumphant endurance of every difficulty. He was able to say, "I can do all things through Christ which strengthened me." The whole tone of his testimony implied that Paul depended on no man. In writing it this way it almost seemed as though he disregarded what the Philippians had done for him. They had helped him by sending Epaphroditus to minister to him, and Epaphroditus had worked for him so hard he almost killed himself. He was "sick nigh unto death." Paul had been so eager to give all the glory for his triumphant experience to his faithful Lord, but now he wanted to make sure they did not misunderstand him. "Notwithstanding ye have well done, that ye did communicate with my affliction" (4:14). To "communicate" is to help another person, to give to another person. We communicate by giving money to the poor and by giving friendship to the lonely. Paul said, "You have done well that you have shared with me, that you communicated with my affliction." This could easily be confusing. At one time Paul wrote, "I can do all things through Christ which strengtheneth me," and now he wrote, "You did well to help me."

To understand this it will be helpful to separate Paul personally from his public ministry as a service. In himself Paul was totally dependent upon Christ alone; he did not need anyone else, and he put his trust in no one else. But in his public ministry Paul carried the name of Christ. It was not Paul; it was Christ who was being preached. Paul was simply the servant who was telling about Christ; therefore, when they were helping Paul as preacher they actually were serving Christ.

Something of this truth can be seen by looking at Jesus of Nazareth as He stood in the courtroom of Pontius Pilate. He was being mistreated, abused by the soldiers, yet He said nothing when falsely accused, "He answered not again." While there Jesus of Nazareth put His trust in God. He depended on God. Even when Peter wanted to defend Him by pulling out his sword, the Lord would not let him do it. That was not the way to meet this crisis. Jesus of Nazareth stood before Pilate's judgment bar trusting in God. When they took Him to the cross He was trusting in God. When He hung on the cross He was trusting in God. He commended His spirit into the hands of His Father in heaven as He died. After His death He was served by Joseph of Arimathea. Although He had put His trust in God, God did not send angels to take Him from the cross; God did not send angels to embalm Him for burial. He was served by Joseph of Arimathea, who asked for His body and placed it in his own grave. He was also served by Nicodemus who came with Joseph of Arimathea with spices to embalm His body. And He was served by the women who stood there in the distance watching Him die.

In other words, although Jesus of Nazareth personally put His trust in God and suffered accordingly, the truth of the matter is that in so doing He was our Savior. He was our Sacrifice, and as such, when Nicodemus and Joseph of Arimathea took care of His body, they were serving God.

This is an important thing for us to remember: the believers who communicated with Paul's affliction were not doing this to Paul as a person, they were doing it to Paul as a preacher. They were doing this to Paul who had brought them the Gospel. What they did to Paul they did as to the Lord, and that is why he could say to them, "Anything you have done for me, you have well done that you did communicate with my affliction." He was depending on the Lord and he expected to suffer. He went all the way, putting his trust in God, so that he suffered even as his Lord had suffered. This was Paul's personal purpose and procedure. When the believers gathered around and communicated with him and helped him, they were serving the Lord.

## Chapter 74

## COMMUNICATED WITH ME

(Philippians 4:15, 16)

*Do you think it is wrong for a minister of the Gospel to talk about money?*

Many sincere believers have different ideas about seeking the blessing of God especially in matters pertaining to money. No doubt there are many factors which cause confusion of opinion and one does not need to be unsympathetic with people who have different views. Practice in supporting the Lord's work differs widely. There is work of the Lord that is done by those who make a pledge and give so much a month; there is work of the Lord that is done by those who respond to a public appeal, an open offering; and there is work of the Lord that is supported by those who send in their money secretly, privately, without anyone asking them to. All of these procedures do occur, and there seems to be no reason to question the sincerity of anyone involved in any of them.

Some feel that the teaching of Jesus of Nazareth about alms-giving should be our guide. "But when thou doest alms, let not thy left hand know what thy right hand doeth" (Matt. 6:3). Any number of people are inclined to prefer that as being the most honoring to the name of Christ. This seems to be a concise statement — the giver should not even think about it. But careful observation reveals that this has to do with giving to poor people — people who are receiving alms on the street. Jesus of Nazareth used this to expose people who gave alms to be seen. It is true there are those who give their money to the poor to be seen, and there are those who give their money to the poor for God's sake. The Lord said there is a difference in the spiritual quality of these acts. The Scripture records also that Jesus of Nazareth noted what people were giving at the Temple; thus it is written in Mark 12:41, "And Jesus sat over against the treasury, and beheld how the people cast money into the treasury."

How shall this teaching be understood? Am I to believe that when I go to church my living Lord sees whether I give a quarter, a dollar, or five dollars, when the offering plate is passed? Yes, I am to realize He sees it, and what is more, He *beholds* it. "And Jesus sat over against the treasury, and *beheld* how the people cast money into the treasury: and many that were rich cast in much." The account goes on to record that He saw a woman cast in two mites and that He called the attention of His disciples to this.

> Verily I say unto you, That this poor widow hath cast more in, than all they which have cast into the treasury (Mark 12:43).

How would He know that? Would it not be that He had noticed what each one gave? He also observed that each one did according to what he had. Should I not, then, think that when I go to church and the offering plate is passed, the Lord Jesus Christ Himself will see my response?

In the history of the church I know that this whole matter has developed in various forms. Some have launched faith projects. One of the most famous of these was the Bristol Orphanage in England when George Mueller sponsored an institution that had at times as many as a thousand orphans in it. All the support came without solicitation. George Mueller issued a statement once a year, which was a balance sheet showing exactly how much money was received and how much was expended. People esteemed this project as a remarkable demonstration of faith. And it was. George Mueller organized it for just that purpose; he intended that it should be a manifestation to the world of the power of prayer. It has served as an inspiration to many earnest believers who want to serve the Lord. But there have been instances when one could almost feel that the people sponsoring a project like that would boast. I have personally heard such testimony: "We never ask anyone to help us."

It seemed almost as if they were patting themselves on the back and saying, "Look at what fine people we are. We don't ask anyone to help us." No doubt there can be a valid emphasis in such direct dependence on God. I have no intention to question anyone about such procedure as far as it goes, but I do not think it should be taken to exclude any other way.

Paul discussed the matter of giving with the believers at Philippi.

> Now ye Philippians know also, that in the beginning of the gospel, when I departed from Macedonia, no no church communicated with me as concerning giving and receiving, but ye only. For even in Thessalonica ye sent once and again unto my necessity (4:15, 16).

Here Paul is saying to them in effect that no church entered into partnership with him except these Philippians. Did he not mention this because he thought it was a good thing, and he wanted them to do more of it? There are various ways to give. A group of believers may get together and decide they want to support an orphanage, or promote a school or college, or a mission project. They may devise a system of solicitation, with opportunities to give. They may invite people to pledge that, during that year, the Lord helping them, they will give a certain amount. At other times a big rally may be held, and in the enthusiasm of a large company of people an offering may be taken. Paul mentioned that these people in Philippi had supported him when he left Macedonia, and went on from there in his missionary journey. Why did he mention this? Is it not true that he wanted such mention to stimulate them? Partnership in the Lord's work is a matter of sharing the resources that I have and accepting the responsibilities that are involved. In all of this I may have in mind that I want to serve the Lord in the best way I possibly can, and one of the ways in which I can serve Him is by giving to His work. We can be sure that the Lord will greatly bless all who give, and who give liberally.

## Chapter 75

## NOT THAT I DESIRE A GIFT

### (Philippians 4:17)

*Can you understand how a minister who does not want to profit personally would yet urge his listeners to give liberally to his ministry?*

Not because I desire a gift: but I desire fruit that may abound to your account (4:17).

In coaching the young believers at Philippi into a manner of life that would give them strength in their faith and increase their joy, Paul came, in the closing part of his letter, to the matter of their giving of their means to support him and his work. Such an emphasis could be easily misunderstood. It certainly is often misunderstood in our day and time. Paul wrote these words, "Not because I desire a gift: but I desire fruit that may abound to your account." He wanted them to prosper spiritually and he knew they would not unless they shared in the work of the Gospel.

People are quick to criticize preachers in anything they do; and this, by the way, actually shows indirectly how sensitive people are to God. If they did not care about God at all they would not bother to say anything about the preacher. But this does not mean that their interest is sound or healthy. The preacher deals with the soul, and people can be conscience stricken about their ungodliness and the neglect of their souls. So it would be natural for them to criticize the preacher, to disparage him, because they feel in this way they can then justify themselves.

Paul understood about human nature and so he laid down a flat denial to protect what he has just said to these believers. This, in effect, is what he said: "I am glad you have started giving again to my support, not especially because I need it. I have learned whatsoever state I am in therewith

266

to be content. Actually I have been both full and I have been empty, I have been up and I have been down, and through Christ I can get along in any situation. I can do all things through Christ who strengthens me. But I am glad that you have started supporting me again, for your sake. You were always generous and there was a time when you were my only support. You were more generous than any of the other churches, and I now want you to continue to have that blessing. And I am not saying this because I want your money, but I want you to be fruitful."

It will be fruit when it is actually the result of "Christ in you." When I am being moved from within to give, that is fruit. By the way, the fruit that you ordinarily expect in connection with anyone being a Christian occurs only in action or in obedience to the Lord. Jesus of Nazareth taught "He that abideth in me, and I in him, the same bringeth forth much fruit: for without me ye can do nothing" (John 15:5). The branch must abide in the vine, and the power of the vine must be in the branch. It is the power, the life that is in the vine, which comes through the branch that produces the fruit. This is the way the Lord would speak about spiritual fruit. When I think of someone giving money to the Lord's work, that money in itself is not the whole story. A man could do that so his wife would like it, or so that he would look good in the eyes of the deacons of the church. But a man could give that money as to the Lord; he could give it to the poor and do that as to the Lord.

There are believers who, when someone comes to the door and asks for an offering for some cause, will actually go to their checkbooks because of the Lord Jesus Christ. They want to serve Him and they have an understanding with Him that when a good cause is presented to them they should share in it for His sake.

> But the fruit of the Spirit is love, joy, peace, longsuffering, gentleness, goodness, faith, meekness, temperance" (Gal. 5:22, 23).

That is a wonderful description of the life that would be called spiritual; but as far as these words are concerned, no one ever sees any one of those characteristics by itself. Consider "gentleness." Do you realize that as far as gentleness is concerned we cannot see it by looking at anyone alone? If we see a man sitting on a chair we cannot see that he is a gentleman, and if we see a woman sitting in her car we do not know that she is a kind woman. But if we see that man deal gently with a child we know he is a gentle person; or if that woman goes out of her way to help someone who is sick, we can see that she is a kind person.

"Goodness" does not come by itself in a package. Goodness occurs in conduct. My conduct may be good or my intentions may be good, or my speech may be good. It is something I do that can be good. Or consider meekness, for example. I cannot see meekness by itself. It is not in some sugar bowl or something like that. Meekness shows up in conduct, in attitude, and in the way I do things. Each of these characteristics in the fruit of the Spirit is to be seen only in conduct. Such fruit can be seen only in action.

Electricity was something that I was fascinated by as a young lad. When I grew up on the farm we had no electricity; it was something I had only heard about and had seen from a distance. I had seen electric lights and was always intrigued by them. In the course of the years I have come to know more and more about it, but to this day I am intrigued by this: if I had our house wired to the electric current, with outlets for all appliances, and did not turn on the current, not one bit of electricity would go through our house!

Now let us think about our spiritual life. I believe in the Lord, I look up to Almighty God and I trust in Him. All about me are people. All about me is the world. I need to realize that if I really want the blessing of God I must do something about souls. I must recognize that it is only as I act toward other people that the grace of God can operate and show up in me. I need to remember the electricity, and then think of the grace of God in me. It will operate only in action when I turn it on. And so with reference to the matter of giving, Paul could say, "It isn't that I want your money for myself, but I want you to give it, because giving your money will actually bring blessing to your soul. It will cause you to prosper in spiritual things."

## Chapter 76

## SACRIFICE OF A SWEET SMELL

## (Philippians 4:18)

*Have you ever thought that the prayers of a believer are actually fragrant as a sweet smell to God?*

> But I have all, and abound: I am full, having received of Epaphroditus the things which were sent from you, an odour of a sweet smell, a sacrifice acceptable, well-pleasing to God (4:18).

These are strong words by the Apostle Paul, and this is the way in which he refers to the benefits that had been brought to him by Epaphroditus. We do not know what that might have been. In our day and time it would probably have been something like money. It may have been clothing or food, but the Philippians had sent support through Epaphroditus.

Have you ever noticed how often we use expressions that refer to our senses when we are indicating our esteem of anything? For instance, we will speak of "a beautiful action." Beautiful refers to sight but we understand that we are approving what was done, when we speak of a "beautiful action." We may say, "That was a lovely word." By that we refer to some statement in conversation, in speech. The word "lovely" refers to appearance but we use it to indicate our appreciation. We may say, "That was a grand description." "Grand" is something big to look at, and we use it to indicate that we were impressed. Perhaps we use such a word, or expression, as "a sweet smile." "Sweet" actually is a matter of taste. Just as when we speak of someone giving a person a "sour" look; that is also a matter of taste. Thus we may speak of a certain person who gives off a "fragrant aroma" in all her contacts; the way she moves among people is just as if you could smell perfume wherever she has been.

In the Old Testament there was use of words like this.

270

There were sacrifices that were ordered for the worship of God in their ritual, and we are told that they were "sweet smelling sacrifices." These were offered in the tabernacle at the altar of incense you will remember. Incense is a sweet smelling fragrance. This was the altar of praise. In the Book of Revelation it is written that certain vials or flasks of perfume were offered up at the altar, which were "the prayers of the saints." All of this gives a background to Paul's use of language here. When he said, "I am full, having received of Epaphroditus the things which were sent from you, an odour of a sweet smell, a sacrifice acceptable, well-pleasing to God," he was indicating that their giving help to Paul was actually an offering to the Lord which was a "sweet smelling sacrifice." It could be termed a thank offering: it was sort of an offering that would be made at the altar of incense.

Now let us note more closely what Paul says: "I have all, and abound." He means to tell these people, "I have everything I need; I am satisfied and running over on every side. My every need is met." Recently I had a letter of request for prayer in connection with a serious need in a certain family. The wife was asking for prayer for her husband. In the course of her letter she said, "I am so glad I do not need to ask you to pray for our material needs. We have been over-abundantly supplied with everything that we need physically." That is the way it was with Paul. He went on to say, "I am full." He meant that he had no desires which were not fulfilled. That is just the language we would have used when as young boys we ate and ate until we could not eat any more. If someone had offered me more food I would have said, "I am full."

Paul deeply appreciated their sending him help, especially by the fine young man, Epaphroditus. He told them that such action on their part was something that God took note of; it was acceptable as a sacrifice to the Lord. They felt they were sending money to Paul, but what they were actually doing was giving money to the Lord, because He had that relation to His servant. The Lord was interested in Paul and He wanted Paul to be taken care of by these obedient Philippians.

When Paul used this expression, "an odour of a sweet smell," he seemed to say it all. There is hardly any way to improve on that. One could speak of that as being fragrant and we would all know what that is like — the smell of a sweet flower. The word "smell" is almost inelegant. It is prosaic, but what else can we say when we smell a rose? Or perhaps a certain kind of lily or any other flower that has a sweet smelling perfume? Paul referred to their conduct, to what they had done for him, as something they had done as to the Lord. It was not done with any idea of substitution for something that had been wrong, like a sin offering: it was not that kind of offering. Nor was it done as something for the Lord which they were under obligation to do. It was done with free will from the heart. They did this thing for Paul because they loved him, and because they wanted him to have their help. Their whole attitude in this matter was pleasing to God.

As far as God was concerned this was like a sweet fragrance, as if they had brought in a bouquet of sweet peas. He was pleased with this; a sacrifice acceptable. Paul used the word "sacrifice" because it was a matter of giving some thing. But what would make it "acceptable"? All through the Bible it is revealed that the sacrifice that comes from a willing heart is the one that is acceptable. The Philippians gave this help in an acceptable fashion because they wanted to. They actually wanted to do this for Paul. He realized that and he is now telling them that their conduct was such in the sight of God, who recognized it as a free-will gift on their part, out of a willing heart. "Well pleasing to God" — Paul adds at the end of the sentence. They did it to Paul, but God saw it; as He always sees what we do for His servants.

"I have all, and abound" Paul wrote. He meant to say, "I have everything I need. I am full. I am entirely satisfied." I have received "of Epaphroditus the things which were sent from you." Their action in doing this was fragrant, just as if sweet smelling flowers had been brought to Paul.

By the way, can you feel as I have been writing this, that here is guidance for our conduct toward other people? Can you realize that the way you treat other people matters to God? If I treat others considerately, thoughtfully, sympathetically, my actions are a sweet smelling fragrance to Him. This is especially true in the way in which I treat those who are seeking to spread the Gospel. Every time I do any one of them a favor the Lord takes it to Himself personally. Whatsoever you do to any one of His servants, is just as if you were doing it for Him.

# Chapter 77

## MY GOD SHALL SUPPLY

### (Philippians 4:19)

*Can you understand how a believer could have freedom from concern for his loved ones?*

> But my God shall supply all your need according to his riches in glory by Christ Jesus (4:19).

This has often been called the most challenging promise in Scripture. And it is a marvelous word. Some have called this "God's blank check." The apostle has been writing this whole epistle to bolster the confidence of the young believers at Philippi. He wanted to strengthen their morale that they might be ready to endure hardship and trouble in the days to come. He was instructing them how to prosper and how to be strong spiritually. He used himself as an example, as a case in point; and he referred to his own circumstances to emphasize that by trusting in God, a believer would be able to endure anything and everything.

Paul had been in distress; he had been in trouble. Even now he was in danger, but for them he wanted them to know there was no need to be distressed about this. There was no reason to be troubled: God would take care of him. He had this confidence, and he wanted them to know that the same God would take care of them and all their people. He urged them to remember this truth.

To be sure, they had been faithful supporters; they had sent money to Paul and helped him in various ways. He appreciated this, and took time to tell them. Their support of him was really an extension of the Lord's arm on his behalf. It was because the Lord Jesus Christ wanted him to be supported that these believers at Philippi had been moved to help him. Now he personally needed nothing more. He appreciated what they had done, and sincerely thanked

274

them; but he was quick to point out, "I did not really need it." Does that not seem a strange way to express himself? The great truth was that he was not really looking to them for help, he was looking to the Lord.

Someone might reflect, "Paul said the Lord was going to help him, but if it had not been for the Philippians, he would not have had any help." But there is a deeper truth: if it had not been for the Lord, the Philippians would not have helped. Paul appreciated what they did, yet he wanted them to know his confidence was in the Lord. While you and I may appreciate all that people do for us, we may know deep down in our hearts that our trust and our confidence must be in the Lord. The Lord not only took care of Paul, but God will take care of all believers and so Paul gives them this marvelous reassurance: "My God shall supply all your need according to his riches in glory by Christ Jesus." Was this because the Philippians were something special? No, this was because Christ Jesus was special. Was this because they were particularly faithful? No, this was because Christ Jesus was particularly faithful. This is the kind of confidence any one of us can have. All parents, brothers or sisters can keep this in mind: we are not being helped from God because we deserve it, or because we earn it. As believers we are being helped because Christ Jesus provides it for us, altogether apart from any merit on our part.

When Paul wrote, "My God shall supply all your need according to his riches in glory," he put the focus back on the Philippians, and on the Lord. Everything they needed that would be asked for in and through the name of the Lord Jesus Christ will be provided. This is God's way of doing things. When Paul wrote, "all your need," he did not mean "all your desires or all your wishes." He was not even saying "all you think you need." No, Paul said just what he meant, definitely, "all your *need.*" I need protection — He will supply it; I need provision — He will supply; I need to be helped day by day — He will take care of me; I need deliverance from the Evil One in my spirit — He will provide it. Then again in my own physical condition I need food, shelter and clothing and I need protection from accidents, from harm: God will take care of me. This is not saying that I will never get hurt or that I will never be hungry, but this is telling me that my need will be provided. When speaking about our needs, sometimes we have in mind what we are trying to do and for that we need strength, blessing. God will define our needs and He will supply them "according to his riches in glory."

The word "glory" does not mean a bright light primarily, or something that is spectacular. The word "glory" is used in the Bible in connection with harvest time. It is "glory" when potentials are realized, when there is the working of Providence for our welfare. That is to "the glory of God." It is the function of the operation of grace when God supplies the grace into our hearts to turn our hearts to Him and give us a desire to be well-pleasing in His sight. All that comes from God and He will supply that, as well as the ministry of the Holy Spirit; because that, too, is a function from God. When God by the Holy Spirit leads us and guides us along the way He wants us to go, all these things belong to the glory of God, the Providence and grace of God, the Spirit of God. Taken all together they produce the glory of God.

Now "riches in glory" refers to how much He is able to do. "He shall supply all your need according to his riches in glory by Christ Jesus." The word "riches" will mean the good things that are for us. When we say "by Christ Jesus" we remember that He is alive now, interceding for us. These good things are going to be done for us, not just because Christ died 1900 years ago, and because Christ came to seek and to save us; it is much more than that. God will do these things for us because Christ Jesus is praying for us now; He is alive now interceding for us.

> Simon, Simon, behold, Satan hath desired to have you, that he may sift you as wheat: but I have prayed for thee (Luke 22:31, 32).

Perhaps there should be a closing word here of warning against presumption. Just because God is going to supply my need does not mean I can go out and spend everything I have. It does not mean to say that I can be loose and careless in my conduct. I will, in praying, be helped to recognize my needs more accurately. I will come before God to pray about something and gradually my own heart and mind will be changed by His grace. This is the confidence that any believer can have. "My God shall supply all your need according to his riches in glory by Christ Jesus."

# Chapter 78

## SALUTE EVERY SAINT

### (Philippians 4:20-23)

*Do you realize that when believers ignore or oppose other believers because they do not belong to their class or their church, they are actually disobeying the Spirit of God?*

As we come to the close of this letter to the Philippians and have followed Paul's line of thought as he has instructed the believers at Philippi how to live, having presented himself as an example, we find that he emphasizes the importance of their friendship with other believers. This is characteristic of the Gospel. "Whosoever will may come" is one of the most wonderful statements ever made. It is to the honor of the name of God that He is no respecter of persons; it is true also of Jesus of Nazareth. People flocked to Him. On one occasion when He was traveling through a certain section of the country some Samaritans were not hospitable to Him; they did not treat Him with courtesy. His disciples asked Him whether they should call down fire from heaven to destroy these people and the Lord Jesus rebuked them, "Ye know not what manner of spirit ye are of for the Son of man is not come to destroy men's lives, but to save them."

It is natural for a man to withdraw from others. But it is sinful for a man to separate himself from others. That whole attitude, so common and so ordinary, "me and my wife, my son John and his wife, us four and no more" is sinful. It is not only natural, it is not only common, it is basically wrong in the plan of God. God created all men. The human, sinful tendency to withdraw from others can actually be seen among believers, when they are not fully mature in Christ Jesus.

278

Each of us at one time or another has seen congregational rivalry. A certain church over here and another church over there will be rivals for new members, and in various other ways will develop between each other a certain hostility, just because they are two different groups. Denominational rivalry is common. One belongs to one group that seem to be more sophisticated, and so is tempted to look down on everyone else. Because another belongs to another group that is active and outgoing and positive in its testimony, he is inclined to sneer about those who seem to be rather formal and ritualistic. That kind of thing is entirely human, and is just as sinful as it sounds. It is class distinction, as when all belonging to one church feel they are in a certain class of society, whereas if anyone belongs to another church he belongs to a different class of society. This is all wrong. Such sinful tendencies are not limited to one group or class.

Pride often is ascribed to the rich, and probably that may be a fair statement, but it is also common among the poor. I do not know of any kind of pride that is more stubborn than the pride of a poor man. It is not uncommon among men to feel that all others are inferior, just as it is not uncommon to see some poor people sneer at the rich: all of this is wrong.

The old song that is so easy to sing and has such an appeal to us, "The old time religion makes me love everybody," is true. Paul emphasizes all of this in writing his closing words.

> Now unto God and our Father be glory for ever and ever. Amen. Salute every saint in Christ Jesus. The brethren which are with me greet 'you. All the saints salute you, chiefly they that are of Caesar's household. The grace of our Lord Jesus Christ be with you all. Amen (4:20-23).

That is the way this epistle closes. Now we should notice that as broad as Paul's outlook was, and as all-inclusive as it was, so that there is a strong, definite aversion to anything like distinctions because they were all believers, at the same time in this letter there is an underlying exclusiveness. For instance, we should note, "Now unto God and *our* Father."

He is not everyone's Father. Right there we must screen some ideas out of our minds.

Have you been asked to accept the easy idea that God is a heavenly Father to all men? In that very idea is nullified the entire significance of the Gospel. If God is the Father of everyone, then Jesus Christ did not need to die — even if someone says to me, "He died for everyone." I know He did, but I know also that not all people have received Him. Here is the truth: "But as many as received him, to them gave he power to become the sons of God, even to them that believe on his name" (John 1:12). They were not the children of God before, but now they had the power to become the children of God. Let us keep that in mind as we listen to Jesus of Nazareth when He spoke to Nicodemus. "Verily, verily, I say unto thee, Except a man be born of water and of the Spirit, he cannot enter into the kingdom of God" (John 3:5). And He went on to say bluntly and plainly, "That which is born of the flesh is flesh; and that which is born of the Spirit is spirit. Marvel not that I said unto thee, Ye must be born again" (John 3:6, 7). That is the plain truth. He is not the Father of all, but of those who are "born again."

When He was speaking to certain people who claimed that Abraham was their Father, and even claimed God as their Father, He said, "If ye were Abraham's children, ye would do the works of Abraham" (John 8:39). "If God were your Father, ye would love me" (John 8:42). "Ye are of your father the devil" (John 8:44). That is the way the Lord put it. That is written right in so many words in the Bible. Someone may say, "I don't believe it." Now that may be and I am sorry because it places that person outside. I can tell the whole world: Christ Jesus came into the world to seek and to save the lost. Shall we think no one is lost? Then He would not have needed to come. Shall we think no one is saved, because He did not get anything done? No, the truth is there are people all over the world who are lost, and there are those who are saved. Every human being must be born again, but those who are born again become the children of God; and now in and through Christ Jesus they are reconciled to God.

"Now unto God and our Father be glory for ever and ever." The word "glory" implies fulfillment of a potential; it implies that what was possible has been done. For instance, the glory of the wheat field is in bushels of wheat; the glory of an apple orchard is the barrels of apples; the glory of a flock of sheep is bales of wool, and the glory of the Lord Jesus Christ is in the fruit that appears to the glory of God. "Herein is my Father glorified, that ye bear much fruit." When it is written, "be glory for ever and ever," the Holy Spirit is saying "Let there be love, joy, peace, longsuffering, goodness, gentleness, meekness, self-control, faith: let there be more and more of that, the fruit of the Spirit, which will glorify God."

We should note again, "every saint in Christ Jesus." "The brethren which are with me greet you." "Not all the brethren, but those which are with me, greet you." "All the saints salute you, chiefly they that are of Caesar's household. The grace of our Lord Jesus Christ be with you all. Amen."

In all this that Paul is talking about there is something inside the family all the way through this epistle; he was talking to believers. When we began our study it was mentioned that we could well have called this "For Christians Only." The entire Book of Philippians is for believers, and it is to believers that these things are said.

It is a wonderful thing to believe in the Lord Jesus Christ. One of the most wonderful things that I can tell everyone anywhere and everywhere is: anyone can come. "Whosoever will may come." "And him that cometh to me I will in no wise cast out" (John 6:37). When I tell you that the Gospel actually produces a group of people who are different from others, that is the truth. Anyone can belong, and when you belong, you are different.